50% OFF Online CPHQ Prep

Dear Customer,

We consider it an honor and a privilege that you chose our CPHQ Study Guide. As a way of showing our appreciation and to help us better serve you, we have partnered with Mometrix Test Preparation to offer **50% off their online CPHQ Prep Course**. Many CPHQ courses are needlessly expensive and don't deliver enough value. With their course, you get access to the best CPHQ prep material, and **you only pay half price.**

Mometrix has structured their online course to perfectly complement your printed study guide. The CPHQ Prep Course contains **in-depth lessons** that cover all the most important topics, **over 950+ practice questions** to ensure you feel prepared, and **over 500 digital flashcards**, so you can study while you're on the go.

Online CPHQ Prep Course

Topics Include:

- Quality Leadership and Integration
- Performance and Process Improvement
- Population Health and Care Transitions
- Health Data Analytics
- Patient Safety
- Quality Review and Accountability
- Regulatory and Accreditation

Course Features:

- CPHQ Study Guide
  - Get content that complements our best-selling study guide.
- Full-Length Practice Tests
  - With over 950+ practice questions, you can test yourself again and again.
- Mobile Friendly
  - If you need to study on the go, the course is easily accessible from your mobile device.
- CPHQ Flashcards
  - Their course includes a flashcard mode consisting of over 500 content cards to help you study.

To receive this discount, visit their website: mometrix.com/university/cphq or simply scan this QR code with your smartphone. At the checkout page, enter the discount code: **TPBCPHQ50**

If you have any questions or concerns, please contact Mometrix at support@mometrix.com.

Sincerely,

SCAN HERE

 in partnership with

Online Resources & Audiobook

Included with your purchase are multiple online resources. This includes practice tests in an interactive format and this book in audiobook format. There is also a convenient study timer to help you manage your time.

Instructions for accessing these resources can be found on the last page of this book.

CPHQ® Study Guide 2025-2026

5 Practice Tests and CPHQ Exam Book for NAHQ Prep [6th Edition]

Lydia Morrison

Interested in buying more than 10 copies of our product? Contact us about bulk discounts:
bulkorders@studyguideteam.com

ISBN 13: 9781637758175

Table of Contents

Welcome.. *1*

Quick Overview.. *2*

Test-Taking Strategies....................................... *3*

Introduction to the CPHQ Exam...................... *7*

Study Prep Plan for the CPHQ Exam............... *9*

Quality Leadership and Integration *13*

    Strategic Planning...13

    Stakeholder Engagement..23

    Practice Quiz 30

    Answer Explanations 31

Performance and Process Improvement *32*

    Quality Improvement Training....................................32

    Quality Improvement Information...............................34

    Quality Improvement Opportunities 35

    Teams, Roles, Responsibilities, and Scope.................36

    Innovative and Evidence-Based Practices...................39

    Change Facilitation...40

    Performance Improvement Methods 41

    Quality Tools and Techniques 46

    Project Timelines and Deliverables.............................48

    Team Effectiveness 49

    Performance Improvement Projects and Solutions 50

    Practice Quiz 53

    Answer Explanations 54

Population Health and Care Transitions................................ **55**

Health Status of Defined Populations...55

Improvement Initiatives...56

Prevention, Wellness, and Disease Management...57

Health Disparities and Equity Within Improvement Initiatives.............................58

Clinical, Cost, Equity, and Social Determinants of Improvement Efforts....59

Care Transitions..60

Care Processes and Transitions..61

Improvement Activities..62

Practice Quiz...64

Answer Explanations...65

Health Data Analytics **66**

Data Management Systems...66

Measurement and Analysis..76

Practice Quiz...82

Answer Explanations...83

Patient Safety **84**

Technologies for Patient Safety...84

Ongoing Safety Evaluations..85

Safety Culture..86

Safety Concepts...87

Safety Principles...87

Safety and Risk Management..90

Practice Quiz...94

Answer Explanations...95

Quality Review and Accountability................................ **96**

Standards, Best Practices, and Other Information..96

Internal and External Requirements 97

Confidentiality of Performance/Quality Improvement Records 104

Quality Initiatives That Impact Reimbursement 106

Practice Quiz 107

Answer Explanations 108

Regulatory and Accreditation *109*

Accreditation, Certification, and Recognition Options 109

Statutory and Regulatory Requirements 111

Organizational, State, and Federal Requirements 113

Survey and Accreditation Readiness 116

Practice Quiz 119

Answer Explanations 120

CPHQ Practice Test #1 .... *121*

Answer Explanations #1 .... *143*

CPHQ Practice Test #2 .... *156*

Answer Explanations #2 .... *177*

CPHQ Practice Tests #3, #4, and #5 .... *200*

Index *201*

Online Resources & Audiobook *205*

Welcome

Dear Reader,

Welcome to your new Test Prep Books study guide! We are pleased that you chose us to help you prepare for your exam. There are many study options to choose from, and we appreciate you choosing us. Studying can be a daunting task, but we have designed a smart, effective study guide to help prepare you for what lies ahead.

Whether you're a parent helping your child learn and grow, a high school student working hard to get into your dream college, or a nursing student studying for a complex exam, we want to help give you the tools you need to succeed. We hope this study guide gives you the skills and the confidence to thrive, and we can't thank you enough for allowing us to be part of your journey.

In an effort to continue to improve our products, we welcome feedback from our customers. We look forward to hearing from you. Suggestions, success stories, and criticisms can all be communicated by emailing us at info@studyguideteam.com.

Sincerely,
Test Prep Books Team

Quick Overview

As you draw closer to taking your exam, effective preparation becomes more and more important. Thankfully, you have this study guide to help you get ready. Use this guide to help keep your studying on track and refer to it often.

This study guide contains several key sections that will help you be successful on your exam. The guide contains tips for what you should do the night before and the day of the test. Also included are test-taking tips. Knowing the right information is not always enough. Many well-prepared test takers struggle with exams. These tips will help equip you to accurately read, assess, and answer test questions.

A large part of the guide is devoted to showing you what content to expect on the exam and to helping you better understand that content. In this guide are practice test questions so that you can see how well you have grasped the content. Then, answer explanations are provided so that you can understand why you missed certain questions.

Don't try to cram the night before you take your exam. This is not a wise strategy for a few reasons. First, your retention of the information will be low. Your time would be better used by reviewing information you already know rather than trying to learn a lot of new information. Second, you will likely become stressed as you try to gain a large amount of knowledge in a short amount of time. Third, you will be depriving yourself of sleep. So be sure to go to bed at a reasonable time the night before. Being well-rested helps you focus and remain calm.

Be sure to eat a substantial breakfast the morning of the exam. If you are taking the exam in the afternoon, be sure to have a good lunch as well. Being hungry is distracting and can make it difficult to focus. You have hopefully spent lots of time preparing for the exam. Don't let an empty stomach get in the way of success!

When travelling to the testing center, leave earlier than needed. That way, you have a buffer in case you experience any delays. This will help you remain calm and will keep you from missing your appointment time at the testing center.

Be sure to pace yourself during the exam. Don't try to rush through the exam. There is no need to risk performing poorly on the exam just so you can leave the testing center early. Allow yourself to use all of the allotted time if needed.

Remain positive while taking the exam even if you feel like you are performing poorly. Thinking about the content you should have mastered will not help you perform better on the exam.

Once the exam is complete, take some time to relax. Even if you feel that you need to take the exam again, you will be well served by some down time before you begin studying again. It's often easier to convince yourself to study if you know that it will come with a reward!

Test-Taking Strategies

1. Predicting the Answer

When you feel confident in your preparation for a multiple-choice test, try predicting the answer before reading the answer choices. This is especially useful on questions that test objective factual knowledge. By predicting the answer before reading the available choices, you eliminate the possibility that you will be distracted or led astray by an incorrect answer choice. You will feel more confident in your selection if you read the question, predict the answer, and then find your prediction among the answer choices. After using this strategy, be sure to still read all of the answer choices carefully and completely. If you feel unprepared, you should not attempt to predict the answers. This would be a waste of time and an opportunity for your mind to wander in the wrong direction.

2. Reading the Whole Question

Too often, test takers scan a multiple-choice question, recognize a few familiar words, and immediately jump to the answer choices. Test authors are aware of this common impatience, and they will sometimes prey upon it. For instance, a test author might subtly turn the question into a negative, or he or she might redirect the focus of the question right at the end. The only way to avoid falling into these traps is to read the entirety of the question carefully before reading the answer choices.

3. Looking for Wrong Answers

Long and complicated multiple-choice questions can be intimidating. One way to simplify a difficult multiple-choice question is to eliminate all of the answer choices that are clearly wrong. In most sets of answers, there will be at least one selection that can be dismissed right away. If the test is administered on paper, the test taker could draw a line through it to indicate that it may be ignored; otherwise, the test taker will have to perform this operation mentally or on scratch paper. In either case, once the obviously incorrect answers have been eliminated, the remaining choices may be considered. Sometimes identifying the clearly wrong answers will give the test taker some information about the correct answer. For instance, if one of the remaining answer choices is a direct opposite of one of the eliminated answer choices, it may well be the correct answer. The opposite of obviously wrong is obviously right! Of course, this is not always the case. Some answers are obviously incorrect simply because they are irrelevant to the question being asked. Still, identifying and eliminating some incorrect answer choices is a good way to simplify a multiple-choice question.

4. Don't Overanalyze

Anxious test takers often overanalyze questions. When you are nervous, your brain will often run wild, causing you to make associations and discover clues that don't actually exist. If you feel that this may be a problem for you, do whatever you can to slow down during the test. Try taking a deep breath or counting to ten. As you read and consider the question, restrict yourself to the particular words used by the author. Avoid thought tangents about what the author *really* meant, or what he or she was *trying* to say. The only things that matter on a multiple-choice test are the words that are actually in the question. You must avoid reading too much into a multiple-choice question, or supposing that the writer meant something other than what he or she wrote.

3

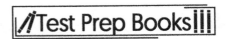
5. No Need for Panic

It is wise to learn as many strategies as possible before taking a multiple-choice test, but it is likely that you will come across a few questions for which you simply don't know the answer. In this situation, avoid panicking. Because most multiple-choice tests include dozens of questions, the relative value of a single wrong answer is small. As much as possible, you should compartmentalize each question on a multiple-choice test. In other words, you should not allow your feelings about one question to affect your success on the others. When you find a question that you either don't understand or don't know how to answer, just take a deep breath and do your best. Read the entire question slowly and carefully. Try rephrasing the question a couple of different ways. Then, read all of the answer choices carefully. After eliminating obviously wrong answers, make a selection and move on to the next question.

6. Confusing Answer Choices

When working on a difficult multiple-choice question, there may be a tendency to focus on the answer choices that are the easiest to understand. Many people, whether consciously or not, gravitate to the answer choices that require the least concentration, knowledge, and memory. This is a mistake. When you come across an answer choice that is confusing, you should give it extra attention. A question might be confusing because you do not know the subject matter to which it refers. If this is the case, don't eliminate the answer before you have affirmatively settled on another. When you come across an answer choice of this type, set it aside as you look at the remaining choices. If you can confidently assert that one of the other choices is correct, you can leave the confusing answer aside. Otherwise, you will need to take a moment to try to better understand the confusing answer choice. Rephrasing is one way to tease out the sense of a confusing answer choice.

7. Your First Instinct

Many people struggle with multiple-choice tests because they overthink the questions. If you have studied sufficiently for the test, you should be prepared to trust your first instinct once you have carefully and completely read the question and all of the answer choices. There is a great deal of research suggesting that the mind can come to the correct conclusion very quickly once it has obtained all of the relevant information. At times, it may seem to you as if your intuition is working faster even than your reasoning mind. This may in fact be true. The knowledge you obtain while studying may be retrieved from your subconscious before you have a chance to work out the associations that support it. Verify your instinct by working out the reasons that it should be trusted.

8. Key Words

Many test takers struggle with multiple-choice questions because they have poor reading comprehension skills. Quickly reading and understanding a multiple-choice question requires a mixture of skill and experience. To help with this, try jotting down a few key words and phrases on a piece of scrap paper. Doing this concentrates the process of reading and forces the mind to weigh the relative importance of the question's parts. In selecting words and phrases to write down, the test taker thinks about the question more deeply and carefully. This is especially true for multiple-choice questions that

4

are preceded by a long prompt.

9. Subtle Negatives

One of the oldest tricks in the multiple-choice test writer's book is to subtly reverse the meaning of a question with a word like *not* or *except*. If you are not paying attention to each word in the question, you can easily be led astray by this trick. For instance, a common question format is, "Which of the following is...?" Obviously, if the question instead is, "Which of the following is not...?," then the answer will be quite different. Even worse, the test makers are aware of the potential for this mistake and will include one answer choice that would be correct if the question were not negated or reversed. A test taker who misses the reversal will find what he or she believes to be a correct answer and will be so confident that he or she will fail to reread the question and discover the original error. The only way to avoid this is to practice a wide variety of multiple-choice questions and to pay close attention to each and every word.

10. Reading Every Answer Choice

It may seem obvious, but you should always read every one of the answer choices! Too many test takers fall into the habit of scanning the question and assuming that they understand the question because they recognize a few key words. From there, they pick the first answer choice that answers the question they believe they have read. Test takers who read all of the answer choices might discover that one of the latter answer choices is actually *more* correct. Moreover, reading all of the answer choices can remind you of facts related to the question that can help you arrive at the correct answer. Sometimes, a misstatement or incorrect detail in one of the latter answer choices will trigger your memory of the subject and will enable you to find the right answer. Failing to read all of the answer choices is like not reading all of the items on a restaurant menu: you might miss out on the perfect choice.

11. Spot the Hedges

One of the keys to success on multiple-choice tests is paying close attention to every word. This is never truer than with words like *almost*, *most*, *some*, and *sometimes*. These words are called "hedges" because they indicate that a statement is not totally true or not true in every place and time. An absolute statement will contain no hedges, but in many subjects, the answers are not always straightforward or absolute. There are always exceptions to the rules in these subjects. For this reason,

you should favor those multiple-choice questions that contain hedging language. The presence of qualifying words indicates that the author is taking special care with his or her words, which is certainly important when composing the right answer. After all, there are many ways to be wrong, but there is only one way to be right! For this reason, it is wise to avoid answers that are absolute when taking a multiple-choice test. An absolute answer is one that says things are either all one way or all another. They often include words like *every*, *always*, *best*, and *never*. If you are taking a multiple-choice test in a subject that doesn't lend itself to absolute answers, be on your guard if you see any of these words.

12. Long Answers

In many subject areas, the answers are not simple. As already mentioned, the right answer often requires hedges. Another common feature of the answers to a complex or subjective question are qualifying clauses, which are groups of words that subtly modify the meaning of the sentence. If the question or answer choice describes a rule to which there are exceptions or the subject matter is complicated, ambiguous, or confusing, the correct answer will require many words in order to be expressed clearly and accurately. In essence, you should not be deterred by answer choices that seem excessively long. Oftentimes, the author of the text will not be able to write the correct answer without offering some qualifications and modifications. Your job is to read the answer choices thoroughly and completely and to select the one that most accurately and precisely answers the question.

13. Restating to Understand

Sometimes, a question on a multiple-choice test is difficult not because of what it asks but because of how it is written. If this is the case, restate the question or answer choice in different words. This process serves a couple of important purposes. First, it forces you to concentrate on the core of the question. In order to rephrase the question accurately, you have to understand it well. Rephrasing the question will concentrate your mind on the key words and ideas. Second, it will present the information to your mind in a fresh way. This process may trigger your memory and render some useful scrap of information picked up while studying.

14. True Statements

Sometimes an answer choice will be true in itself, but it does not answer the question. This is one of the main reasons why it is essential to read the question carefully and completely before proceeding to the answer choices. Too often, test takers skip ahead to the answer choices and look for true statements. Having found one of these, they are content to select it without reference to the question above. The savvy test taker will always read the entire question before turning to the answer choices. Then, having settled on a correct answer choice, he or she will refer to the original question and ensure that the selected answer is relevant. The mistake of choosing a correct-but-irrelevant answer choice is especially common on questions related to specific pieces of objective knowledge.

15. No Patterns

One of the more dangerous ideas that circulates about multiple-choice tests is that the correct answers tend to fall into patterns. These erroneous ideas range from a belief that B and C are the most common right answers, to the idea that an unprepared test-taker should answer "A-B-A-C-A-D-A-B-A." It cannot be emphasized enough that pattern-seeking of this type is exactly the WRONG way to approach a multiple-choice test. To begin with, it is highly unlikely that the test maker will plot the correct answers according to some predetermined pattern. The questions are scrambled and delivered in a random order. Furthermore, even if the test maker was following a pattern in the assignation of correct answers, there is no reason why the test taker would know which pattern he or she was using. Any attempt to discern a pattern in the answer choices is a waste of time and a distraction from the real work of taking the test. A test taker would be much better served by extra preparation before the test than by reliance on a pattern in the answers.

6

Introduction to the CPHQ Exam

Function of the Exam

The Certified Professional in Healthcare Quality® (CPHQ) exam is required for all candidates seeking Certified Professional in Healthcare Quality® certification. Earning this certification demonstrates one's competency in healthcare quality, dedication to the profession, and ability to improve outcomes across the care continuum. It also can add to a professional's credibility and can distinguish the professional in the field. The National Association for Healthcare Quality (NAHQ) designed the CPHQ to promote professionalism and excellence in the field of healthcare quality. To date, over 11,000 professionals in healthcare quality have achieved certification.

The tasks and objectives defined on the CPHQ content outline are designed based on a job task analysis conducted every three to five years. This job task analysis examines the practice and skills of professionals in healthcare quality. Professionals in healthcare quality are defined as those who have on-the-job experience in conducting and/or managing healthcare quality activities such as performance and process improvement, coordination of care, risk management, patient safety, population health, the analysis and measurement of data, performance and quality improvement, and compliance with healthcare regulations. Healthcare quality professionals use administrative, information management, and evaluation skills while performing one or multiple of these functions.

After the job task analysis is conducted, those tasks deemed significant to healthcare practice along the care continuum, including acute care, long-term care, home healthcare, managed care, behavioral health, managed care, and other common care settings, are included in the CPHQ exam. It is recommended that candidates have at least two years of direct experience as a healthcare quality professional. However, there are no formal eligibility requirements to sit for the exam.

Test Administration

Candidates can register online for the exam at www.nahq.org or through a paper form. Candidates must complete an application and pay for the exam, after which they will have 90 days to schedule and take the exam. The exam is offered in a computer-based format online, with online proctoring, or at more than 300 PSI testing locations around the United States. Some international sites are available as well. Test takers can take the exam Monday through Friday. Evening and weekend availability may be offered. Two forms of valid ID with the candidate's name and signature, one of which must include a current photo, are required to gain entrance into the exam center or to begin the online exam.

Candidates who successfully pass the exam will receive a printable certificate, a digital badge, and information about recertification approximately 2 weeks after the date of administration. Candidates who wish to purchase printed certificates and physical CPHQ pins may do so at www.nahq.org. The Certified Professional in Healthcare Quality® credential remains valid from the date the digital badge is received through a period of two years beginning the on January 1 of the calendar year beginning after the exam was passed.

Retakes are permitted for candidates who fail to pass the test, although a new application must be submitted, and test takers must wait 90 days to reapply. No more than three attempts may occur in 365 days, and if a candidate fails after the third attempt, he or she must wait a full year to retest. Candidates with documented disabilities can receive accommodations according to the Americans with Disabilities

Act. PSI must be notified of the requested accommodations at the time of application and scheduling and must receive written verification of the disability and requested accommodation at least 45 days prior to the desired appointment date.

Test Format

The CPHQ contains 140 multiple-choice questions, of which 125 are scored. The remaining 15, which are randomly scattered throughout the exam, are used to gauge their worth for inclusion in future versions. Of the scored questions, approximately 23% are recall questions, which require the test taker to demonstrate their knowledge of specific concepts or facts applicable to the field. The majority of the questions, 57%, are application questions, which evaluate the test taker's ability to interpret and apply given information to a posed situation. Lastly, 20% of questions are analysis questions, which require the test taker to problem solve, integrate information, or use their judgement regarding one or multiple situations. Test takers are given three hours to complete the exam. The following table provides the domains on the exam and the number of scored questions for each major domain:

Domain	Number of Questions
Quality Leadership and Integration	19
Strategic Planning	
Stakeholder Engagement	
Performance and Process Improvement	27
Population Health and Care Transitions	11
Health Data Analytics	26
Data Management Systems	
Measurement and Analysis	
Patient Safety	18
Quality Review and Accountability	16
Regulatory and Accreditation	8

Scoring

An unofficial score report with the pass/fail status is available at the testing site upon completion of the exam. Even those candidates who "pass" must wait to use the CPHQ designation until after the certificate and official results are received. Unofficial score reports also include the number of correct answers and raw scores indicating general performance for each of the major content areas. Raw scores are scaled based on the difficulty of the question, which enables scores to be compared across different exams.

Study Prep Plan for the CPHQ Exam

1 **Schedule** - Use one of our study schedules below or come up with one of your own.

2 **Relax** - Test anxiety can hurt even the best students. There are many ways to reduce stress. Find the one that works best for you.

3 **Execute** - Once you have a good plan in place, be sure to stick to it.

One Week Study Schedule		
Day 1	Quality Leadership and Integration
Day 2	Performance and Process Improvement
Day 3	Population Health and Care Transitions
Day 4	Patient Safety
Day 5	Regulatory and Accreditation
Day 6	CPHQ Practice Test #1
Day 7	Take Your Exam!

Two Week Study Schedule			
Day 1	Quality Leadership and Integration	Day 8	Patient Safety
Day 2	Stakeholder Engagement	Day 9	Quality Review and Accountability
Day 3	Performance and Process Improvement	Day 10	Regulatory and Accreditation
Day 4	Performance Improvement Methods	Day 11	CPHQ Practice Test #1
Day 5	Population Health and Care Transitions	Day 12	CPHQ Practice Test #2
Day 6	Health Data Analytics	Day 13	CPHQ Practice Test #3
Day 7	Measurement and Analysis	Day 14	Take Your Exam!

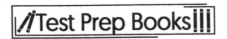

One Month Study Schedule					
Day 1	Quality Leadership and Integration	Day 11	Health Data Analytics	Day 21	Answer Explanations #1
Day 2	Establishing Priorities	Day 12	Measures	Day 22	CPHQ Practice Test #2
Day 3	Stakeholder Engagement	Day 13	Describe Data and Examine Relationships...	Day 23	Answer Explanations #2
Day 4	Consultative Support for Quality...	Day 14	Patient Safety	Day 24	CPHQ Practice Test #3
Day 5	Performance and Process Improvement	Day 15	Safety Event/Incident Reporting	Day 25	Answer Explanations #3
Day 6	Teams, Roles, Responsibilities...	Day 16	Quality Review and Accountability	Day 26	CPHQ Practice Test #4
Day 7	Performance Improvement...	Day 17	Practitioner Performance Evaluation	Day 27	Answer Explanations #4
Day 8	Team Effectiveness	Day 18	Regulatory and Accreditation	Day 28	CPHQ Practice Test #5
Day 9	Population Health and Care Transitions	Day 19	Communication with Accrediting...	Day 29	Answer Explanations #5
Day 10	Health Disparities and Equity Within...	Day 20	CPHQ Practice Test #1	Day 30	Take Your Exam!

Build your own prep plan by visiting:

testprepbooks.com/prep

As you study for your test, we'd like to take the opportunity to remind you that you are capable of great things! With the right tools and dedication, you truly can do anything you set your mind to. The fact that you are holding this book right now shows how committed you are. In case no one has told you lately, you've got this! Our intention behind including this coloring page is to give you the chance to take some time to engage your creative side when you need a little brain-break from studying. As a company, we want to encourage people like you to achieve their dreams by providing good quality study materials for the tests and certifications that improve careers and change lives. As individuals, many of us have taken such tests in our careers, and we know how challenging this process can be. While we can't come alongside you and cheer you on personally, we can offer you the space to recall your purpose, reconnect with your passion, and refresh your brain through an artistic practice. We wish you every success, and happy studying!

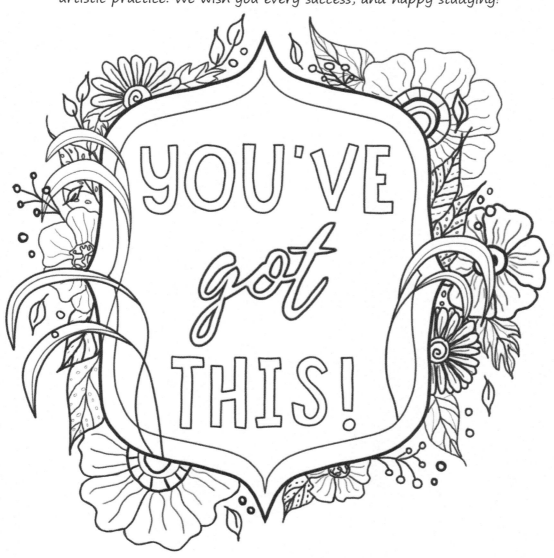

Quality Leadership and Integration

Strategic Planning

Organizational Improvement Opportunities

The Healthcare Quality Professional (HQP) must ensure that all recommendations they present to their organizations leadership team have an evidence-based foundation. Before making any recommendations, the HQP must review their organization's data for workplace performance, client or patient outcomes, or other analogous data as appropriate to the healthcare organization. Processing this data is important because it is through this review that the HQP can identify elements in the organization's operations that require additional support, fewer resources, or adjustment to achieve targeted operational outcomes—for example, reviewing procedure notes to ensure that every surgeon reports verbally confirming a patient's name, age, and the scheduled procedure to reduce errors in a hospital's surgery department.

Once the organization's performance data has been reviewed, the HQP must determine appropriate recommendations for the leadership team. The exact recommendations may vary widely. Some factors include the organization's structure, scope of operations, and mission and core values. For example, the specific recommendations made to a hospital's surgery department will likely look very different from those made to an outpatient psychiatric care office. Despite these differences, the basic process of creating recommendations for leadership is similar.

Recommendations need to cohere with the organization's goals and respond to the analyzed data. If a recommendation is not based in quantifiable evidence, the HQP is at risk of making an "apples to oranges" type of error. For example, data about infection rates after surgical procedures probably isn't good evidence for changing a hospital's policy for emergency use of manual restraints. Valid recommendations advocate for a change in the organization's operations based on evidence that change is necessary and that the recommendations ought to improve the targeted inadequacy.

After providing recommendations to the leadership team, it is important for the HQP to repeat this process. Quality improvement is a continuous process with which the HQP is involved. Yearly iteration of data analysis and improvement recommendations is important to confirm that any actions agreed upon by the leadership team had their desired impact.

Finally, it's also important for the HQP to be aware that at times "no action" is the correct recommendation. Change is important when striving for continuous quality improvement. If analysis of the organization's outcome data indicates that operations are meeting or exceeding their targeted objectives, the HQP ought to identify this success to the leadership team and work with them to help the organization maintain the positive trajectory.

Development of Action Plans and Projects

Facilitating development

A **facilitator** plans, guides, and manages group events to make sure that the meeting's objectives are reached and that all members become involved, clearly express their thoughts, and agree on a solution. A good facilitator needs to be objective; they must take a neutral stance on the topics discussed and instead focus on managing the group process.

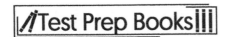

The first step to a successful meeting is defining what the meeting should achieve. This ought to be done even before sending out meeting invitations, because determining a clear objective will help delineate who will need to be present at the meeting, how long the meeting should last, and what should be on the meeting's agenda. The facilitator should also pause before sending a meeting invite to evaluate whether or not a meeting is the best means to achieve the stated objective or if they should pursue a different technique (e.g., observation, workshops, interviews). Finally, knowing and articulating the desired outcome of a meeting sets expectations for the meeting and can also be used to measure the success of the meeting and any outcomes resulting from the meeting. If the outcomes achieve the stated goal, then the meeting and its subsequent effects were a success.

The facilitator should limit the group to a number between 5 and 20 people. This will ensure that the facilitator will only select participants who are actually necessary for the meeting, while also being respectful of stakeholders' time. Persons who have expressed an interest in the topic, people with power, and people with knowledge of the task at hand are all good choices for team members.

Preparation for meetings is essential. The facilitator should have a clear and concise agenda, get the information out well in advance of the meeting, and it may be necessary to personally brief attendees. If there is a possibility of conflict, the facilitator must understand why in advance and have a plan to deescalate any conflict.

The facilitator must assign a scribe who can also help with any logistical items. Ensure that the meeting room is booked and large enough, equipment (projector, flip-charts, slides) is available and working, and that the facilitator has notes and anything else needed for the meeting.

Group process is the method used to of manage group discussion, receive input from all participants, and have the event arrive at a successful conclusion. Optimal facilitation enables the group to generate ideas, solutions, and decisions. To do this, facilitators design the group process and provide tools that will help the group arrive at that outcome. The facilitator is responsible for guiding the group process to achieve a productive outcome. Ideally, there must be strong participation among group members, they must arrive at a consensus, everyone's input should be acknowledged and used in developing ideas, solutions, and decisions, and all participants should share responsibility for the results.

The facilitator must also make sure that all questions, actions, and outcomes are documented and properly handled. The task of recording group process may also be delegated to a scribe, to free up the facilitator to more easily handle other tasks during the event. The following items must be considered when facilitating a group event:

- Whether there should be open discussion or a structured process
- If variety of topics needed can be covered
- Whether enough ideas and solutions can be generated
- The facilitator's own ability to get everyone's involvement and buy-in
- The number of participants
- The nature of the topics being discussed
- The type of involvement needed
- The background and positions of the participants
- How well the participants understand the subject and other members
- The time available

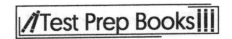

There are many organizational devices that a facilitator can use to help the meeting run smoothly:

- Ice Breakers, to ease group contributions
- Multivoting, for choosing fairly between multiple options
- Brainstorming, for producing many ideas
- Role Playing, to prepare for difficult situations
- Small group discussion
- Paired listening
- Eisenhower matrix (Urgent/important grid)
- Pros and cons list
- Plus-Minus-Implications list

The last step in preparing for group events is to consider how the meeting will be run and organized. It's beneficial to set ground rules for the event so that the meeting stays under control, people respect each other's ideas, and that questions are handled appropriately. The facilitator should also plan some ground rules ahead of time to present at the start of the meeting. To ensure the meeting runs smoothly, there are several things an effective facilitator should do:

- Set the scene. Give participants an overview of the meeting, including the agenda and objectives. Ensure that everyone knows their role and the purpose of the event.

- Get things flowing. Have all participants introduce themselves and use icebreakers to positively kickstart the event.

- Keep up the momentum and energy. Intercede as the event progresses and energy levels change. Keep participants attentive and focused on the discussion.

- Listen, engage, and include. Set a positive example for participants by staying alert, actively listening, and staying engaged and interested. This also enables the facilitator to intervene if needed.

- Monitor checkpoints and summarize. Stay on top of schedule, let participants know what's been covered, and tell them what will happen next. Frequently summarize the event, and only intervene if necessary.

- Record, aggregate, and address actionable output. The facilitator is responsible for making sure the ideas, solutions, and outcomes from the event are recorded. They should gather the event's output and share it with the group, and will need to ensure that action is taken from event outcomes.

- Refresh the group on the discussion thus far, maintain group focus, and keep progressing towards the objectives. If the facilitator is unsure that the recordkeeping is accurate to the discussion, they should get clarification before moving on.

- Provide follow-up after the meeting to make sure that actionable items are addressed, and that the proceedings arrive at a successful conclusion.

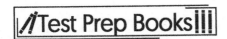

A good agenda may only have a few action items. It is better to focus on broad objectives first and drill down to more specific objectives. As an example:

- Brainstorm session: What worked well this year and what didn't? (15 min)
- Determine priority items down to top five (10 min)
- Action plans for the top 3 (20 min)
- Questions/concerns/next steps (10 min)

The final step in a successful meeting is follow-up. Without clear action items, delegation, and dates for implementation and review, even the best meeting will have no lasting effect. Making sure that these items are in place before a meeting ends will h elp ensure useful and complete follow-up.

When a decision is made to initiate a performance or process improvement project, healthcare organizations typically begin by reviewing all areas of weakness. Primarily, those areas are determined by reviewing the business goals, mission, vision, and values of the organization, along with the associated **key performance indicators (KPIs)**. The basic framework of the project is built on this needs assessment. It is also necessary to determine the **critical to quality measures (CTQs)**, which are the aspects of a business process or product that must be met in order to satisfy the consumer. Once a significant list has been compiled, the team can begin to define the problem.

Ideally, organizations seeking to maintain a high level of excellence should consider evaluating the internal **voice of the business (VOB)**. The VOB reflects the specific needs and concerns of the healthcare organization as a business and may include concerns such as profit, growth, and competitiveness. When designing an appropriate process flow for a client-centered service, it will be crucial to determine the must have aspects of that service according to the customer, or the **voice of the customer (VOC)**. The consumer's voice is the outward image of the business and the reputation that the business has earned among consumers. Building on the external VOC and the internal VOB, the project management team must work collaboratively to ensure that performance and production waste are eliminated, while simultaneously improving overall organizational efficiency and revenue. When standards and policies that were originally created to satisfy the customer according to the CTQs are not consistently met, the business begins to falter. It is important to ascertain whether the projected business goals meet or exceed the VOC and VOB, or whether they have conflicting interests.

When the business's needs do not match the customer's needs, resources can become exhausted. The team will conduct a needs assessment based on the priority of CTQs to calculate how projected goals from previous quarters differ from current results. These needs assessments are performed throughout the company and on all crucial processes and procedures. Specialized departments that handle more intricate issues may have a more stringent process and procedure assessment schedule. Apparent gaps in outcomes related to the VOC and the VOB must be addressed and the staff retrained in an effort to standardize policies, procedures, and processes. Addressing CTQs enables the project management team to focus on the problem.

Strategic Quality Plan

Each healthcare organization develops a strategic quality plan in order to guide the organization through the process of setting the right quality initiatives. Without a strategic plan, the organization will jump from one temporary fix to another. Each organization must create a team of quality professionals who can be trusted to ensure that quality products and services are delivered to all customers. If the organization has only one person with the responsibility and knowledge of quality, that person will need

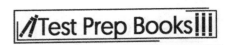

to create and educate a team of individuals who can take responsibility for the management of quality within their jobs.

The strategic quality planning process consists of two phases: research and strategy. The **research phase** includes everything necessary to collect and analyze data before the strategic quality planning starts. The **strategy phase** incorporates the steps needed to develop the actual plan. Every initiative must be tied to the key business processes and their performance indicators. Without this step, there would be no real impact on the balance sheet.

The first task of the strategic quality planning team is to examine the existing strategic plan. All team members must understand all of the corporate strategies. The quality strategies they develop must align with and support accomplishing corporate goals. During the research phase the team will evaluate all of the quality initiatives that the organization has used in the past, along with those they will use in the present. They will research and evaluate the significance of tools like Kaizen, reengineering, Six Sigma, and project management. They also need to calculate the cost of quality and compare it to their desire to aim for quality awards.

The team will then determine the answers to these questions:

- What initiatives have been used before?
- What was successful or unsuccessful?
- Why were some of initiatives successful and others not?
- What learning will come?
- Will the learning allow us to reduce the things that prevent success?
- Will it increase the factors that created success?

As a result of the thorough analysis, the team will eventually abandon some initiatives and choose others. They may want to revisit unsuccessful initiatives that they decide might have been done incorrectly or at the wrong time.

The initiatives must meet organizational needs, but they must also address customer needs. Customer satisfaction results can identify problems and opportunities. The performance of managers, executives, and employees can be assessed by reviewing customer satisfaction. The **voice of the customer (VOC)** can be obtained through customer surveys, interviews, and focus groups. The results of VOC can point out which quality strategies might help drive new product and service development. Service delivery and competitive positioning can also be improved by listening to VOC. Customer satisfaction levels cannot be determined until the customer's expectations and priorities have been stated.

It is also essential to involve employees when developing quality strategies. Employee input, such as voicing challenges, concerns, and ideas, can give additional insight to issues. It also ensures employee buy-in during the strategic implementation stage, which ties the quality development into action plans that impact employees directly.

Benchmarking is another way for the strategic quality planning team to decide how they can improve their internal quality processes, products, and structures. When they know what their competitors are doing, they can incorporate lessons learned into the development of their own quality strategies. During the strategy stage, the team must create their own vision of organizational quality and develop the strategies to achieve it. This may be a challenge since it is difficult to anticipate the future of healthcare. For this reason, some teams are more comfortable focusing on clear, short-term goals than on long-

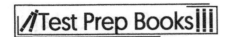

term visions that could be incorrect. The team must understand both present and future needs so they can align their organization with appropriate quality strategies.

Once the team has set their ideal vision, the team needs to develop and/or update their organizational quality policy. This policy must clarify the overall goal, mandate, and objective for quality. The quality policy should be a brief statement that shows the organizational commitment to quality. With this policy, the organization can ensure that all employees are aware of, aligned with, and support the organization's intentions regarding quality management. The team then creates an operational effectiveness plan, starting by developing objectives that will meet each quality strategy. Detailed action plans are then used to detail how the objectives will be carried out.

Action Plans

An action plan should be more than just a list of what activities to carry out. An ideal action plan should answer some basic questions by including the following items:

- A time frame (When will it happen?)
- Assessment of the existing capacities, to identify missing capacities (How will it be done?)
- A cost evaluation (How much will it cost?)
- Identification of the actors (Who will take part?)
- Appropriate mechanisms to track and evaluate progress (Why/What for?)

In other words, an action plan should answer the five W's and one H: who, what, when, where, why, and how.

Each objective in an action plan needs to have a clear purpose and well-defined outputs. The action plan should be used in a logical framework, which shows the interventions taken to develop statistics. The framework consists of a few components:

- Overall objective: The broad development impact brought about in part by the project

- Outcome: The development outcome after the strategy's implementation, especially the predicted benefits for target groups

- Outputs: The direct and tangible results to be delivered, which are largely controlled by project management

- Activities: The actions that must be performed to produce the expected results

- Indicators: Connected to the objective-oriented planning and measure how the objectives, purpose, results, and activities will be accomplished

An action plan should be well-defined and used daily by the team leader to manage the actions, expenses, and timeline of a project. Additionally, it should be used in monitoring and evaluating the project's strategic implementation, making adjustments as needed, and assessing the results.

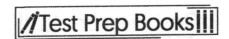

Example of an Action Plan

Goal 1	Action Step Descriptions	Party/Dept Responsible	Date to begin	Date due
Write your goal statement here				
List resources and desired outcomes				

Goal 2	Action Step Descriptions	Party/Dept Responsible	Date to begin	Date due
Write your goal statement here				
List resources and desired outcomes				

Goal 3	Action Step Descriptions	Party/Dept Responsible	Date to begin	Date due
Write your goal statement here				
List resources and desired outcomes				

Goal 4	Action Step Descriptions	Party/Dept Responsible	Date to begin	Date due
Write your goal statement here				
List resources and desired outcomes				

Establishing Priorities

Each healthcare organization must prioritize monitoring various aspects of care according to its unique situation and types of care provided. The focus should be on the areas of care that are provided most frequently, those which are considered high risk, and any areas of care that are particularly problematic for the given organization. Screening methodologies and peer review can both help organizations pinpoint where their priorities should be and avoid wasting resources attempting to monitor all aspects of care all the time. An organization's leadership must also ensure that their teams are up to date on the best definitions of high-quality care and are committed to constant improvement by utilizing review programs that are continuous, priority-oriented, and effective. The 80/20 rule must also be acknowledged and investigated. All indicators and criteria used to monitor care must be consistent with

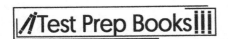

current state-of-the-art practice. Leaders must invest time and funds to improving diffusion of current clinical knowledge to practitioners. They must be equally aware that substandard care may occur and seek new ways to improve that care.

Establishing priorities for monitoring aspects of care is particularly important in light of the numerous efforts to control healthcare costs and the effect of those cost-control measures on healthcare quality. Consumers are increasingly interested in quality comparisons between healthcare plans and healthcare providers, and are also becoming more aware of the aspects of care that are most important to their individual situations.

One effect of this growing consumer-orientation in healthcare is that care is increasingly provided outside of hospitals and other inpatient settings. The quality of care in settings such as ambulatory care, home care, rehabilitation centers, specialized outpatient service centers, etc. directly impacts the ability of hospitals to provide quality inpatient care, and the quality of inpatient care also affects the ability of providers in other settings to provide quality care. Providers in all healthcare settings must coordinate their efforts and track patient care across an illness or episode of care to track and improve quality outcomes rather than focusing on the quality of one setting alone. Quality evaluation is a critically important element of healthcare service and must be a priority for staff at every level of all healthcare organizations.

Despite best efforts, mistakes and issues can and will occur in healthcare settings. These events must be carefully evaluated and continuously monitored in order to devise processes that will eliminate, or at least minimize, such events and improve care. Various methodologies are available to assist healthcare organizations in identifying areas that need the most improvement in quality of care. For example, a **Pareto analysis** could be used to illustrate how a relatively small number of areas account for majority of variation. By finding the most costly departments, there are areas that can be focused on. This provides healthcare organizations a starting point for improving quality, beginning with the processes that have the largest variation in quality. Setting and agreeing upon priorities allows healthcare providers to efficiently reduce variations and improve care.

Quality Governance Infrastructure Activities

An HQP's role in their organization's quality improvement process is to develop or advise on the development of policies and procedures, perform audits ensuring that these are being followed by employees, and train other employees of the organization on how to effectively provide quality improvement data.

Whether an HQP is involved in the creation of an organization's policies and procedures will vary from organization to organization. In some cases, the level of involvement depends on the HQP's job title. The HQP may be responsible for creating and implementing procedures but not policies. However, at any organization the HQP ought to advocate for their involvement in the creation of policies and procedures concerning the quality of healthcare outcomes, at least in an advisory capacity.

Policy is high-level—and sometimes abstract—guidance implemented by an organization's leadership team. Policies direct how the organization's operations will meet its mission while remaining true to the organization's values. Policies are fulfilled through specific **procedures** developed by staff members who are experts in a particular field—such as the HQP—and in a leadership or management role in the organization. Procedures are then implemented by other employees in the course of performing their duties.

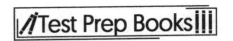

The policies or procedures for which an HQP is typically responsible delineate how the organization's staff generate data about operational outcomes as part of the quality control process. When developing a new policy or procedure, the HQP's directions must be specific, brief, and intentional. The policy or procedure should not generate meaningless data. Rather, the new data should be useful when evaluating if operations are accomplishing the leadership team's strategic objectives. The policy's or procedure's text ought to be brief and precise. Straightforward and simple directions reduce the risk of incorrect implementation by employees—and incorrect implementation leads to incorrect data. Finally, the new policy or procedure should describe why collecting the data is important. If the quality control data cannot be justified as meaningful to the organization's improvement, it should be excised to reduce administrative overload.

As part of the annual analysis of the organization's healthcare quality, the HQP should perform an audit of internal operations. This is not a financial audit but rather an audit of the organization's quality assurance procedures. If an individual, group, department, and so forth, is not generating the appropriate data, the HQP needs to intervene or pass that information along to an appropriate member of the leadership team. The audit is not data analysis. The audit's purpose is to determine that the requisite data has been collected.

Depending on the organization, it may also be the HQP's task to train employees to implement quality improvement procedures. Whether this is necessary will depend on the procedure that is used. Specialized training is not necessary for distributing a paper or digital questionnaire but may be necessary if that same questionnaire is provided to the recipient of services through an interview. Throughout, it is important for the HQP to develop new procedures to be as simple as possible. This reduces the training needs of the organization and allows employees to focus more time and energy on serving the healthcare organization's clients or patients.

Strategic Goals Quality and Safety

A well-researched quality plan will provide clear directions for the organization to move forward. Every healthcare organization begins with a goal of caring for the sick and encouraging the health of the well. Strategic planning moves the organization onto a specific track that will ensure that the goals are all accomplished. Although healthcare organizations improve the health of their patients as one piece of their mission, strategic planning enables them to develop a well-organized plan built on the stability of the team. It is essential that the organizational mission and vision align with the goals of nationally recognized standards of care.

The planning team must also ensure that quality and safety activities are in sync with the strategic quality planning process. Strategic and operational goals have to be reviewed by all team members. Aggregated data can then be scrutinized for trends that could become critical success factors. Identified trends are often used to create **key performance indicators (KPI)**, the measurable results that will decide if the goals and objectives the team sets can be obtained.

The **Centers for Medicare and Medicaid Services (CMS)** has taken the lead in the national goal of transforming healthcare delivery. That goal aims to "meet the person-centered goals of each individual in creating a healthcare system that fully engages persons and families in the design, delivery and

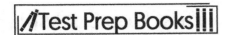

evaluation of care." In 2022, CMS published the National Quality Strategy for Healthcare. The strategy outlined the objectives and outcomes for action to realize eight broad, interrelated goals:

- Goal 1: Embed Quality into the Care Journey
- Goal 2: Advance Health Equity
- Goal 3: Promote Safety
- Goal 4: Foster Engagement
- Goal 5: Strengthen Resiliency
- Goal 6: Embrace the Digital Age
- Goal 7: Incentivize Innovation and Technology Adoption to Drive Care Improvements
- Goal 8: Increasing Alignment

There are also six strategic pillars intended to guide the actions of CMS. Healthcare organizations and CMS must strive to ensure that each of these pillars is incorporated into the eight goals listed above. The pillars are:

- Advance Equity: remove the barriers to health equity that are inherent in our healthcare system
- Expand Access: extend the Affordable Care Act and ensure access to excellent and affordable healthcare for all
- Engage Partners: work with various partners and local communities to make sure that healthcare solutions meet their needs
- Drive Innovation: encourage innovation to overcome the problems within our healthcare system and make sure that healthcare is focused on meeting the needs of individuals
- Protect Programs: use resources wisely to ensure the longevity of the programs
- Foster Excellence: build inclusive, constructive workplaces and strive for excellence in every area

The National Quality Strategy was further enhanced in 2022 with the updated **CMS Meaningful Measures**, which identifies key target areas where measuring and improving outcomes will provide significant benefits for patients and their families while also reducing the burden on clinicians and providers. Meaningful Measures 2.0 has five complementary goals:

- Put patients at the center of making beneficial healthcare choices by focusing on patient-led quality measures and ensuring transparency.
- Utilize measures of quality care to encourage equity in healthcare and to close any identified gaps.
- Encourage improved quality measurement through the Meaningful Measures Initiative.
- Use additional payment programs and public reporting to support continued improvement.
- Introduce digital systems and advanced data analytics to increase the efficiency of quality measures.

The strategic quality planning team must establish and monitor methods to avoid or reduce the mitigating factors associated with all of the listed items, including high-risk procedures and patient-care services. When preventing mistakes, such as during surgery, both the goals and activities must be clearly defined in a strategy known as **mistake-proofing**. This involves developing the necessary countermeasures to solve any problems before they actually occur. Mistake proofing is designed to prevent issues that are identified in advance as to what could possibly go wrong. Steps can then be taken to ensure that they do not go wrong.

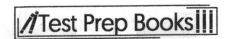

The data associated with implementation must be periodically reported to the governing board, in compliance with fiduciary duty-of-care regulations. The **fiduciary duty-of-care rule** involves assurances that the board members are acting in good faith, in a prudent and reasonable fashion, and making decisions that are in the best interests of the organization. This regulation allows the board time to prepare a prompt response or adjustment to any detected errors or concerns. Once any errors are addressed, the initiatives can be reintroduced, and follow-up comparison data are gathered. The organization's ability to adhere to this cyclical evaluation process is the best quality indicator for positive safety outcomes. The chart below shows a few examples of CMS objectives and possible outcomes.

Objectives	Desired Outcomes
Improve support for a culture of safety	• Improved application of safety practices involve all team members, patients, and families and assure that individuals' voices are heard • Organizations exhibit strong leadership that educates and empowers the workforce to recognize harm and increase reporting of errors and potential errors • Consumers have increased access to understandable health information • Expanded use of evidence-based services and primary care • Disparities in care are eliminated
Reduce inappropriate and unnecessary care	• Healthcare organizations continually assess adverse events in accordance with evidence-based practices • Healthcare cost reductions are attributable to the reduction of unnecessary, duplicative, and inappropriate care • Disparities in care are eliminated
Prevent or minimize harm in all settings	• HACs, Provider Preventable Conditions (PPCs), and healthcare-associated infections (HAIs) are reduced • Medication error rates are improved • Falls are decreased • Visibility of harm is improved in all settings • Expanded use of evidence-based services and primary care • Person and family access to understandable health information is increased • Disparities in care are eliminated

Stakeholder Engagement

Identifying Resource Needs

When the leadership change agent identifies the need for specific resources, it is essential that the findings be communicated to the rest of the leadership team and the Board of Directors. Staffing and technology needs necessary to perform basic medical-related functions are all upper level decisions with a clear policy. Leaders must be effective resource managers in order to align the organizational mission, values, and goals with the needs of the employees and surrounding community. Internal staffing models can leverage the talent pool against the acuity of the workload of any given unit.

The AHRQ has developed a health information technology initiative to bridge the gap between technology and healthcare. Leadership must consider how social media and other technologies have become a part of the patient culture. Creating a social media presence increases the visibility of the health system and offers opportunities to publicize health information on a global scale. Once consent is obtained, health information in the form of emails and text messages can be sent directly to patients.

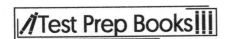

Telemedicine is also a rapidly growing option for patients with mobility issues or those in remote areas that have a difficult time attending in-person visits.

The **Health Information Technology for Economic and Clinical Health (HITECH) Act**, which was signed into law by President Obama in 2009 as a component of the American Recovery and Reinvest Act of 2009, supports and expedites the adoption of EHR-provided incentives to those providers who adopted the implementation and use of EHR systems through 2015. The HITECH Act increases the accessibility and exchange of protected health information and supports the electronic exchange of health information using EHR information. Under this act, patients or their appointed designees can gain access to their medical charts in an electronic format. This access enables patients to view their medical history and provides an enhanced method for information sharing among providers.

Providers and organizations must report security breaches related to electronic PHI as soon as it occurs, or they will face civil and/or criminal penalties. The HITECH Act also calls for physicians and hospitals that have meaningful use attestation to perform a HIPAA security risk assessment. To move between the three stages of meaningful use, providers must demonstrate the ability to function within each of the stages for two years before they can proceed to the next one.

Quality and Safety Culture

Effective program evaluation begins with an in-depth assessment of all aspects associated with the safety of the organization. The role of a healthcare quality professional is the evaluation and ongoing review of the quality of patient safety within healthcare settings. A focus on safety is not merely the avoidance of errors. Patient safety has to be considered in every aspect of care. The healthcare quality professional confirms which policies and procedures are practical, which are outdated or ineffective, and which need to be revised.

The primary goal of patient safety is the prevention of harm through the methodical analysis of previously harmful events. This is accomplished through the systematic review of those policies and procedures both directly and indirectly related to patient safety. For example, when evaluating the provision of bedside care in a hospital setting, it is essential to assess the official and unofficial procedures of the nursing staff. This can be accomplished through shadowing randomly selected nurses and healthcare providers on multiple shifts, medical record reviews, and incident reports. Is the patient handoff conducted at the bedside, or does it frequently occur at the nurse's station? Do nurses scan the patient's wristband with each scheduled administration of medications? It is also important to ensure this culture of safety is apparent not only to clinical staff, but also to ancillary providers and the patients themselves.

Initially, the healthcare quality professional examines the organization's core mission and values. One of the most influential aspects of promoting a culture of patient safety is to assess the attitude exhibited by organizational leadership. It is the leadership team that will ultimately develop the core culture. The primary goal of this portion of the assessment is to determine if the organizational culture is an accurate reflection of the initial vision of the organization. How clearly are the core values articulated to the staff? Do the policies and procedures reflect the proposed core mission and values? How does the leadership team respond to incidents that contradict the organization's core mission and values? What actions have been taken to perform periodic internal evaluations of the staff? Healthcare quality analysts must ascertain if an actual culture of safety exists within the organization and how visible it is to patients and staff. The next step is to ensure that the culture is reinforced and find ways to enhance it.

24

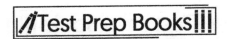

Policies and procedures enacted by healthcare organizations to ensure patient safety typically include factors that meet The Joint Commission National Patient Safety goals. The Joint Commission established the **National Patient Safety (NPS)** goals in 2002 and implemented them the following year. This nationwide effort instituted a set of uniform, realistic, and specific goals that could be consistently applied and measured in every healthcare setting. National Patient Safety goals have set the standard for excellence and are set annually. Several of the most important goals applicable in every healthcare setting include: identifying patients correctly, using medications safely, preventing infection, identifying patient safety risks, and improving staff communications.

Each goal requires that the leadership create an atmosphere of patient-centered care, with a focus on the interdepartmental teamwork necessary to maintain the safety of the entire patient population. Any breech in patient security should be noted, along with recommendations on the necessary adjustments. Accreditation assumes that every healthcare agency seeking recognition is interested in developing the types of programs, policies, and procedures that focus on evidence-based, clinically appropriate care. Physicians, nurses, and other healthcare providers view the accreditation of an institution as a sign of excellence. Other benefits can include the fact that many local and state governments reward healthcare organizations for being recognized through expedited licensure, waivers through Medicare and Medicaid, third-party reimbursement, and improved access to more lucrative managed care contracts.

Leadership Teams in an Organization's Culture of Quality

It is a well-known fact that when the leadership team functions effectively, performance improves. As the central organizing body of the organization, leadership has an obligation to deliver all of the functions of administration, including:

- Ensuring cohesion
- Defining vision and values
- Creating and executing strategy
- Ensuring alignment
- Engaging stakeholders
- Developing talent
- Managing performance
- Building accountability
- Ensuring succession
- Allocating resources
- Crafting the culture
- Delivering results

The leadership team is the organization's center. The business's performance is dependent upon how effective the leadership team is. The leadership team must give particular focus to defining key processes, implementing them with efficiency, studying the results, and then redesigning the processes in order to achieve the desired ends more effectively. Additionally, strategic communication must be consistent and deliver the message in a way that results in organization-wide understanding. Leadership must be actively involved in daily conversations and be engaged enough to unite people around a common cause. This reduces uncertainty and keeps people focused. It also leverages the power of leadership decisions in shaping beliefs and behaviors.

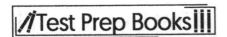

Leaders take discernment and strategic direction and transform them into goals and objectives. Systems for performance accountability can clarify what is expected of people. Only then can consequences or rewards be aligned with actual performance. Ideally, each process should be simple, efficient, and responsive to the situation and needs of a particular organization. Where applicable, processes may also need to be globally adaptable. Establishing and optimizing operational performance is a journey that never ends.

For the best leaders, the goal is **transformational leadership**. Transformational leaders use four key characteristics—charisma, inspiration, individualized consideration, and intellectual stimulation—to inspire confidence and to encourage employees to visualize a better future. Transformational leaders question the status quo and coach employees to develop to their full capability. Ultimately, transformational leaders and their followers form a symbiotic relationship that encourages motivation and honesty for everyone.

Values-based leadership is a perspective on people, philosophy, and processes. Values-based leaders grant authority to their subordinates and lead by example. They believe in the ideas of liberty, equality, and natural justice. Some characteristics of values-based leadership are respect for followers, integrity, clear thinking, vision, listening, inclusion, and trust. Values-based leadership often produces social change. The needs of the followers are more likely to be satisfied, which may ultimately change the beliefs and behavior of the followers. Values-based leadership provides strategic unity and allows independent initiative.

Mechanistic organizations are those that have highly complex structure. They are extremely formalized and centralized. Employees of mechanistic organizations are encouraged to perform routine tasks and rely heavily on programmed behaviors. Mechanistic organizations are generally slow to respond to the unfamiliar. They provide fewer opportunities for employees to exercise initiative and generally suppress the individual differences expressed by leaders and followers.

On the opposite end of the spectrum, **organic organizations** are flexible and adaptive with emphasis on lateral communication. Organic organizations utilize experts and knowledge rather than position and authority, and they offer fluid responsibilities rather than rigid job descriptions. Information is exchanged rather than handed down as instructions, and fewer constraints are imposed on the activity of members, encouraging the expression of individual behavior.

Promotion of Quality and Safety

Senior leaders recognize that engaging stakeholders at every level of program development increases their interest and commitment as well as the likelihood of developing a successful program. If this is done well, stakeholders will begin to invest in long-term support for the program. Hospitals generally have multiple methodologies for engaging stakeholders. Three of the most successful strategies are finding "champions," leaders who will actively and visibly support both the program's initial phases and its long-term sustainability; building strong relationships with stakeholders and ensuring that they are kept up-to-date and receive frequent communications; and clearly communicating the outcomes of the program under development.

Champions assist with program growth and development and encourage program stability. These leaders must be stakeholders with a significant commitment to the program who are also highly respected by their peers. These individuals should have the authority to grant the time and resources necessary to design and launch programs, as well as authority over areas that will be affected by the

26

changes from those programs. Program developers will be able to rely on the expertise and experience of these champions for help with program planning and design. The champions are also extremely helpful in promoting the program and ensuring its continuation and sustainability. They also help manage other stakeholders' expectations. Program champions can offer feedback by identifying areas for clarification and by giving input on potential initiatives and will also be in an excellent position to help program staff understand how other stakeholders may view preliminary evaluation results. Champions can be drawn from many different groups, including State and national agencies, state government, the provider community, patient advocates, and patients themselves. Input from the provider community is particularly important during the planning and designing stages as they can give expert advice on the clinical side of the program. Clinicians can also become champions and serve as ambassadors to their patients.

A team may include a primary care provider (PCP) champion. The PCP champion is a team member with a personal interest in improving a clinical process. This person may also assist in analyzing the program's metrics, to determine the success of different areas of the program, identify which areas are in need of improvement, and come up with solutions for those areas.

Ongoing **communication** encourages stakeholder support. Frequent and direct correspondence between stakeholders and program staff ensures that stakeholders have correct and up-to-date information about the program. Because program staff are the key contacts for the program, stakeholders will have a direct pipeline through which they can discuss all questions or concerns. After a program is implemented, continued stakeholder support depends on regular communication about the program's successes, failures, and any new plans that are being considered or introduced.

Managing expectations to maintain continued stakeholder support is primarily achieved by communicating program successes and outcomes to the stakeholders. To be successful, outcomes must be reported from the beginning of the program's implementation and updated frequently. It is particularly important to consider what outcomes and measurements will be most useful for each stakeholder group.

CMS developed an emergency preparedness checklist for healthcare facilities that has 70 tasks and gives guidance for developing emergency plans. Healthcare facilities are required to have disaster preparedness manuals and protocols that specify the steps to follow in the event of one of the following:

- Weather emergencies (tornado, hurricane, thunderstorms, etc.)
- Earthquakes and situations with power loss
- Infectious disease outbreaks
- Bomb threats
- Active shooters
- Bioterrorism

Community-based organizations work closely with case managers, physicians, and other members of the healthcare team to coordinate care, so it is important to include these organizations in all disaster preparedness planning. Community organizations working at a local level can promote patient empowerment and self-management. These community vendors can provide a variety of services, including support groups or financial assistance.

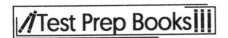

Consultative Support for Quality Improvement

It is essential that the leadership team of a healthcare organization work closely with the clinical staff regarding their roles and responsibilities. The three most crucial aspects are credentialing, privileging, and quality oversight. All clinical staff are required to meet stringent competency guidelines surrounding the specific competencies for each role. **Credentialing** includes allowing a licensed or certified medical professional to provide care within their scope of practice. **Privileging** includes an evaluation of the practitioner's actual performance and qualifications. In healthcare, for a particular provider to become eligible for reimbursement, they must meet a specific set of requirements regarding their educational preparation, clinical experience, and competence. The leadership team must maintain strict **oversight** of all medical staff by periodically verifying that each individual is qualified to perform their assigned duties. Privileging functions as an internal quality measure for patients. They can trust that the care they receive is from providers who have demonstrated excellence in clinical practice set by the medical governing board of the organization.

Risk management is the process of identifying actual (and potential) hazards and developing efficient, cost-effective plans to prevent them from occurring. A sentinel event is an adverse incident that has led to, or has the potential to lead to, a catastrophic outcome. Sentinel events require an immediate intervention. After any workplace accident or near miss, it is mandatory to complete an incident report. Within this report are the variables that caused or assisted the problem. Individuals involved are interviewed, the scene is examined, and management is notified.

During the root-cause analysis, the risk-management team utilizes the answers found in incident reports and interviews to determine the main cause of the sentinel event. The focus then changes from the problem to the solution and the leadership team collaborates with the risk-management team to dialogue about gaps in procedures, policies, workforce, and/or environment that need to be addressed. The primary objective in this step is to prevent future occurrences of a similar nature, while preserving the factors that did not contribute to the problem. The best changes to implement are feasible, efficient, and cost effective.

Inter-Professional Teamwork

The HQP plays an important role in contributing to a supportive workplace culture because they typically are not assigned to work for a specific department. Rather, the HQP's role is interdepartmental because monitoring the organization's quality of care is a task that can't be achieved through attention to a single partition of the organization. The most comprehensive way for the HQP to integrate a supportive *esprit de corps* is establishing a personal habit of seeking collaboration and inclusiveness when interacting with all levels of the organization.

Meaningful collaboration must be sincere. The HQP has an opportunity to encourage good communication and collaboration through the leadership aspect of their job duties. Inviting employees from every department—and from a variety of levels of each department—to discuss new policies and procedures concerning the quality of the organization's healthcare increases emotional investment in the workplace. In general, the people who work with a healthcare organization want to feel they are a useful part of that organization. Inviting staff into the rulemaking process facilitates a culture of collaboration throughout the organization.

In addition to encouraging feedback on the HQP's policies or procedures, a culture of mutual support can be encouraged within the healthcare organization through inviting collaboration in setting the goals

28

of the healthcare quality assurance program. Listening to frustrations, victories, and stressors among the staff of a given department helps the HQP ascertain what problems are perceived by the employees. This social component provides insight that may be difficult to identify with data. When seeking to determine how best to improve the organization's operations, the HQP should not rely wholly on data or employee self-reports but rather combine these strategies.

The HQP must be sure that any feedback and suggestions solicited from the organization's employees is given due consideration. Meetings without intent of using the relayed information are counterproductive to creating this organizational culture. Instead, the employees will feel the HQP—or other individuals involved with quality assurance and leadership—do not listen to their concerns. If an employee presents a question, concern, or complaint about an aspect of the organization's healthcare quality, it should be addressed directly and in good faith, even if the topic is not presently one that the organization has the time or resources to address. Acknowledging failures—such as insufficient resources—often encourages a supportive culture due to the honesty shown by upper-level staff members.

Practice Quiz

1. Several employees make a similar recommendation concerning practitioner scheduling in a hospital's emergency department. The HQP determines that the hospital does not have sufficient resources to act on the suggestion. Which response best encourages a supportive culture in the organization?

    a. Refrain from response until additional resources have been obtained to avoid reducing employee morale.

    b. Respond that the organization is working on implementation, but it may take some time.

    c. Respond that the organization doesn't have sufficient resources to implement the suggestion.

    d. Ask employees for suggestions for improvement that can be accomplished with the organization's current resources.

2. Which of the following stakeholders in a healthcare organization has the least weight when providing opinions on how to improve the organization's quality of care?

    a. Donors

    b. Front-line staff

    c. Department management

    d. Leadership

3. What benefit can be gained by serving as a team leader?

    a. Communicating with other team leaders and directors

    b. Being able to supervise and direct the work of others

    c. Reaching the endpoint of professional learning and growth

    d. Gaining knowledge about the business and operations

4. Which role assists the team when disputes arise in a project, encourages members to voice their opinions, and helps the parties involved move beyond an impasse by collaborating effectively?

    a. Project champion

    b. Process owner

    c. Facilitator

    d. Sponsor

5. Which of the following is NOT a difference between strategic and operational goals?

    a. Operational goals are short-term, whereas strategic goals are long-term.

    b. Operational goals are concerned with creating new and sustainable improvements, whereas strategic goals are concerned with the execution of best practices.

    c. The heads in charge of setting and meeting operational goals are often more involved with the day-to-day operations of a healthcare facility, whereas the heads of setting and meeting strategic goals are more often involved in management.

    d. Strategic goals are often designed to align with a company's mission, whereas operational goals are often designed to align with a company's strategic goal.

See answers on the next page.

Answer Explanations

1. D: Honesty and outreach during collaboration with the organization's employees are the best strategies to foster an environment that encourages teamwork. Choice *A* is incorrect because lack of response can incorrectly message the HQP's indifference to employee suggestions. Choice *B* is incorrect because it is dishonest. Choice *C* is incorrect because the response does not invite the employees to continue contributing ideas.

2. A: Donor opinions have the least weight because the organization's employees are healthcare workers with professional education and credentials. Some donors may have professional expertise, but as a category they are not considered experts. Choices *B, C,* and *D* are incorrect.

3. D: Gaining knowledge about the business and operations, such as financial information, is a benefit of being able to serve as a team leader. This can be rewarding—both personally and professionally. Choices *A* and *B* are incorrect because communicating with others, supervising, and directing work are specific job duties a team leader would engage in and not examples of a benefit gained by serving in this role. Choice *C* is incorrect because an HR professional should never reach the endpoint of their professional development but should always strive to continue learning and growing.

4. C: A facilitator is the individual who assists the team when disputes arise in a Six Sigma project, encourages members to voice their opinions, and aides the parties involved to move beyond an impasse by collaborating effectively. The project champion essentially owns the project. They are charged with ensuring the project's success and representing the organization's interests. This individual is involved in the activities of project selection, project kickoff (in conjunction with the project leader), and providing overall support to and communicating with the project team. The process owner is the individual who's responsible for the business process which is the focus of the Six Sigma project. Finally, the sponsor is the senior executive who's supporting the Six Sigma movement within the company.

5. B: Operational goals, as the name implies, are goals concerned with the general operations of a healthcare facility. Therefore, they are often more concerned with the maintenance of best practices than the introduction of new strategies. On the other hand, strategic goals are more concerned with an organization's long-term goals and often involve the testing and introduction of new strategies. Therefore, Choice *B* is correct.

Performance and Process Improvement

Quality Improvement Training

Despite a busy and fast-paced work environment, leaders at medical facilities must continuously train their employees. **Training** solidifies the existing skills of each employee and helps them improve in areas where they lack experience. Effective training programs identify specific areas where employees can improve in order to address them properly and allow every staff member to become both independent and competent in their roles. Effective training increases employee confidence in their abilities and knowledge, positively impacts performance across the board, and encourages the introduction of new ideas and methodologies.

Training must include information regarding personal and patient safety practices. The consistency of hospital policies improves when everyone is aware of current regulations for the organization and the healthcare industry as a whole. Studies have reported that one of the reasons nurses quit is due to poor education programs. Employees are more likely to remain satisfied if they receive training, because it encourages teamwork among staff members. Proper training helps everyone feel appreciated and that their hard work is being acknowledged.

Senior leaders must be able to create or replicate programs that work effectively with all learning types and are designed specifically for the organization. Training programs should be customized to address the specific needs of the organization as well as the needs of individual employees. This can best be achieved by including knowledgeable staff in the planning process for training programs. Their knowledge and experience are invaluable resources both for what should be included in a training program and for pitfalls to avoid. Leaders should also take advantage of technology by using new methods of teaching, such as simulation and just-in-time training. Screensavers and signs throughout the facility can also provide passive learning opportunities.

Leaders must be mindful that the efficacy of each program also needs to be improved. Inefficient or ineffective programs wastes money, time, and human resources. Leaders must assess the needs of the employee for a specific training and define the organization's training objectives before anything else is done. Surveys, patient feedback, performance reviews, and observations from team leaders or immediate supervisor can all be used to determine the educational needs of employees. Needs assessments for employee training should be performed to create the training program's goals, which will later help define performance expectations. Only after they know their objectives and what method will be utilized for training, can they move to the design, creation, and implementation of the program.

Methods of instruction can be lectures, written materials, SIM labs, just-in-time (JIT) training, seminars, or workshops. Some training will be short, and others will be extended. The location and times should fit easily into the employee workday. A training and development program is most effective when it is designed to meet the organization's goals and improves the skills and competencies of employees.

Finally, each healthcare organization must clearly outline the expected training outcomes. These can be measured through various methods, including performance tests and other evaluations. The results of these evaluations must then be considered carefully and any problems they identify must be corrected in the training program. Without this final step, it will be impossible to know whether or not the training has achieved its goals.

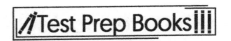

The leadership team of any healthcare organization is tasked with the development of strategies that improve the quality of current processes. It is necessary to eliminate waste, redundancies, and risks while working to expand currently successful strategies. Clinical excellence can only be obtained by developing processes that enhance the quality of healthcare delivery. Models of clinical excellence should be reviewed in order to determine the best model to utilize.

Knowing these positives and negatives and understanding how employees might react to both, the leadership team must provide the education and training in a way that is non-threatening while fostering employee buy-in. There must be a component that explains what benefits the employee will receive from participating in the training. Leaders must also incorporate change theory and project management processes into the training.

Training cannot simply be a leadership-oriented process, however. Unless it becomes habitual for employees at every level of a healthcare organization, training will fail to achieve its full effectiveness. Most organizational change is not maintained because it is not tied into the current culture, or it is so different from the culture that employees do not embrace it. These sorts of barriers should be identified early in the planning process and solutions should be incorporated from the very beginning of a training program. Continuous evaluation and feedback will help identify any continuing problems with implementation and any other issues that were not adequately addressed at the planning stage.

The **National Health Service Sustainability Model** is one example of a continuous quality improvement methodology that outlines four tools for identifying barriers to the continuation and success of quality improvement projects and improving the processes themselves. The first two tools are process control and performance boards, which communicate the results of improvement processes to both leadership and healthcare staff. The third tool is standard work, which is an outline of the current best practices for a given job. This outline also ensures that any improvements are implemented across the board and applied to all areas of patient care. The fourth tool is improvement huddles, short, frequent meetings that allow staff to anticipate and prevent problems, assess current performance, and build the habit of continuous improvement.

The leadership team developing each training must utilize all the tools available to deliver a quality education product. One particularly helpful tool that project managers can use to track their projects is regularly scheduled meetings where those involved in a project can exchange information about the project's progress. The project manager should often review several project elements during these status meetings:

- Task updates
- Schedule status update (behind or ahead of schedule?)
- Budget status update (under or over budget?)
- Quality/scope status update (maintaining desired scope/quality levels?)
- Current or anticipated issues (changes, risks, resource issues, etc.)
- Next steps

In order for the project manager to provide up-to-date information to the leadership team, status meetings should be held on a regular basis. The complexity of the project, the number of team members, and the amount of detail needed all affect the length and frequency of the meeting.

Successful meetings provide the project manager with timely updates on tasks and they let the team recognize milestone achievements, share information, and bring up any new problems. Unsuccessful

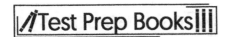

meetings tend to fail in those similar areas. Typically, they are poorly planned, lack preparation, and don't correctly prioritize items. These meetings do not receive useful input from all team members, and often fail to manage their time wisely.

Dysfunctional meetings also significantly disrupt progress of the project itself. Aside from obvious negative effects to the schedule, budget, and quality, dysfunctional meetings also lower the project manager's credibility. Because the project manager is typically viewed as responsible for the effectiveness of status review meetings, when meetings don't go smoothly, or aren't relevant or efficient, the team members may view the project manager as incompetent.

Quality Improvement Information

The final task involved in the development of performance, process, and quality standards involves the dissemination of the on-site survey findings within the organization. This part of the process is the most critical facet of the maintenance of performance standards. There can be no uniformity in the application of the results of the new and improved processes if there is no dissemination of the results. If staff members are not made aware of the findings of the organizational self-assessment, they cannot be expected to adhere to them.

Once the survey has been completed and the organization has been privately notified of the results, the information is made available to the public. Similar organizations, patients, and even prospective clinical and ancillary staff can readily review the information. The Agency for Healthcare Research and Quality benchmarks for quality indicators remain central to the maintenance of a culture of commitment to quality and safety. This competitive benchmarking allows the organization to closely monitor and compare the progression of proposed changes to the current processes with their competitors subsequent to their separate on-site survey.

Recent changes noted in the 2018 TJC survey process indicate that the decision categories include: accredited, accredited with follow-up survey, preliminary denial of accreditation, and denial of accreditation. All results, favorable or not, must be provided to the organization in an effort to promote transparency, responsibility, and accountability. The leadership team must utilize all of the information contained in the summary to guide the discussions and generate the momentum necessary to maintain any changes to current processes. Follow-up surveys for those that have received a designation other than accredited will typically occur within two months. When preliminary denial requires the organization to provide additional detail, the organization must provide the information within ten working days. If approved, the organization will become accredited. If no progress has been made, the organization may request a formal appeal with the review board to dispute the findings.

It is necessary to include ongoing staff training after the successful completion of the survey process. Without this, continued quality improvement is not sustained. Leadership must do more than simply encourage clinical staff to personally initiate continuing education. In order to remain current on industry standards, employees must be directed to the website of the accrediting entity to complete specific continuing education credit modules.

The Joint Commission is an approved provider of continuing education credits by the majority of professional organizations, including but not limited to: The Accreditation Council for Continuing Medical Education (ACME), Accreditation Council for Pharmacy Education (ACPE), and American Nurses Credentialing Center (ANCC). Clinical leadership should also consider attending the webinars and trainings offered by the accrediting entity. The training modules review pertinent information regarding

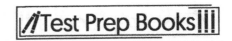

each standard, along with industry-specific rationales, and are essential for those involved in the survey process.

For organizations able to achieve accredited status through The Joint Commission, the journey is far from over. As previously mentioned, the procurement of accreditation for the entities that garner reimbursement are most valuable for sizable healthcare organizations. This is due to the federally deemed status that accredited organizations enjoy. For example, accomplishing accreditation through an entity with comparable or more stringent requirements, like The Joint Commission, enables a healthcare organization to waive the survey and certification process with CMS while continuing to remain eligible for federal reimbursement. The organization will receive a federal Condition of Participation certificate of compliance, either through governing entities like TJC or state auditors acting on the behalf of CMS. Despite the fact that each accrediting body has its own reaccreditation cycle, it is incumbent upon healthcare organizations to maintain a state of constant readiness.

Leadership must work diligently with clinical managers to encourage all employees to adopt a culture of safety. This can be accomplished internally through the dissemination of monthly risk reports to managers, to be shared during team meetings. Additional options include quarterly safety newsletters, rewards to top performers who exceed safety standards, and surveys regarding questions or concerns about quality.

Quality Improvement Opportunities

Identifying ways in which a healthcare organization's operations can be improved is an important role for the HQP. This is achieved through the first three steps of the Six Sigma methodology's **DMAIC** process: **defining** the organization's desired outcomes, **measuring** the current outcomes, and **analyzing** the data's relationship to operational processes. The final two steps are **improve** and **control.** These concepts are used when implementing identified opportunities. The precise results of each step will vary, depending on the healthcare organization the HQP works for, but the basic method used remains universal.

The defined outcome of improvement processes needs to be specific so that the outcome is measurable. A broad, nonspecific outcome, such as "healthier patients" or "speedier completion of the treatment program," is not an actionable goal. Rather, the HQP needs to identify data-driven metrics— for example, completion of an inpatient alcohol treatment program in an average of thirty days, reduced from forty days. This gives a specific goal that the HQP can devise quality improvement processes toward achieving.

Once the objective is defined, the HQP must determine how process toward that goal can best be measured. The purpose of measurement is to focus on the present. How is the healthcare organization currently performing? After understanding the healthcare organization's current outcomes, the HQP has the data necessary to analyze current operations. The HQP might implement a variety of measurement systems, depending on the type of operations the healthcare organization performs and the procedures currently in place for data collection. During analysis, the HQP organizes the raw data to come to conclusions about current outcomes.

One example is reviewing procedural notes for thirty days of operations in the surgery department to determine the total number of instances in which the patient developed an infection after surgery. Once the reports have been reviewed, the HQP determines the percentage of patients who had an infection

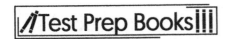

and begins reviewing the reports more closely. Their goal is to determine what common causes, if any, can be found from procedure to procedure.

As an HQP, managing a healthcare organization's limited resources is another important facet to quality improvement. The HQP's job is not just to use DMAIC to identify target areas for improvement but also to determine the degree of importance of these objectives. A useful tool for deciding which outcome is most important to improve is the **prioritization matrix.** This matrix is a tool that considers each of an organization's healthcare quality objectives from the perspective of **urgency** and **impact.** The HQP's analysis should consider urgency and impact from the perspective of the people receiving services from the healthcare organization—not with a focus on what would be convenient or cost-saving for the organization. This is an important principle of quality patient-first healthcare.

An objective is urgent if achieving it is time-sensitive—for example, revising an organization's safety procedures to follow new regulatory guidance, which will come into effect in sixty days. Due to the timeline and the possible legal consequences if the organization does not abide by the regulations, this task is quite urgent.

An objective is impactful if achieving it will improve the quality of client care. For example, reducing wait times in a hospital's emergency department by 20 percent speeds the ease with which patients receive potentially life-saving care. This is very impactful to the organization's healthcare quality.

Urgency and impact can sometimes overlap in the field of healthcare. Taking corrective action to counteract a sudden increase in mortality rates during surgery is an example of a task that is both urgent and impactful.

One common process development tool to quantify urgency and impact is a **SIPOC diagram.** This diagram defines each step of a process before it's implemented in terms of suppliers, inputs, processes, outputs, and customers (SIPOC). It ensures that all resources are in place when needed and notes critical inputs that are the most important.

When determining where to spend an organization's resources, the HQP should use the principles of the prioritization matrix. This helps them decide which objectives to achieve first due to their combined high urgency and impact. Of the two factors, impact is more important because it has a direct relationship to the quality of care. Thus, the HQP should weigh an objective's impact more highly than its urgency if deciding between multiple objectives that they rate similarly on the matrix.

Teams, Roles, Responsibilities, and Scope

It is often necessary to periodically evaluate processes to eliminate waste, remove redundancies, and reduce risks, while working to expand on the gains of currently successful practices. The implementation and evaluation processes include several key items. Key stakeholders and business leaders in healthcare organizations have an expectation of sustainable change, so the best approach is to be both innovative and imaginative. Once the parameters and goals of the project have been clearly defined, defects can be rooted out and eliminated. If the tactics are successful in their implementation, the end result will help to encourage agency-specific changes aligned with the mission, goals, and values of the host organization. The team seeks out opportunities to add value to the consumer experience and improve the overall experience.

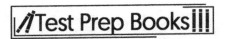

In the rapidly-changing healthcare marketplace, intermittent evaluation of the effectiveness of an organization's culture is critical. Organizational excellence cannot be built if the departments, teams, and employees are not immersed in a culture that recognizes the importance of performance improvement standards. When the staff expects to be evaluated and rewarded for adherence to performance standards, the organization can become more competitive. It is also necessary for the leadership team to model being an effective team player. This top-down approach reinforces the company culture of competence and excellence. Moving from individual to collective accountability requires significant skill. Team-building efforts must result in a cohesive team. It is crucial to qualify and quantify the effectiveness of team members, in order to emphasize the importance of a team approach to improving current policies, procedures, and processes. When employees feel that their contribution is linked to the mission, values, and goals of the host organization, they are more likely to accept responsibility for their results.

It is necessary to confirm the depth and breadth of each team member's knowledge base. Since direct management staff are typically well aware of the individual skill sets of their employees, they are frequently notified when the CPHQ professional must build a reasonable candidate pool for projects. Once assembled, the candidates are dispatched to their respective teams and the real work of team building can begin.

One particularly effective team-building technique is **Bruce Tuckman's model**. This model for team building focuses on forming, storming, norming, performing and adjourning. Initially, the manager will begin **forming** the team. The primary goal in this phase is to encourage discussion among colleagues. Team members are chosen based on the areas of expertise necessary to achieve optimal results. Together, the team members will create the framework of the performance improvement plan (PIP). Next, the manager will need to quiet and calm the **storms**, or the naturally-occurring conflicts between different team members' communication styles. The goal of this step is to explain the stages of the process and confirm that each team member is aware of their expected contribution.

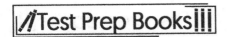
Mutual trust in the team is built as each team member begins to recognize their separate and collective strengths. Norming is next. **Norming** is when team members come to recognize each other's strengths and resolve their differences. Members are encouraged to assume responsibility for their assigned roles. The manager acts as scaffolding, keeping the team members on task and fostering more collaboration. The next stage in Tuckman's model is defined as **performing**. During this phase, the manager can begin to take a less direct role and delegate activities to team members. Essentially, letting them do it by themselves builds each team member's confidence, competence, and skill set, which will cement individual accountability. **Adjourning** is when the project comes to a close and the team moves on, appreciating and reflecting on their growth as a team.

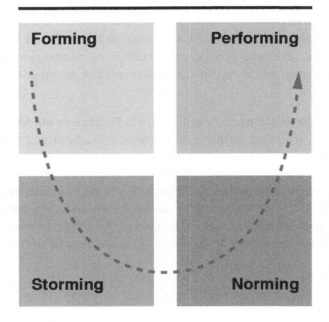

Four stages of team development

Councils and Committees

In order to develop quality initiatives, the healthcare organization must designate quality-improvement councils and committees to build the foundation of excellence. The **American Healthcare Association (AHCA)** was established in 2012 in an effort to improve the quality of patient care in post-acute and long-term-care facilities. This initiative focuses on the achievement of favorably measurable outcomes by March 2021 in four specific areas:

- 10% reduction in hospitalizations
- 10% increase in overall customer satisfaction
- 15% increase in functional mobility outcomes
- 10% reduction in the administration of antipsychotic medications

These specific changes will improve the quality of care delivered and positively impact patient experiences. SMART goals are used to tie the safety activities to the strategic planning process. Roundtable discussions with members at each level of the healthcare team often reveal gaps in care that need to be addressed. Conducting quality strategy meetings may lead significant insights that can

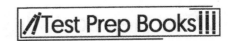

be used in the quality plan. During brainstorming sessions, council members look for viable options to reduce variations in quality by eliminating unnecessary or wasteful process steps. As an example, a SMART intervention for each safety initiative may involve several options: hourly rounding on every patient by nursing staff; fall precautions based on age, history, and medications; and remote access to the electronic health record (EHR) so physicians may readily view status changes. Each committee can be tasked with creating realistic methods to integrate the plan into current processes.

Innovative and Evidence-Based Practices

Innovation is the process of developing new ideas, methods, or actions that improve upon a predecessor. Innovation in healthcare aims to improve current processes, policies, or standards that are outdated or inefficient in an effort to improve outcomes. Advances in technology have changed the ways healthcare teams research, retrieve, and spread information. It is necessary to identify current trends that will show where, why, and how to allocate resources. The leadership team must be able to use predictive analytics and move toward innovative solutions. Progress cannot exist without innovation.

One of the primary responsibilities of the leadership team is to remain informed of the fluctuations in industry standards. These changes can provide the foundation for continued innovation in each particular healthcare organization. To ensure that they remain up to date, some organizations may wish to create specific positions for leadership in strategy and innovation, while others may prefer to have the entire leadership team take on this responsibility.

Two of the most promising healthcare innovations of this decade include telemedicine and predictive technologies. **Telemedicine**, or **telehealth**, has reformed healthcare delivery across the country. Providers can now conduct patient assessments, prescribe medications, and collaborate with other medical professionals remotely, via Skype, telephone, email, and secure chatrooms. Distance health eliminates the constraints of geography and mobility, and allows providers access to increasing numbers of previously underserved populations.

Predictive technologies, like patient analytics and medical informatics, help healthcare organizations remain ahead of the curve. Moving beyond the basic EHR, predictive analytics can create a multilingual medical record system. Although efficient, most systems do not communicate with each other. EHRs at two different offices may have software that cannot communicate with each other. This complicates the process and moves further away from a paperless system. Creating a standardized medical software or multilingual software that translates any data into useable information is required to create a more cohesive EHR system. Information technologists have started working on these issues. Other future innovations include the use of 3D printers to create prostheses, implantable devices, surgical tools, and instruments.

During this process, it's important for the HQP to not just review the available information but to also ask themselves if the available information is sufficient to form actionable conclusions. At times, the correct result from reviewing quality control data is that the HQP requires more information. One noteworthy flaw in such analysis to be wary of is **survivorship bias.** This bias occurs when an analyst focuses on successful outcomes, seeking to determine why they succeeded, and overlooks examining why unsuccessful outcomes failed.

If the HQP determines that they have insufficient data to provide valid suggestions for improving the organization's operations, it is important that they suggest implementation of additional quality control techniques. This supports continuous improvement of the quality of the organization's operations. Some common methods of additional data collection include employee reviews, requiring additional documentation detail, discharge interviews with people the organization serves, and anonymous surveys for both employees and people served to provide feedback.

Change Facilitation

Organizational leaders must have a specific skill set in order to lead and facilitate change. They need good business judgment, strategic insight, comfort with uncertainty, social intelligence, self-awareness, and people management skills in order to thrive. Change management must be a core competency because embracing change and taking risks are requirements for healthcare. The most effective method of facilitating change includes a combination of theories and stages of change.

There are many different theories related to behavioral change and the stages that an individual goes through in order to achieve lasting change. A few of these theories are detailed here.

The **Transtheoretical Model** focuses on the thinking process a person goes through even before the active process of change begins. This model has 6 stages:

- **Precontemplation** occurs when a person has not started thinking about change and may be oblivious to any need for change.

- **Contemplation** happens when a person is still not ready to make change but is beginning to think about it and may intend to make changes in the foreseeable future.

- During the **preparation** stage, the person is prepared to make changes in the immediate future and begins to actively get ready to make changes, such as through creating plans and setting goals.

- **Action** happens when a person makes clear and decisive changes.

- **Maintenance** occurs when the changes are sustained and become enduring habits that continue for a significant period of time.

- **Termination** occurs when the person has overcome both unwanted behaviors and the temptation to return to them.

Lewin's model of change has three distinct stages: unfreeze, change, and refreeze. Just as an ice cube can be melted, remolded, and refrozen, this model theorizes that the same process works with people seeking change. The first stage, **unfreeze**, involves looking at a situation and recognizing the need for change. It is helping people challenge their current attitudes, habits, or behaviors, in order to make a persuasive case for why change is needed. During the next stage, **change**, new methods are sought, examined, and accepted. Finally, during the **refreeze** stage, these new habits and behaviors are solidified.

In Kotter's 8 step change theory, the first step is to **create urgency**, or to make use of a crisis situation in order to emphasize how urgently change is needed. The next step is to **form a coalition**, which is a team of professionals and family members who will work together to support the person making a change. After that it is important to **create a vision and strategy for change**, with goals and objectives, and then **communicate the vision** to all those who are involved in the process. The next step is to identify and

40

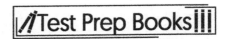

remove obstacles that might stand in the way of a person achieving the goals they set. The sixth stage is to create short-term wins by recognizing and encouraging the small behavioral changes that are achieved. Once these small steps have been acknowledged, it is easy to build on the change, turning the small changes into bigger, long-lasting changes. The final step is to anchor the change, making the changes a permanent part of life.

As it applies to healthcare management, diffusion can be defined as the passive and unplanned spread of new practices. Dissemination occurs when new practices are actively spread; this usually involves specific and carefully planned targets and methodologies. Implementation occurs when those practices are adopted and integrated within a healthcare setting. The spread concept refers to the rate at which newly disseminated ideas or innovations are adopted and implemented. Leaders, acting as change agents, must always be prepared to employ these tactics to facilitate the changes necessary to improve the overall quality of care.

The Diffusion of Innovation theory states that innovations in healthcare spread over time, in five distinct and predictable phases: knowledge, persuasion, decision, implementation, and confirmation. Acting as the change agent, leaders must identify the innovators within the organization and appeal to them in the preliminary stages of the new project, providing knowledge about the concept. It is important to focus on the relative advantage, or benefits, of adopting the new idea over the old. Change agents must also consider ways to persuade innovators of the trialability of the concept, or it if can be implemented on a trial basis, without full commitment. It is essential to confirm that the chosen innovators will communicate their decision to implement the new strategy to stakeholders within the organization. As the use of the new concept or technology spreads within the organization, its implementation will phase out previous behaviors in favor of progress.

Performance Improvement Methods

As mentioned earlier, there are four terms that apply to starting a new process or method in an organization:

- **Diffusion** occurs when new practices spread passively, without deliberate implementation.

- **Dissemination** occurs when new practices are deliberately implemented and actively spread. Plans for dissemination usually identify a target audience and outline specific methodologies.

- **Implementation** occurs when those practices are adopted and integrated within a healthcare setting.

- **Spread** refers to the rate at which newly disseminated ideas or innovations are adopted and implemented.

One key principle is that quality insurance cannot be a one-and-done effort. No matter how good and thorough the implemented methodologies are, healthcare processes must be continuously evaluated

41

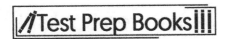
and improved in order to continue to provide quality of care. Lessons learned can be used to shift strategy and try new interventions.

Plan-Do-Study-Act Model

PDSA

One of the most useful healthcare improvement models is the PDSA cycle, illustrated in the figure above. PDSA stans for Plan, Do, Study, Act – the four fundamental elements of any improvement plan or methodology. These four steps lay out a continuous cycle of evaluation and improvement, based on the idea that all elements of a healthcare system are interdependent, and even small changes in one area can have large effects across the system. The PDSA cycle provides a straightforward methodology that involves staff at every level of a healthcare organization in the process of discovering problems, coming up with solutions, and then testing the new systems. Because it involves the providers who use the healthcare systems on a daily basis as well as the organization's leadership, this model provides the greatest likelihood for systemic, continuous, and successful improvement in quality care.

The original version of this model was developed in 1950 by Dr. W Edwards Deming as the PDCA model (Plan, Do, Check Act). However, Deming and others later proposed the PDSA model because the *Study* phase was more effective than the original *Check* phase of the PDCA model. Deming felt that there needed to be additional reflection on the results of early testing.

42

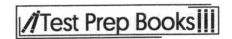

The four parts of the PDSA model are explained below.

Plan

The first step in the PDSA cycle focuses on defining goals, developing a strategy, and determining the measurements for success. When using PDSA to improve a healthcare process, the first step is to identify possible goals and strategies to implement. Each goal must be specific, measurable, and feasible. Having the goal clearly articulated will support communication across the healthcare organization and will ensure that each staff member knows the objective.

The second part of the Plan step is to develop a strategy that seem likely to achieve the stated objective. This strategy must consider potential barriers to implementation as well as the likelihood of achieving the stated goal. For example, are there any cultural issues or organizational compatibility issues that will make a given strategy difficult to implement? The strategy must also be streamlined to directly suit the specific problem being addressed. Utilizing input from staff, patients, and members is a good way to achieve this portion of the Plan step.

The third part of the Plan step is to lay out the measurements that will determine whether or not the strategy was successful. It is vitally important to pay attention to the desired outcome and make sure that the success metrics will actually measure whether or not that outcome has been achieved. Tools such as control and run charts, dashboard reports, and tables of aggregated data are all means by which the success metrics can be presented and assessed.

Do

The second step of the PDSA cycle is where the plan is implemented. This involves preparing a written action plan for the healthcare organization that states the goals and strategies developed in the Plan step. It should also include specific action items necessary for the implementation of the strategies and a calendar that ensures various actions are completed in the correct order and that the overall timeline is feasible. Utilizing the Gantt chart format is extremely helpful at this stage. It is also important during this step to ensure that the measures to be taken directly address the key elements of the improvements that the organization wishes to make. There should not be so many measures that they overwhelm the organization's staff, but there should not be so few measures that the organization does not have sufficient information to track the success of the changes made.

Study

The third step of the PDSA cycle is where the results of the plan are measured to see if they are successful or if there are additional issues and areas that need improvement. Small-scale testing is particularly useful at this point because it allows for corrections in smaller teams or areas before a plan is implemented more broadly. It is also easier to implement incremental modifications to a plan in a smaller area rather than throughout the organization as a whole; with small-scale testing, every element of the plan is more responsive to change and can be more easily measured, and if a plan does not work it the failure will not be organization wide. The primary element in this step is to study and review the results of the small-scale testing and adjust the plan as necessary to achieve the stated goals. Once the small-scale testing is a success, the plan can more easily be implemented across the entire organization. An additional benefit of achieving success with small-scale testing before wider implementation is that enthusiasm and positive word-of-mouth acknowledge early successes, which will most likely encourage participation and engagement across the organization when it is time for wider implementation.

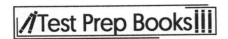

Act

The fourth step of the PDSA cycle brings the cycle full circle by evaluating what has been learned throughout the process and using it to adapt and alter the goals, methodologies, action items, etc., or, if necessary, go back to the drawing board and revise the current initiative or compose a new initiative altogether. Implementation is expanded to reach sustainable improvement. While all of the other steps are necessary, the Act step of the PDSA cycle is the most important element of ensuring continuous improvement and is the area where healthcare organizations focus the majority of their time.

The PDSA cycle is a flexible methodology that can be customized to fit the needs of any organization. There is no set length of time that a cycle must take; instead, that is left up to the particular organization. Additionally, while are no rules for frequency of monitoring, most organizations choose to monitor either monthly or quarterly.

Lean model of continuous improvement

Identify

Opportunities in the process workflow

Review

How changes work for the team?

Plan

How can the current process be improved?

Execute

Implement changes

Six Sigma and Lean

Lean Six Sigma is a fact- and data-based quality improvement philosophy that prioritizes the prevention of events over detection. The method improves customer satisfaction and the bottom-line by reducing or eliminating process variations, inefficiencies, and cycle time. Additionally, it encourages the use of workflow standardization to gain a competitive business advantage. Every employee should be involved in Lean Six Sigma because it can be applied to any process where variations or waste are found. The Six Sigma methodology treats all forms of work as processes that are able to be defined, measured, analyzed, improved, and controlled. Processes can be described in terms of their inputs (x) and outputs (y), and if their inputs are controlled, the outputs will be as well. This allows a process to be quantified and expressed mathematically as $y = f(x)$.

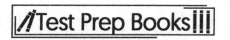

Continued progress in the field of quality improvement has blurred the line between Six Sigma and Lean. The term "Lean Six Sigma" is being used with increasing frequency because both Six Sigma and Lean offer benefits in process improvement. The Six Sigma philosophy is focused on eliminating variations and improving control in processes; it achieves these goals through quantitative methods including statistical data analysis and the process of designing and testing experiments and hypotheses. Lean, on the other hand, is focused on removing waste and inefficiencies and promoting work standardization and flow; it achieves these goals through continuous quality improvement, visual controls, and organization. Both process improvement philosophies aim to provide customers with the best quality, value, delivery, and nimbleness.

Lean has been used by top organizations to maximize their efficiency and effectiveness, reduce waste, and map value streams to gain enhanced understanding of their throughput. Organizations using Six Sigma assign teams to handle clearly-defined projects that will directly benefit their bottom line. Training in statistical thinking is provided to all levels of the organization and key individuals are given further training in advanced statistics and project management. Practitioners of the Lean Six Sigma approach must participate in a series of certification levels, known as belts. Each level signifies the practitioner's knowledge, training, and expertise. A Master Black Belt coaches black belts and green belts. A Black Belt coaches project teams and leads problem-solving projects. A Green Belt helps with data collection and analysis for Black Belt projects and leads Green Belt projects. The Yellow Belt acts as a member of the project team and reviews process improvements and the White Belt works in problem-solving teams as a beginner.

Six Sigma utilizes many qualitative and quantitative tools for process improvement, including statistical process control (SPC), control charts, process mapping, root cause analysis (RCA), and failure mode and effects analysis (FMEA). The main methodology Six Sigma uses is **DMAIC**, which stands for define, measure, analyze, improve, and control. This method lays out the steps for Six Sigma practitioners to follow, which begins with determining the problem and concludes by laying out long-term solutions. Although DMAIC is not the only methodology used by Six Sigma practitioners, it is by far one of the most common, and as such it is well-recognized. Six Sigma says that QI (quality improvement) is a continuous process that is required to maintain the gains from a project. The target for quality performance in Six Sigma is only 3.4 defects or failures per million occurrences.

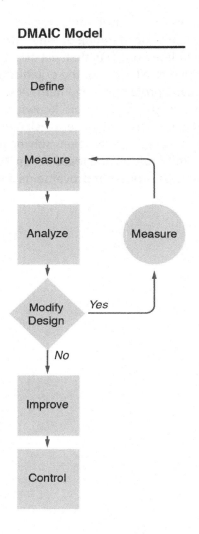

Quality Tools and Techniques

When creating a blueprint for current policies and procedures, it is necessary to consider the most appropriate tools for the job. Depending on the scope of the project, the size of the organization, and the goals, the project management team must use certain tools to measure a baseline and terminal success. One of the most integral tools of an effective project management team is a commitment to cooperative and collaborative teamwork. Most project management teams use tools in the early phase of the project to define the limits of the intervention. Each rung of the process ladder is summarized or

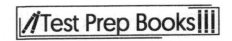

identified. The team creates the high-level process map, adding each individual facet of the processes as needed. The map reveals which steps need improvement. The process maps are typically designed as a visual representation of the current processes, in an effort to find areas of redundancy and lack of value to the customer. This is always necessary to accomplish the goal of the project. Using clearly-labeled process maps, the team determines the basic definitions of the variables involved to accurately measure the problem.

An alternate form of program evaluation involves a more outcome-based method. Most CPHQ professionals work to determine how any given process in the system might fail. **Failure mode and effect analysis (FMEA)** seeks to uncover ways that business leaders can most effectively operationalize the efforts of frontline staff. The purpose is to find solutions before they become necessary. This form of program evaluation uses a qualitative approach to better understand and prevent future and ongoing threats to patient safety. The actual staff must be involved, as they can help to identify gaps in the practical application of the results. Both actual and perceived failures in practice are examined. Three questions are asked and answered:

- What is the severity of the effect on the customer?
- How often is this event likely to occur?
- How easily can the customer identify the problem?

Each category is ranked according to potential effect, severity of the effect, potential cause and probability of occurrence, and detection severity. Ranked in severity from 1 to 10 by the team, they are placed in descending order to begin the brainstorming portion of the problem-solving process. The assembled team will then begin working to create solutions to the identified problems. Wherever the actual failures are ranked as a 5 or greater, the risk assessment team will target how to implement the most effective solutions. The strategy continues with the team developing an action plan for erroneous or unnecessary steps in the current processes. As the momentum builds, more solutions become apparent.

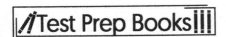

One final format for depicting statistical data is the **fishbone**, or cause and effect diagram. Named precisely due to the shape, this diagram focuses largely on depicting the precipitating factors, or performing root cause analysis, for an event or outcome. Those root causes can then be separated into more meaningful categories. Practitioners can then periodically engage in the brainstorming and process mapping necessary to clarify potential solutions during each phase of the project. This format for evaluating the effectiveness of current processes is also useful in achieving results aligned with the objectives and value drivers of any organization.

Example of a Fishbone Diagram

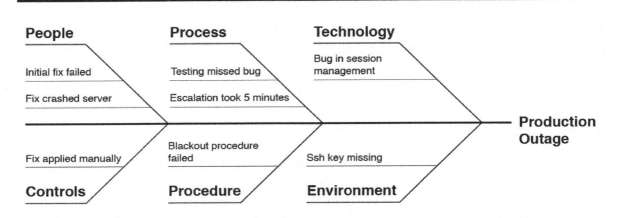

Project Timelines and Deliverables

Successful performance and process improvement requires the team to participate in monitoring of the timeline and deliverable objectives. As previously mentioned, the project team needs to determine the most necessary aspects of the initiative and align them with performance metrics. When performance metrics are reviewed, the focus can shift from problem-focused to solution-focused. The apparent gaps in outcomes related to the VOC and the VOB must be addressed and the staff retrained in an effort to standardize policies, procedures, and processes. The primary goal for process improvement in program evaluation is for the team to maintain the gains achieved by identifying statistically significant processes across the organization. The value added to the customer's experience is of paramount importance. This will encourage staff adherence to new process changes, thereby ensuring continued compliance and less variation. This continuation of the define stage of the DMAIC model encourages the team to ask a series of questions as listed below. The subsequent answers will be the driving force behind all the project charter initiatives.

- Which objectives must be accomplished first?
- What are the tangible deliverables for this project?
- What is the current state?
- What is the vision for the future state?
- How frequently will progress towards the goal be evaluated?
- How exactly will progress towards the ultimate goal be measured?

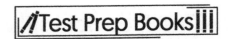

- What is the final due date for the project?
- What are the value-added benefits to the customer?

Simply put, performance and process improvement techniques focus on delivering value to the customer.

Performance and process improvement is essentially a game of remove and replace. Antiquated or ineffective processes are removed, and they are replaced with activities designed to increase the likelihood of success. The assembled project management team must define the projected outputs, or deliverables, to be received by the customer. Next, the team must determine whether the effort of the staff to implement the new processes is outweighed by the reward delivered to consumers. The cost-benefit analysis is an activity used in the Lean Six Sigma methodology as a way to determine the true costs of a potential solution compared to the actual benefits. It is frequently necessary to conduct a cost-benefit analysis at the start of the project charter, during the define phase, and throughout implementation of the project.

While working toward creating a cohesive plan of action, the key managers and decision-makers must be well aware of the KPIs. KPIs can best be defined as measurable data that will further indicate whether the goals are attainable. These performance measures enable the team to operationalize success. When considering what may go wrong, the team must determine whether the individual actions in the newly developed processes are logical. If the steps are too complex, they may be abandoned in favor of old habits. For this reason, mistake-proofing is used, which entails developing the necessary countermeasures to solve any problems before they actually occur. Although each activity in mistake-proofing can build on the previous step, the steps are also independent. Finally, the timeliness of the resolution of the PIP is crucial. Each initiative should have a measurable timeline, but performance improvement in the organization as a whole is an ongoing commitment to excellent performance. When performance improvement projects are considered as fluid in nature, it becomes evident that the periodic evaluation of their effectiveness is mandatory.

Team Effectiveness

It's important to keep track of team attendance. Late arrivals, early departures, and unusual patterns of sick days are all indicators that a team member's not meeting their maximum potential. There are several possible reasons for low attendance, including poor motivation, health issues, and burnout. These absences may put additional pressure on the rest of the team that has to pick up the slack for missing members. It's ideal to address issues of understaffing and overwork as early as possible to avoid risking the team's health and happiness.

It's crucial that team members are able to finish their work on time. Ideally, they must be able to effectively prioritize tasks and have a thorough understanding of the time and resources available to them to complete their work efficiently. It's also important for organizations to identify team members that take initiative. Individuals who frequently take initiative are better suited for fast-paced workplaces that need employees to quickly adapt to changes and be proactive. Although it can be difficult to measure initiative-taking, the team leader may quantify how often a team member takes initiative. The most important, but most difficult, metric to define is the quality of a team member's work. Those who are invested in their work are more likely to achieve high levels of success, and it's important to recognize these achievements.

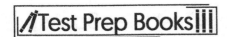

Performance Improvement Projects and Solutions

Methods for Evaluating Success

The effective evaluation of performance and process training begins with the determination of the most accurate and appropriate method of measuring success. The team may need to return to the data-collection phase if data are unclear. The analysis phase will reveal the data associated to the problems identified in the define stage of this methodology. If it is determined that there are several identified areas for improvement, the leadership team must scrutinize the data to verify the most crucial areas in need of improvement. These key areas will encourage the team to isolate the primary root causes for a deeper dive into analysis.

One of the primary tools utilized in the analysis phase is the **Pareto chart**. This quality-control tool helps to emphasize the most impactful problems in order to allocate the appropriate amount of resources to rectify the problem. The **Pareto diagram** is a graphic representation of the data collected to aid in the visualization of the frequency and root causes of deficits associated with the current processes.

Although the data may not actually meet the basic 100% with regard to total distribution, the data will clearly indicate the most significant variables. This display of the results will help to both quantify and qualify the variables. Pareto charts allow the leadership team to focus on operations that deliver on, rather than detract from, the value of the services provided. The data gleaned from the Pareto chart can be the foundation of the process-improvement initiative. Once the team is aware of which problems to address, the next step is to develop creative solutions. Through the internal benchmarking exercise, the team can look at departments in-house with similar issues and subsequent successes. Identifying the top performers in similar roles to participate in staff retraining is essential. Colleagues can normalize the new processes and demonstrate their effectiveness.

The competitive benchmarking option suggests looking to organizations with similar concerns that have succeeded in improving their outcomes. This is particularly effective among healthcare organizations that already possess or are seeking to obtain comparable accreditation. This task can be accomplished through reviewing the publicized summary of a competitor on the website of the governing body.

Diffusion

A strong commitment to improving processes and employee performance improves the organization's ability to compete in the healthcare marketplace. Evaluating the success of performance improvement measures is integral to the maintenance of project management. Best practices of performance improvement include a willingness to seek a better understanding of the VOC, or voice of the patient, as well as the VOB. It is the critical examination of the answers to these questions that will guide the expansion of the process improvement implementation from general to specific goals and change the level of difficulty for measuring the effectiveness of the interventions from problematic to less challenging. It will always be more advantageous to consider the importance of adding to, rather than detracting from, the value delivered to customers.

Developed by Everett Rogers in 1962, the **theory of the Diffusion of Innovation** tries to explain how ideas and technology spread over time. Innovation is the action or process of developing a new idea, methodology, or action that improves on its predecessor. As it applies to performance improvement, diffusion can be defined as the passive and unplanned spread of new practices. This diffusion is said to occur through a **five-step decision-making process** containing the following steps: knowledge, persuasion, decision, implementation, and confirmation.

- **Knowledge**: When the individual is exposed to a new idea but lacks information about it.
- **Persuasion**: The individual is interested in the new idea and pursues information about it.
- **Decision**: The individual weighs the advantages/disadvantages and a decision is made about whether or not to accept the new idea.
- **Implementation**: The individual uses the new idea during this stage and determines its usefulness.
- **Confirmation**: The individual decides whether or not to continue using the new idea.

Effective performance improvement techniques involve training all groups in the organization. Managers must always remain diligent and remain aware that the responses of the process innovators, early adopters, and the early majority will most likely determine the success of the newly developed process and performance expectation. Once it has been determined which of the newly developed process modifications have been adopted, and to what degree, it will be necessary to determine their success.

The most necessary step in evaluating the success of process improvement is the execution of the pilot study. Participants in the pilot study need to be polled regarding their overall experience with the processes, the software, and any unexpected outcomes. It is crucial to engage with the members of the team, both individually and as a group. Which participants were responsible for encouraging other team members to endorse, adopt, and execute the process changes? Who are the process champions? How long did it take to integrate the changes in with current procedures? What, specifically, did the innovators perceive to be most effective? In what ways did the proposed process changes fail? During the improve phase of the DMAIC model, the goal is to assimilate all the ideas into a strategic plan that prioritizes opportunities for improvement. Additionally, the goal is to amend all processes associated with changes, including any process flows and job aids. Questions must be asked and answered in order for the team to adequately determine the most logical steps to document the agreed-upon process changes and improvements.

Document Results

The ultimate goal for the team professional is to empower the organization's leadership to improve their employees' performance. Strategies that are no longer effective in bringing out the best in their employees must be replaced. Performance improvement planning also requires the team to collaborate with the leadership team and guide the development of a multidimensional approach that capitalizes on the internal strengths of the organization and minimizes weaknesses. During the control phase of the DMAIC model, the team needs to implement strategies to determine the sustainability and benefits of the newly defined processes. The team looks for feasible answers to the questions asked in the improve phase.

Monitoring and reviewing the process improvement project consists of assembling the team to review all the findings associated with the pilot study and the subsequent brainstorming sessions. Lessons learned through streamlining the ill-fitting portions of the new process will be applied. The project manager must periodically assess whether the team is on task, and it is also crucial to collect the lessons learned during each phase. This is most effective during the break-out brainstorming sessions, and once the managers have been trained on the newly developed processes.

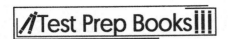

The evaluation team will also return to review the issue logs and initiate thought process mapping, to further eliminate wasteful steps. How will gains be maintained? Have periodic process audits been established to assess the use and effectiveness of the solutions to ensure that staff do not revert to previous activities? In what ways have the results been leveraged to prevent occurrences of similar issues in all departments impacted by the problem? What is the most effective display of the findings? In an effort to prevent a recurrence of previously identified defects, the team must verify that the outcome of their action plan is functional, and they must further validate that the outcomes are aligned with the predetermined targets. Verification refers to testing that the proposed solution produces the desired outcome, while validation is a process that ensures that the outcome actually solves the problem. Once the results of the initial project are confirmed, a new project is identified, and the process begins again with the next identified issue of the organization.

The team must maintain an awareness of the nature of performance and process improvement. The goal is to train the leadership teams on the best practices to conduct performance and process improvement reviews periodically, utilizing the most effective methods. Once proficient in the Lean Six Sigma methodology, trained leaders become trainers themselves. The professional accountability and adherence to ongoing performance and process improvement measures afford the chosen organization the opportunity to remain competitive in the healthcare marketplace.

Practice Quiz

1. What diagram is used to brainstorm all possible causes of a problem in order to sort ideas into categories that ultimately lead to a solution?
   a. Plan-Do-Check-Act (PDCA) cycle
   b. Fishbone diagram
   c. Quality planning road map
   d. Value stream map

2. Which is NOT one of the five principles of lean thinking?
   a. Empowerment
   b. Flow and pull
   c. Employee satisfaction
   d. Perfection

3. Susan is preparing her team's department objectives that will be used to create individual goals and accomplishments for her employees' performance reviews. What should Susan ensure that each of these objectives includes?
   a. What the employee thinks should be changed in the department
   b. Specific, measurable, achievable, relevant, and time-bound aspects
   c. Professional growth, development, training, and learning opportunities
   d. Recognition and appreciation for previous performance and accomplishments

4. During which stage of team development might a team member be impolite when expressing frustrations about expectations toward another team member?
   a. Performing
   b. Storming
   c. Norming
   d. Forming

5. During a Failure Mode and Effects Analysis (FMEA), each category is ranked by all EXCEPT which of the following?
   a. The potential cause and probability of occurrence
   b. The cost of rectifying the cause
   c. The severity of the effect
   d. The potential effect

See answers on the next page.

Answer Explanations

1. B: The fishbone diagram is used to brainstorm all possible causes of a problem so that ideas can be sorted into categories that ultimately lead to a solution. The Plan-Do-Check-Act (PDCA) cycle is an ongoing evaluation of procedures and managerial policies leading to continuous improvement, and it is made up of four stages. The quality planning road map provides a more detailed approach to the activities associated with each of the three processes within Dr. Joseph M. Juran's Trilogy. Finally, a value stream map is a visual means to identify and analyze a specific business process within a company.

2. C: Employee satisfaction is not one of the five principles of lean thinking. The five principles include: value, creating a value stream, flow and pull, empowerment, and perfection.

3. B: Susan should ensure that each objective includes the SMART aspects: specific, measurable, achievable, relevant, and time-based. Without these aspects, an objective may not be met, or the status could be unknown. By including the SMART aspects, there can be a clear understanding of performance expectations. Choice *A* is incorrect because all language should be well-written, clear, concise, and specific, but without SMART aspects, there could still be misunderstandings as to what is to be accomplished. Choices *C* and *D* are inaccurate because professional development and recognition should be separate items contained within a performance review, distinct from performance objectives. If a training opportunity is to be an objective for an employee, the item should be written as an objective, containing the SMART aspects.

4. B: During the storming stage of team development, a team member may be impolite when expressing frustrations about expectations toward another team member. During the performing stage of team development, team members find it relatively easy to be part of the team and can be seen taking on various roles and responsibilities as needed. During the norming stage, the team members begin to grow closer to one another and respect the team leader as an authority figure. Finally, during the forming stage, members have a great deal of uncertainty about the team's leadership, structure, and purpose.

5. B: When conducting a FMEA, each category is ranked by potential effect, severity of the effect, the potential cause and probability of occurrence, and detection severity. The cost of fixing the potential issue is not considered. Ranked in severity from 1 to 10 by the team, the categories are placed in descending order to begin the brainstorming portion of the problem-solving process.

Population Health and Care Transitions

Health Status of Defined Populations

The health status of a population refers to a group of people's overall health and well-being. A population's health status can be measured using a variety of data and resources. Some indicators include mortality rates, life expectancy, quality of life, housing conditions, morbidity rates, occurrence of chronic diseases, and access to healthcare services. Reviewing these indicators provides insight into the behaviors of people within that population and is therefore an important part of measuring a population's health status.

Vital statistics are used to quantify information about births, deaths, and marriages within a population. They also provide important demographic information such as gender, age, and race. Tracking this kind of data provides a foundation for public health officials to identify areas of improvement. For example, analyzing mortality and morbidity rates by tracking deaths and causes of deaths over time allows public health officials to assess the effectiveness of policies and interventions currently in use. Mortality rates of specific diseases, such as diabetes or cancer, can also be examined to determine treatment options and disease prevention strategies that could be improved.

Examining a population's demographic characteristics allows targeted interventions and policies to be established when health disparities and inequities are identified. For example, analyzing demographic data could include reviewing certain racial or ethnic groups for specific diseases and higher mortality rates. Public health officials could then explore potential causes (such as limited access to healthcare services) and aim to create interventions that promote health outcomes. Primary sources for obtaining vital statistics data include birth/death certificates, census data, and data from state health departments. These sources are critical to proper understanding of a population's health status and areas where interventions may be needed.

Types of health outcomes data include the prevalence of certain health conditions and a person's quality of life. By monitoring the prevalence of specific health conditions, public health officials can identify areas where prevention and treatment options can be improved. For example, one could track health outcomes by reviewing rates of infectious diseases (such as influenza) and identifying more at-risk populations with which to implement targeted interventions with the goal of reducing spread and transmission of the flu. In addition, health outcomes data can be used to analyze a person's quality of life. To do this, areas of focus could include the number of visits to an emergency department, subsequent hospitalizations, and a patient's outcomes. Two resources that can be used to analyze health outcomes data are national health surveys and electronic health records (EHRs). National health surveys, like the National Health and Nutrition Examination Survey, collect data on health outcomes. Similarly, EHRs contain detailed information regarding a patient's health status and treatment outcomes. Both tools can be used to track health outcomes over time, which further assists public health officials as they work to improve health outcomes.

Environmental data should also be reviewed because it analyzes a person's health by examining housing conditions and air/water quality. Water contamination or air pollution can contribute to respiratory illnesses or other health problems that negatively affect a population. In addition, different climates contribute to specific health concerns (e.g., diseases spread by mosquitoes or heat-related illnesses). Housing conditions are also important to consider as they can have a significant impact on health. Poor housing conditions can lead to asthma and other respiratory illnesses. The Environmental Protection Agency (EPA) has state and local departments that collect and monitor environmental data. Public health officials can use such data to understand a certain population's unique health status and develop interventions to improve the population's health.

Improvement Initiatives

The CDC describes population health as a flexible, multidisciplinary approach to healthcare that enables health departments to implement local changes using various policies. The goals of population health management are to identify, address, and improve health outcomes of individuals throughout a community using improvement initiatives. Some examples of these initiatives include providing health education, engaging family members in patient care, and implementing health programs.

Providing education on healthy behaviors assists individuals in making knowledgeable decisions about their health. The National Institutes of Health (NIH) defines health behaviors as actions an individual takes that affect their overall health. These are actions that lead to better health, such as eating more nutritious foods, increasing physical activity, and decreasing disease risk by reducing alcohol or tobacco intake.

Some ways that health education can be integrated into improvement initiatives include promoting public health campaigns, hosting health fairs, and providing online resources. The purpose of a public health campaign is to promote healthy behaviors that both improve health and prevent disease. The NIH provides many resources and models that can be used to better inform the community. A few sample public health campaigns provided by the NIH include: Move Your Way, Learn More Breathe Better, and Take Good Care. These programs could be promoted throughout the community via social media, billboards, or radio ads. Similar to public health campaigns, health fairs provide individuals with health resources at a community level. Health fairs are useful ways to share health education through prevention screenings, demonstrations of healthy habits, and other initiatives that raise awareness of health risks. Such education is a valuable tool that can encourage individuals to implement healthy behaviors. Another way to empower individuals to take control of their health is through online resources. Online resources include webinars, interactive tools, and educational videos. The CDC, NIH, and American School Health Association each provide different resources and are just a few of the many options available online for health education.

Involving family members in a patient's care is another strategy that may be used to manage population health. It provides support to the patient and allows family members to feel more connected. As such, it's important for healthcare workers to communicate clearly to both the patient and their family members when providing education. Family members who ensure that the patient is exercising, eating well, and taking their medications are a valuable resource to the patient. These actions contribute to better health management, fewer adverse effects, and improved health outcomes.

Implementing health programs is another effective population health management strategy that helps improve health outcomes. Health promotion programs can be integrated by implementing new wellness programs, incorporating health education into existing programs, and using digital tools. Wellness programs are great resources that can be implemented in workplaces, schools, and community centers. For example, programs might promote physical exercise, healthy eating, or disease prevention. Each of these programs can be adjusted to meet each specific population's needs. Incorporating health education into existing programs is another way to improve health outcomes. Programs that help individuals manage chronic diseases like diabetes and heart disease already exist, but there is room for

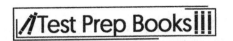
improvement. Patients with chronic diseases could also be educated on maintaining a healthy weight or reducing stress. This approach allows patients with existing conditions to further improve their heath. Lastly, digital tools, such as smartphone apps and wearable devices, are especially helpful when integrating health promotion. These resources help engage younger populations who may otherwise not be reached due to barriers such as limited resources or lack of access. The overall goal of implementing health programs is to achieve the best health outcomes for individuals and communities.

Prevention, Wellness, and Disease Management

Prevention, wellness, and disease management are essential components when providing improvement initiatives to individuals and communities. Prevention is a frontline solution for implementing healthcare initiatives because it attempts to promote healthy behaviors and outcomes. The goal of prevention is to decrease occurrence frequency and severity of diseases within a community. A few examples of prevention include immunizing, encouraging physical activity, promoting healthy eating, and implementing screening programs.

Immunizations have been proven to help protect populations from illnesses like polio, influenza, and measles. Promoting vaccines is one of the most effective methods to prevent the spread of communicable diseases. One way to accomplish this is through the use of immunization campaigns. The World Health Organization (WHO) provides examples of these campaigns, whose overall goal is to deliver as many vaccines as needed to targeted individuals. Screening programs could be included during immunization campaigns as they are simple tools that can detect a variety of illnesses. One way to implement them is by providing individuals with risk assessments, which can screen for various types of cancer or chronic illnesses based on a person's family history, age, and medical history. These screenings provide simple, effective ways to improve health outcomes.

The CDC states that physical activity not only helps a person feel better, but it also promotes better sleep, decreased stress, and reduced risk of chronic diseases. Encouraging physical activity is a valid way to promote better health outcomes. Healthy eating provides similar benefits and should also be promoted throughout the community. Some ways to promote healthy behaviors include implementing policies that encourage physical activity and healthy eating as well as increasing the accessibility of healthy food options. An example of a workplace policy that promotes physical activity and healthy eating could be the initiation of a wellness program that might include offering healthier food choices in the cafeteria or providing access to exercise facilities. Likewise, education on healthy behaviors should be presented to the public (whether in the workplace or other community locations) to provide resources and encouragement for implementing a healthier lifestyle.

Wellness is another component of improvement initiatives because it encompasses the overall health and well-being of an individual. Instead of focusing specifically on an illness or condition, it emphasizes a balance between mental, physical, and emotional health. Some strategies that could be used for improving wellness include teaching stress management and providing mental health support. Stress is known to have adverse effects on a person's physical and mental health; as such, learning to manage one's stress through relaxation and other coping techniques is important. Likewise, providing resources for mental health, such as therapy or counseling, should also be included in wellness initiatives. Sustaining these healthy behaviors reduces the risk for chronic illnesses and contributes to a healthier lifestyle.

Lastly, disease management provides a person with resources to manage chronic conditions like heart disease, diabetes, or asthma. Learning to manage these illnesses can prevent further complications and improve a patient's quality of life. A coordinated approach for disease management is comprised of early detection, treatment, and monitoring. Some disease management strategies include educating patients, providing medication management, and coordinating care. Coordinating care is a team-based approach that can include physicians, nurses, therapists, and/or pharmacists. Learning to manage a chronic condition takes time and effort from both the patient and their healthcare provider. Having healthcare providers work together allows patients to better understand their treatment plan and the best ways to monitor their current condition. By incorporating these strategies, the quality of care for patients with chronic conditions can be improved.

Health Disparities and Equity Within Improvement Initiatives

Health equity can be defined as a lack, or absence, of avoidable or unfair disparities in health outcomes between different groups of people. One of the most important concepts to understand in this section is the social determinants of overall health. Non-medical factors, such as income, housing, education, and accessibility of healthy food all influence the health outcomes of individuals in different groups. Healthcare organizations should not only recognize the social determinants of health, but also address these health disparities to promote health equity.

Additionally, it is important to note that the concept of health equity is not the same as health equality. Health *equality* refers to the same standard of care being provided to every patient, without regard to their background or general circumstances. The issue with a health equality approach is that there is no room to consider that different groups of people possess different health needs and might require varied approaches to achieve the same level of physical health. In contrast, health *equity* refers to the idea that each individual must be provided the necessary resources and support, with regard to individual circumstances, to ensure that they have an equal opportunity to achieve good health.

Several available techniques can promote health equity and address health disparities when it comes to healthcare improvement initiatives. Cultural competency training is one of these commonly used techniques. Cultural competency training refers to educating healthcare professionals to help them understand and respect the beliefs and cultural backgrounds of each individual patient. Improving understanding of a patient's beliefs can help ensure that all patients receive proper care regardless of their background. Health literacy intervention is another effective technique. Health literacy interventions involve providing information to patients so that they can make informed decisions about their health. This information is most commonly offered through written materials in plain language that sometimes include visual aids to explain complex medical concepts.

Focusing on population health in conjunction with patient or individual health can assist organizations in addressing health disparities and promoting health equity. Population health encompasses the health of entire communities rather than individual patients. Another effective approach is to implement targeted interventions aimed at directly reducing health disparities in marginalized communities. These interventions can be achieved through community partnerships that identify the unique health needs of the given population and subsequently tailor interventions to address those needs. Additionally, healthcare organizations can become more accessible by establishing mobile clinics, transportation services, and telemedicine programs to lessen barriers of geographical distance or lack of transportation. Organizations can also offer language interpretation services to ensure that language and cultural differences do not keep patients from receiving appropriate care.

Healthcare organizations must be willing to engage in complicated discussions about race, ethnicity, and other factors that contribute to health disparities between different communities. This means not only

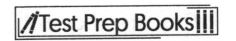

acknowledging health disparities but committing to taking action to mitigate those disparities moving forward.

Clinical, Cost, Equity, and Social Determinants of Improvement Efforts

Improvement efforts in healthcare are greatly influenced by examining and using clinical, cost, equity, and social determinants of health (SDOH) data. It is important to analyze these methods as they each contribute to the improvement of healthcare.

Clinical data include medical measures pertaining to the patient, which include a patient's diagnosis, treatment, and outcomes. Using clinical data can help healthcare providers recognize trends, patterns, and any areas of improvement within the healthcare system. Analyzing cost data assists in identifying areas where savings can be made. These healthcare service areas include direct costs that are specifically associated with a department or patient (such as procedures, medications, etc.) and indirect costs (such as information technology support and administrative resources). Equity in healthcare is described by the CDC as each person having an equal and fair opportunity to achieve their highest level of health. Equity data analyze how healthcare systems use their resources across various populations, including those with disabilities or who are disadvantaged in another way. Analyzing this data is important in order to identify areas of improvement to promote health equity. SDOH data include nonmedical factors, such as a person's education, income, housing, etc., all of which contribute to their overall health. Like health equity data, SDOH data help to determine causes of disparities and possible improvements.

There are several strategies that healthcare organizations may use in order to drive and monitor improvement efforts, including collecting and analyzing the data mentioned above, creating interventions to address areas of improvement, and monitoring any improvements made from the analyzed data. Healthcare data can be collected in multiple ways, such as through the use of electronic health records (EHRs) and patient surveys. EHRs are patient records that can be used to monitor and assess patient outcomes. These records also contain demographic information, which is helpful in analyzing SDOH. EHRs allow healthcare providers to determine areas of improvement and create specific interventions. Patient surveys are another method of collecting data that can be used to gauge a patient's satisfaction, access to healthcare, and overall health outcomes. Surveys can be sent electronically to a patient once discharged from a clinical setting and are valuable to the receipt of timely feedback. Analyzing this data allows healthcare providers to create patient-focused interventions and identify any areas needing improvement.

Addressing areas of improvement can best be done by implementing evidence-based guidelines, improving healthcare access to marginalized populations, and by reducing costs. Implementing evidence-based practices is helpful when areas of inconsistency have been found. To help eliminate inconsistencies, educational training could be provided to employees to ensure that each member of the healthcare team is providing the same care for each patient. This would help healthcare workers recognize a patient's condition and ensure that they receive the recommended screening or treatment needed. Assisting marginalized populations often includes providing education and ensuring that each patient is informed of any available programs. Some examples of such programs include vaccination clinics, screening programs, and health promotion in the community (i.e., smoking cessation programs). Analyzing cost data is essential if healthcare organizations hope to reduce expenses. The goal of this intervention is to ensure that costs are reduced without compromising patient outcomes. A simple example of this is to replace high-cost medications with lower-cost options.

None of these interventions can be beneficial unless the progress is monitored over time. Monitoring improvement efforts allows healthcare organizations to see if goals are being reached and if any adjustments are needed based on the results. To provide high quality, equitable, and cost-effective care, it is necessary to incorporate these interventions and ensure that improvement efforts are being made.

Care Transitions

Organizational leaders in healthcare must work diligently to develop activities which engage in healthcare promotion and the overall continuation of care of the populations they serve. An **episode of care (EOC)** is defined as all medical services for one individual patient, for a specific medical condition, from the onset of symptoms to the end of the final treatment. **Episode-based payments**, also referred to as **bundled payments** or **value-based care**, were introduced as a payment system in an effort to contain costs. This payment system is a contrast to the traditional **fee-for-service system**, which involves physicians receiving payment based on the number of patients that they care for, or the number of procedures they order. Bundled payments can be defined as a single payment made to cover the costs of the treatment provided for any given service. Led by the **America's Health Insurance Plans (AHIP)**, this initiative was established to encourage payers to employ a set of core measures to utilize during reporting. The Core Measures include the following: Cardiology, Gastroenterology, HIV and Hepatitis C, Medical Oncology, Obstetrics and Gynecology, Orthopedics, Pediatrics, Accountable Care Organizations, Patient Centered Medical Homes, and Primary Care. It is important to note that the primary purpose of reporting significant findings is the adherence to specific standards of excellence.

A **standardized shift handoff** can provide a seamless transition between two different medical staff members who are providing care for the same patient. It can provide detailed and crucial information about the patient and the case. It also indicates official responsibility has moved from one provider to another. This provides a clear mechanism for accountability for oversight of specific tasks. All healthcare facilities have their own internal handoff protocol, with formal handoff training for new staff, ongoing training for established staff, verbal handoff protocols, written handoff forms, and consequences for employees who do not meet handoff standards.

External handoffs occur within two separate healthcare entities or during different transitions of care. Unless the two systems involved have similar procedures, external handoffs can be prone to errors. Standardizing a process may occur through a written checklist, a process flowchart, meaningful acronyms, or an audit tool for staff members to follow. Handoff errors can occur when established standard operating procedures are ignored, written poorly, or are too broad for the scope of the procedure. Errors in handoffs can also occur if medical staff are rushed, are unsure of the team members they are working with, or if they receive incorrect information at any time during the patient stay.

According to the CDC, a **transition of care** occurs when a patient moves between settings of care. A **setting of care** is any location where a patient receives medical care and may include hospitals, primary care and specialty care facilities, outpatient surgery centers, long-term care facilities, rehabilitation facilities, and even home healthcare. As the responsibility for patient care transitions from one healthcare professional to another, or from healthcare professionals to patients themselves, adverse events and miscommunications are more likely to occur. To avoid problems with transitions of care, it is necessary to have both clear and effective provider communication and complete patient understanding

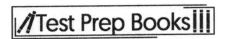

of discharge instructions. Patience and clarity on the part of healthcare providers is particularly important because patients are often confused and vulnerable during complex discharge processes. One beneficial process during transitions is the **IPASS** system; IPASS is a mnemonic that stands for Illness severity (I), Patient information (P), Action list (A), Situational awareness and contingency plans (S), and Synthesis by the receiver (S).

Successful transitions require care coordination and logistical planning to reduce the risk of health complications that could lead to readmission, adverse events, an increase in healthcare costs, or a greater length of stay. A successful transition plan includes, at a minimum, scheduling and keeping appointments, effective medication management, and ongoing medication reconciliation.

Care Processes and Transitions

Many stakeholders are involved during the entire care process and patient transition. These stakeholders include the patient, healthcare providers, caregivers, administrators, and various community organizations. Most patients wish to be involved in their care, and their opinions and preferences should be taken into account when providing care. Doing so will help optimize the care process as treatment is tailored to each patient individually. "Healthcare providers" is a broad term used for many workers, including physicians, nurses, physical therapists, speech therapists, social workers, etc. Each of these providers is responsible for a different aspect of patient care. When healthcare providers work together, they optimize the patient's care process as well as any transition of care that the patient may experience.

Caregivers, such as friends, professional aids, and family members, are also an important part of the patient care process. Caregivers provide a unique view of the patient as they are often involved in the patient's care on a day-to-day basis and know their individual needs and preferences. Administrators include hospital or clinic managers and directors who play a key role in patient care. They are responsible for mainstreaming each patient transfer and ensuring that the care process is as efficient as possible. Community organizations are institutions that contribute to patient care outside of a hospital or healthcare facility. These organizations may include outpatient physical therapy, rehabilitation services, or home health services. These institutions help to improve the patient care process once a patient is discharged, and they allow a patient to receive the care they need once they return home. Each of these stakeholders plays a valuable role in the patient care process by working together to ensure the best results for the patient.

Optimizing patient care involves providing proper education once a patient is ready to be discharged home. Discharge planning includes a collaboration between healthcare providers, and it should comprise of education targeted to the patient and the patient's family upon leaving the facility. Ensuring that the patient understands the requirements for discharge is vital to ensuring the highest quality of care. Trainings for healthcare professionals can be employed to ensure that proper education is given to patients and family members.

One way to improve patient care among healthcare providers is by cross-training employees. This optimizes the care process by increasing employee flexibility, decreasing employee burnout and workload, improving productivity, and enhancing collaboration amongst healthcare providers. Employee flexibility is improved as healthcare workers are able to perform a variety of tasks and fill in where needed. Healthcare worker burnout can be reduced by dispersing the workload evenly among employees. Cross-training allows for greater productivity by ensuring that each healthcare provider is

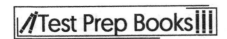

providing the highest level of care to patients. Overall, cross-training contributes to greater success in the workplace while improving the quality of care given to patients.

Utilizing the resources listed above, healthcare providers can collaborate with stakeholders to identify areas of improvement in order to optimize care processes and transitions within healthcare to ensure the highest quality of care.

Improvement Activities

Social determinants of health (SDOH) have been described by the CDC as nonmedical factors that contribute to and influence a person's health outcomes. These factors include where a person is born, grows up, lives, and works; their age; and any other social factors that may affect their health. While these dynamics vary based on the person, they are each interconnected and have a substantial impact on health outcomes. Identifying improvement activities allows healthcare professionals and organizations to address any healthcare biases, and it encourages healthier outcomes for all involved.

Some key SDOH factors that could be integrated into improvement activities include health behaviors, healthcare access and quality, education, and economic stability.

Exercise, diet, medication adherence, substance/alcohol use, and regularly visiting a physician are all examples of health behaviors. Access to healthcare facilities and the quality of care received are areas that may be challenging for many people. These two determinants of health greatly rely upon a person's access to a primary care provider. Many Americans do not have insurance; therefore, the challenge to receive health services or medications is great. Increasing insurance coverage for people who fall into this category is essential to improving a person's overall quality of life. However, this may not always be possible, and other community resources should be recommended. The importance of educating patients on these resources, such as applying for low-cost government healthcare, must be encouraged in order for people to improve their health.

Education is another key factor that contributes to a person's health. While education may seem like a basic aspect, there is a strong correlation between obtaining a higher education and receiving better healthcare. Gaining a higher education often means a better salary (with benefits such as health insurance), which allows for greater access to healthcare. Similarly, economic stability and a person's income or employment status also contribute to their health outcomes. When people experience economic instability, they are more likely to have increased levels of stress and anxiety, both of which influence their health and wellbeing.

Healthcare workers are often required to address these issues; therefore, it is imperative for workers to be trained to recognize areas of improvement. SDOH factors should be addressed throughout the entirety of a patient's stay (during admission and discharge) at a healthcare facility, or anytime they visit a clinic. Trainings should be held to ensure that all healthcare providers are asking the same questions and are able to provide necessary patient education. Screening tools may be implemented to standardize this process and make it more efficient. Using a screening tool at the beginning of a patient's care allows healthcare providers to understand what help and resources should be provided to the patient. Educating patients plays a major role in improving a patient's quality of care and health outcomes. Patients should be provided with readily available resources, such as social service agencies, local health departments, and community-based organizations, that will go beyond what a clinic or hospital can provide once a patient goes home. These resources are better equipped to address any underlying SDOH factors.

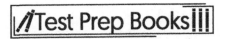

The Institute of Medicine defines care coordination as a strategy to improve the safety, efficiency, and effectiveness of the American health system. Ideally, this strategy shares information throughout various health organizations to provide a stronger continuity of care. For example, this method would imply that a patient's preferences and needs are relayed from one entity to another. Teamwork is essential because each healthcare provider must be able to manage a person's care in order to avoid delays that could further contribute to social disparities and any other SDOH factors.

Practice Quiz

1. Which of the following is a reason for a public health official to analyze environmental data?
    a. A certain population has an increased risk of diabetes.
    b. A certain population has higher levels of emergency department visits.
    c. A certain population is experiencing a surge in asthma diagnoses.
    d. A certain population has a lower risk of heart disease.

2. A healthcare provider is instructed to include family members when teaching about a patient's condition. What is the overall purpose for including family members?
    a. To assist the patient in managing their health condition
    b. To help sympathize with the patient
    c. To assist the healthcare provider in taking care of the patient
    d. To increase the patient's medication compliance

3. A healthcare provider notices an inconsistency in treatment for several patients with the same diagnosis. Which intervention would best improve patient care?
    a. Notify the healthcare organization's administrator.
    b. Suggest hosting a training to ensure that all employees are providing the same level of care.
    c. Inform the patient of their treatment options.
    d. Provide the patient with a survey regarding the treatment they have received.

4. External handoffs between healthcare entities can be common. Which of the following is a frequent error during external handoff?
    a. Reviewing the patient's plan of care with the healthcare provider who will be caring for the patient next
    b. Providing a written report, in addition to a verbal report, for the next healthcare provider
    c. Using a systematic checklist provided by the facility for handoff
    d. Providing the report to the first healthcare provider available

5. Social determinants of health are key factors that affect a person's health outcomes. Which area of assessment best helps the provider identify a patient's SDOH factors that need addressing?
    a. The patient's height and weight
    b. Needs of the patient's family members
    c. The patient's current occupational status
    d. Any prescriptions that the patient needs to have refilled

See answers on the next page.

Answer Explanations

1. C: Choices *A, B,* and *D* are incorrect because they relate more to vital statistics and health outcomes data. Choice *C* is the correct answer since it reflects a disease that could be related to an environmental factor.

2. A: Choice *B* is incorrect because it does not help improve the patient's outcome. Choice *C*, while helpful to the provider, is incorrect since it is not the main purpose of involving family members. Choice *D* is helpful to the patient and could be a possible outcome when including family members; however, it is not the overall goal of including family members and is therefore incorrect. Choice *A* is the correct answer because it describes the overall purpose for including family members in education about a patient's healthcare.

3. B: Choice *A* is incorrect because it passes the responsibility to someone else and does not address the problem. Choice *C* is helpful, but it is not a specific intervention to assist in solving this problem and is therefore incorrect. Choice *D* is incorrect as it is a form of collecting clinical data, which does not apply to this situation. Choice *B* is correct because it is a specific intervention to help improve patient care.

4. D: Choice *A* is incorrect since reviewing the plan of care is an appropriate action. Choice *B* provides two ways for a correct report to be given. Choice *C* is a consistent way to communicate handoffs. Choice *D* allows for error in handoff as the first healthcare provider available may not be the primary caregiver for the patient; therefore, it is the correct answer.

5. C: SDOH factors are nonmedical factors that influence a patient's health outcomes. Choice *A* is a medical factor that does not currently need to be addressed; therefore, it is incorrect. Choice *B* is incorrect since it does not relate to the patient directly. Choice *D* may be helpful, but it is not the best option to be addressed in order to better help the patient. Choice *C* is the correct answer because it provides insight as to how the healthcare provider can best assist the patient's nonmedical needs.

Data Management Systems

Data Management Systems for Quality Improvement

Providing exceptional medical care to patients requires that protected health information be safeguarded. The **Health Insurance Portability and Accountability Act (HIPAA)** of 1996 is a federal statute requiring all entities who care for patients to protect their medical records as protected health information. The portability portion focuses on protecting patient rights to maintain health insurance coverage in the event of a loss of, or change in, employment status. The accountability portion of the bill covers how patient health information is guarded. Medical records are to be stored so that access is limited, and strict confidentiality is maintained. HIPAA protections cover all documentation that could reveal diagnoses, treatments, payments, and any other related medical information. Violations of the HIPAA laws may result in severe financial and legal sanctions on the offending organization. Employees who violate HIPAA laws are generally terminated.

Advances in technology continually inform how personal health information (PHI) is entered, stored, and retrieved. Patients must provide their written consent before release of PHI. Healthcare organizations must make each patient aware of the protections and limitations to their PHI policies whenever possible.

It is the HQP's responsibility to ensure that their organization's data management system is both **efficient** and **effective.** This means that the data management system provides sufficient information to the HQP for them to be able to analyze and create valid improvement proposals (effectiveness) while also not consuming excessive administrative and front-line staff time (efficiency). Although it is generally preferable for the HQP to work within context of the organization's existing data management systems—because the benefits of a system's change are generally outweighed by the cost of training staff on the new system—a modernization transition to digital data management may be necessary in some organizations. Digital data management is, generally, more efficient in the long run due to its ease of access and the data analysis tools available in most current systems.

The specific data management software used will vary from organization to organization; however, it is important for the HQP to be familiar with industry-wide forms of data management. These include **electronic health records (EHRs)** documenting patient medical records, **population health management (PHM)** software to identify high-risk patients, and **clinical decision support systems (CDSSs)**. These types of systems are used by the HQP to quickly gather data about an organization's operations for the sake of improvement analysis.

With the advent of the EHR, data management professionals within healthcare realized that they must remain attentive to its advantages and disadvantages. The digitizing of EHRs has led to more efficient recordkeeping and increased compliance with documentation standards. It has allowed multiple user access. The leadership team must ensure the PHI is protected through multiple firewalls and gradations of PHI access. In addition, protocols and policies must be in place to prevent and detect security breaches. Accreditation entities also require specific strategies and policies to manage PHI. Any failures in this area are damaging to an audit and could slow or derail accreditation efforts. The leadership team

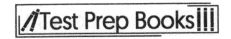
must work continuously to ensure that the healthcare organization remains compliant by guarding all aspects of PHI.

Industry standards for data management—and, more generally, quality management—are determined for healthcare in the United States by the **Centers for Medicare & Medicaid Services (CMS)** and affiliated regulatory and nongovernmental agencies. Quality management standards in healthcare and a variety of other industries are supported through the work of the **International Organization for Standardization (ISO).** Although ISO standards are not regulatory standards, adherence to their quality management principles is common industrial practice, including in the healthcare industry. The most important standard for an HQP to be familiar with is **ISO 9001.** This standard describes operational practices that can be adopted in nearly any industry or workplace context to facilitate planning and support quality improvement.

The most important regulatory standard for data management in the United States is the **Health Insurance Portability and Accountability Act,** commonly known as **HIPAA.** HIPAA sets standards for protection of privileged health information and is enforced by the Department of Health and Human Services. It is the HQP's responsibility to ensure that their organization's data management system remains in compliance with HIPAA regulations. This requires verifying that a release of information was signed each time the organization releases patient information and ensuring that identifying information is removed from data prepared for analysis and that both digital and analog security measures are implemented to prevent unauthorized access to privileged information. The HQP should evaluate their organization's data security requirements annually to ensure patient confidentiality.

Any use of data for quality improvement initiatives must not reveal patient information. For example, an oncologist's office could present data about the total number of patients treated for colon cancer and the percentage of all patients who were in remission. However, they could not name specific patients who had gone into remission and patients whose cancer remained malignant.

Data Collection Plans

The **Institute for Healthcare Improvement (IHI)** has a free data collection plan that healthcare organizations are encouraged to use. As stated previously, shamelessly stealing from the best practices of others is considered a best practice in healthcare. **Simple data collection planning** is one process outlined by IHI to make sure that the collected data is helpful, accurate, and can be gathered effectively. In particular, it strives to avoid collecting useless or unreliable data and also works to avoid processes that are overly costly or time-consuming. Simple data collection planning has the following benefits:

- The data contains current, accurate information that is useful for the improvement process under review.

- Common data collection errors can be avoided.

- The data collection process is streamlined to avoid wasting time and money collecting useless data or repeating unhelpful or failed tests.

The IHI Simple Data Collection Plan

1. Begin your data collection planning by answering these key questions:

- What question do we need to answer—why are we collecting these data?
- What data analysis tools do we envision using to display the data after we have it?
- What type of data do we need in order to construct this tool and answer the question?
- Where in the process can we get this data?
- Who in the process can give us this data?
- How can we collect this data with minimum effort and chance of error?
- What additional data do we need to capture for future analysis, reference, and traceability?

2. Keep the following points in mind when planning for data collection:

- Seek usefulness, not perfection! Remember, data for improvement are different from data for research. Confusing the two can slow down improvement work. We need data that are "good enough" to permit us to take the next step in improving a process. These data are for learning, not judgment.
- Data recording must be easy. Try to build it in to the process under study. Use sampling as part of the plan to collect the data.
- Design the form with the collector's needs in mind.
- Minimize the possibility of errors.
- Provide clear, unambiguous directions.
- Use existing data whenever possible.

3. Develop your plan by answering the following questions:

- Who will collect the data?
- What data will be collected?
- When will the data be collected?
- Where will the data be collected?
- How will the data be collected?

4. When you developed a method to collect the data, test it with a few people who will be collecting the data and incorporate their ideas for improving the data collection plan.

- Be aware of the cost of collecting the data relative to the benefit gained from having it.
- Teach all of the data collectors how to collect the data correctly.
- Record what went wrong during the data collection so that learning can take place.
- Audit the data as it comes in for accuracy and completeness. Correct errors early.

Measuring Development

Once the mission, goals, and values of a healthcare system have been evaluated, the leadership team creates a project charter. The project charter is specifically defined to serve as a written file that is a roadmap for process improvement. This written agreement usually includes the primary reason for the project, the goal and scope of the project, expected budget, and roles of each member of the team. Measurement is an essential part of testing and introducing changes. By using a variety of measures, a team can identify if the changes being made will be an improvement.

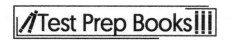
Outcome measures tell the organization how the system impacts the health and wellbeing of patients and shows the impacts on other stakeholders such as payers, employees, or the community. Some examples of outcome measures are:

- For diabetes: Average hemoglobin A1c level for diabetic patients
- For access: Number of days to the third next available appointment
- For critical care: Intensive Care Unit (ICU) percent unadjusted mortality
- For medication systems: Adverse drug events per 1,000 doses

Process measures indicate how well the parts of a system function and whether the team is making steady improvements. Examples of process measures include the following:

- For diabetes: Percentage of patients whose hemoglobin A1c level was measured twice in the last twelve months
- For access: Average daily clinician hours available for appointments
- For critical care: Percent of patients fully attended to during scheduled proactive rounding

Balancing measures examine a system from all sides to ensure that changes intended to fix one problem do not cause new problems elsewhere. A couple examples of balancing measures are:

- For reducing time patients spend on a ventilator after surgery: Make sure reintubation rates are not increasing
- For reducing patients' length of stay in the hospital: Make sure readmission rates are not increasing

The leadership team must decide where to set the thresholds on their goals and objectives. Benchmarking with competitors and national organizations is a good starting point. Literature review for pertinent data will also give clues where the best thresholds need to be set. As an example, numerous studies have been done on C section rates, so when looking at these rates within an organization, a standard threshold limit can be easily determined. Similarly, infection rates, patient satisfaction, and readmission rates are easily located for benchmarking.

Tools and Techniques

As stated earlier there are numerous internet sites where quality tools, plans, processes and guidelines are free to use. Using these tools helps to standardize the quality process and decreases the time spent collecting data. The leadership team is frequently tasked with gathering and compiling health-related data, validating, analyzing, and drawing specific conclusions regarding how to address noted deficiencies. The task at this stage is to select the most appropriate tools for gathering data as well as the tools used to analyze the data once collected.

Data can be either quantitative (numerical), or qualitative (descriptive). Quantitative data can be either continuous or discrete. **Discrete data** has finite values that can be counted. **Continuous data** has an infinite number of steps, forming a continuum with up to infinite precision. Some examples of discrete data include the number of children in a household, number of languages a person speaks, and number of people sleeping in statistics class; there may only be certain numbers of these (i.e. there cannot be one and a half people sleeping in class). Some examples of continuous data include the height of children, mass of cars, speed of trains. For example, a child's height could be 4.5 feet, or it might actually be 4.50003 feet.

There are seven fundamental tools used to evaluate quality, developed by a professor of engineering at Tokyo University named Kaoru Ishikawa.

The seven indispensable tools are:

1. **Cause-and-effect diagram** (also known as an Ishikawa or fishbone chart): A chart which identifies several possible causes for an issue and sorts them into useful categories.

2. **Check sheet**: An organized form used to collect and analyze data; a general-purpose tool that can be used for a wide range of activities.

3. **Control chart**: A graph used to study how a process changes over time. A control chart begins with a time series graph. Control charts use a central line as a visual reference to aid in identifying shifts and trends. This is known as the process location. Upper and lower control limits (UCL and LCL), also referred to as the process dispersion, are made from available data and placed equal distances from the central line.

4. **Histogram**: The graph used most often to show frequency distributions, or how often each different value in a data set occurs.

5. **Pareto chart**: A bar graph that illustrates which factors have the most significant impact. Also called a distribution diagram.

Example of a Pareto Chart

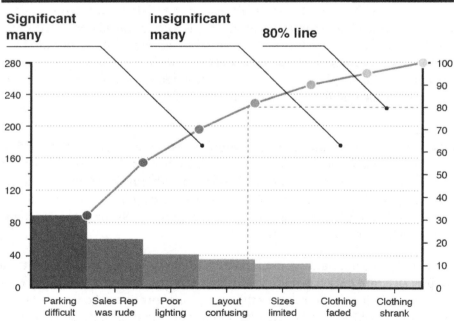

6. **Scatter diagram**: A graph that combines pairs of numerical data, using one variable per axis, to identify relationships in data sets.

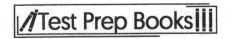

7. **Stratification**: A technique that separates data gathered from a variety of sources so that patterns can be seen.

Example of a Stratification

Day	Mon	Tue	Wed	Thu	Fri	Sat	Sun
Frequency - Late in Office	4	2	1	0	0	0	0

In addition to the basic 7, there are numerous other types of quality tools available for use. Free samples of the five why's, Gantt charts, x bar and R charts, z score, and others are all available on quality websites.

Sampling Methodology

Bias occurs when the estimated result of your analysis is different from the true value of the statistic you are measuring. There are several reasons bias might be present, including sampling errors, measurement errors, or unrepresentative samples. **Sampling error** is the tendency of sample statistics to not perfectly represent the population. Error does not necessarily mean there was a human error or mistake. Even with a relatively large sample, some small amount of sampling error will still be present, because it's only part of the population. If a statistic is completely unbiased, the average of all statistics from all samples would average the true population parameter.

Measurement error occurs when the data gathered does not match the real values. For example, you might survey several people to find whether they support or oppose a bill. However, if the survey is worded poorly, some individuals may unintentionally respond with the opposite of their position. There are several sources of measurement error in statistics, including how a question is presented, the phrasing in a questionnaire, the method used for gathering data from respondents, and the surveyor's record-keeping system.

Sampling methods can be classified into two categories: probability and nonprobability.

Probability Sampling

Probability sampling is when a small group, or sample, is randomly selected from a larger group or population. The key element of probability sampling is that every member of the large group has a known and equal chance of being selected for the sample group. This ensures that any information gathered about the sample group will provide accurate statistical inferences about the larger population.

Simple Random Sampling (SRS)

Simple random samples are designed to provide an unbiased analysis of a larger population. To make sure that the random sample truly is random, it is vital that every member of the larger population is equally likely to be selected for the sample group.

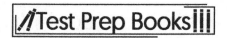

Stratified Sampling

Stratified sampling is used when a researcher wants to make sure that every group in a population is accurately represented in the sample group. To do this, the larger population is first divided into **strata**, or groups, based on a variety of variables, depending on the traits the researcher is examining. These traits can include age, gender, ethnicity, income bracket, job role, etc. Simple random sampling or systematic sampling is then used to draw the members of the sample group from each stratum. This methodology is especially helpful when analyzing a heterogenous population that can easily be divided into fairly uniform strata.

Cluster Sampling

Cluster sampling divides populations into heterogenous groups called **clusters** that, ideally, have characteristics similar to those of the larger population. (Note that clusters are very different from strata – clusters should be heterogenous and represent the population as a whole while strata should be homogenous and represent only a portion of the population.) Random samples are obtained from a limited number of these clusters. While this method is useful for obtaining data from large or widespread populations, it does have two weaknesses. First, it is very difficult to determine whether or not a cluster accurately represents the entire population. Second, clusters may be dramatically different from each other, which could potentially skew the gathered data.

Systematic Sampling

Systematic sampling is a probability sampling method which selects samples members from the population using a random start point and a recurring interval. This is called the sampling interval, which is calculated by dividing the population size by the desired sample size. For example, to sample 125 people out of 1,000, every eighth member of the population would be selected for the sample. For systematic sampling to be considered random, the start point must also be random and the interval must be decided before sampling. It is also important to make sure that there are no hidden or underlying patterns in the population list.

Multistage Sampling

Multi-stage sampling also divides a population into clusters; however, unlike cluster sampling, the clusters in multi-stage sampling are further subdivided into smaller groups across multiple stages of sampling. This is also known as multi-stage cluster sampling. This sampling method takes large clusters of a population and divides them into smaller clusters in multiple steps to simplify the data collection process. If the same sample size is considered, multi-stage sampling is not as accurate as simple random sampling, but it reduces the cost and time requirements of data collection.

Non-Probability Sampling

Non-probability sampling should be avoided because it introduces many potentially biased sources and it does not accurately represent the population as a whole. Instead of random samples, it uses voluntary samples and haphazard (convenience) samples. These kinds of samples are selected by hand, not at random, and thus they cannot be explained statistically. These common mistakes have disastrous results on the accuracy of sampling.

Projects targeting the improvement of defective processes in healthcare service delivery will require the collection of raw data at various points in the process. Once the project charter has been developed and the appropriate analytical tools have been chosen, the project management team will need to determine how often to collect the data in order to confirm that the appropriate amount of information has been gathered. This step entails asking several fundamental questions. Some of the most crucial include: Where will the data come from? How will we gather the data that we need? What are acceptable intervals within which to collect the necessary data? How will we know when we have what we need?

Measures

There are three types of quality measures that are used to evaluate and compare healthcare organizations: structural measures, process measures, and outcome measures. **Structural measures** indicate the healthcare organization's resources for providing quality care. In particular, it focuses on features such as the organization's capacity, systems, and processes. For example, a structural measure might compare the ratio of nurses to patients, the percentage of physicians who are board-certified, whether or not the organization maintains registers of patients with certain conditions, and what type of electronic medical record system the organization uses.

Process measures review the effectiveness of patient care and are the most common publicly reported healthcare quality measure. They focus on the healthcare activities actually done for patients and are often based on best practice recommendations for various procedures and conditions. For example, a process measure might track the percentage of women who get regular mammograms, the percentage of diabetes patients with controlled diabetes, or the percentage of patients with hypertension who get regular blood pressure checks. Process measures give patients an easy way to find out what treatment they will receive based on their condition, thus educating the patients and encouraging compliance with their treatment plans.

Outcome measures look at a healthcare organization's outcomes of care, which are the results of the patient's healthcare procedures on the patient's health. They would include statistics such as surgical mortality rates and/or complications, the rates of successful pregnancies resulting from the various procedures at a fertility clinic, and the percentage of hospitalized patients who are readmitted. While outcome measures seem to be the best quality measure available, results are often skewed by circumstances outside of the healthcare organization's control. **Risk-adjustment methods** can help correct for some factors, but the process is not yet advanced enough to prevent misleading or inaccurate healthcare quality reports.

Healthcare leaders are always aware of comparative data and benchmarking so they are in the best position to identify and select measures for their organization. High volume processes, error prone processes, safety measures and others that are mandated by CMS or a parent organization can result in an organization monitoring several dozen measures each year.

Quantitative and Qualitative Data

When an organization collects its own new data, despite attempts to avoid errors, there can still be mistakes. Because of this, organizations need to validate their data by checking for bad data. When using data from outside sources (e.g., the CDC), it should still be checked after it's been put in the format that the organization intends to use it in. There are a lot of unintentional mistakes that can occur when importing or exporting data, which makes the data validation step one of the most important pieces of data collection and analysis. Data validation should be performed before the data is used in any way by a healthcare organization.

Throughout the data validation process, the leadership team must always be asking whether the results make sense. Common procedures to validate continuous variables include checking the minimum and maximum values, the mean, and the median. For example, when working with hospital data, one of the variables may be how long a patient has lived at their current residence. The first items to check are the minimum and maximum values for how long they've lived at their current address. If the results had a minimum of 0.05 years and a maximum of 47 years, those would be reasonable results. Some patients will have lived at the same location for a long time, while others may have recently moved in. If, instead of those results, the minimum was 50 years and the max was 4.7 years, it would be obvious there's an error in the data. There might have been some mathematical mistakes or data entered incorrectly.

When collecting and validating data, two main checks should be routinely done: confirm whether the data was downloaded correctly, and see if the data was imported into the right format for your analysis software. These are both steps where data mistakes can easily happen. **Cross tabulations**, which display the frequency with which each combination of variables occurs, are often useful when validating data because it allows you to identify combinations that shouldn't occur. Regardless of how much effort is made towards creating a good data collection system, there will always be some errors. These must be fixed during data cleaning, which can be an expensive, complicated, and time-consuming process, but it is necessary for any project that handles data.

Quantitative data (information that can be measured) include continuous data and discrete data. **Continuous data** have an infinite number of values that form a continuum, such as temperature, height, weight, length, and time. **Discrete data** have finite values that can be measured, such as the number of students taking a math class, the number of responses to a survey, and the number of golf balls in a bucket. One should include continuous data measurements whenever feasible because slight changes in date and processes may not be measurable in discrete data but may be observed in continuous data. Furthermore, discrete data require larger sample sizes in order to achieve equivalent risk levels.

External Data Sources for Comparison and Benchmarking

Benchmarking is another method that allows for the analysis of healthcare delivery, trends, and best practices. Benchmarks are useful in that they permit the comparison of apples to apples. This is especially true when audits are internal to an organization. Benchmarking allows the comparison of results with state, regional, or national organizations that are similar in structure. For example, the average length of stay or number of bed days may be a metric that is monitored and even tied to the performance of an organization. Industry benchmarks in managed care organizations include the following:

- Acute-care admissions per thousand
- Acute-care bed days per thousand
- Skilled nursing bed days per thousand
- Home care admissions per thousand
- Home care visits per thousand

The benchmarking exercise can also help to identify processes that have an opportunity for improvement. The exercise supports monitoring of consistency in practice, while also enabling compliance with quality standards. Patients, caregivers, providers, payers, and a variety of other participants in the patient's care should be a part of evaluating their experience. Their feedback is critical in the evaluation of the overall effectiveness of a program.

The leadership team decides which benchmarks are appropriate for their organization and metrics. In most cases the benchmarks are standardized or mandated, as in Joint Commission benchmarks or

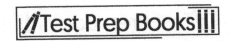

national quality and patient safety benchmarks. Internal benchmarks are those that the organization determines are important trends to monitor.

Scorecards and Dashboards

A **scorecard** is a type of report that measures an organization's performance and compares it against its projections and goals. Modern scorecards are sophisticated software solutions. The scorecard utilizes the organization's data to evaluate the success and failure of **key performance indicators (KPIs)**. If used correctly, scorecards can be an extremely valuable tool. Scorecards allow organizations to assess their current objectives and progress, evaluate trends, and maximize efficient use of resources.

Scorecards started out as a simple framework for measuring performance but have become a robust system for management and strategic planning. Scorecards give performance measurements on daily activities for every part of an organization. Senior management create the vision and strategies which are passed to every part of an organization. These are then used by departments to set objectives and goals, assign responsibilities, and create accountability. Additional training should be given if necessary, in order to help employees meet their department's new goals.

Dashboards provide a focused view of summaries, key trends, comparisons, and exceptions. Ideally, a dashboard's design will be simple, have minimal distractions, and provide meaningful data for businesses to make quick and informed decisions. Dashboards are created using multiple reports and make it easy to compare and contrast reports or examine a variety of data sets together. Scorecards may also be used as part of a dashboard to ensure the accuracy of the reports.

Example of a Dashboard

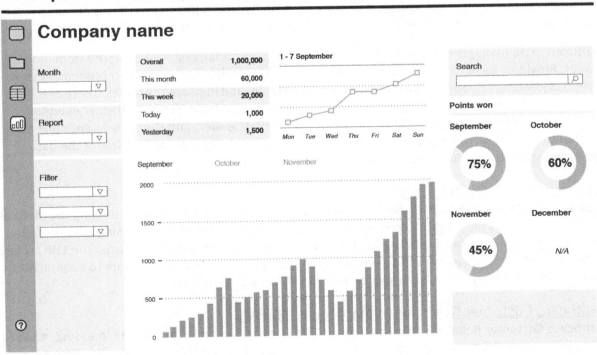

The laws around data are evolving. Privacy is a state of being that every organization must take responsibility for. Each organization must cloak its daily habits using a **VPN (virtual private network)**

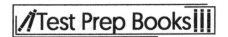

connection. A VPN service will scramble the signal so that identity and location are at least partially masked from trackers. A VPN will substantially reduce how much the world can observe the organization's online habits. Some of the most common reports used on a dashboard are new item trends, 52-week profit analysis, and exception reports.

Measurement and Analysis

Organization, Analysis, and Reporting

The amount of healthcare data available can seem overwhelming. Healthcare leaders need to drive their organizations to work with a more data-oriented mindset. Administrators and physicians must be diligent when collecting patient data, marketing departments need to utilize data-based outreach, and patients must become more involved in their own healthcare. Everyone in the healthcare industry needs to be involved to make data management a priority.

As the healthcare industry moves aggressively toward outcome-based reimbursement, all healthcare entities need to remodel their operations to focus on affordable, effective and accessible service delivery. Leaders will need to develop strategies to reduce costs and improve collaboration to face the challenges posed by ever-evolving threats to their IT systems and data. It's important to find new ways to efficiently manage people, processes, and technology to deliver integrated and effective care, as well as efficient business services.

The healthcare organization must also be able to adapt to new regulatory requirements and to rationalize and integrate systems in the wake of mergers and acquisitions or consolidation of payers and providers. Strategic thinking about the application of new technology is crucial to improving IT cost-efficiency and quality. Without a strategic approach, organizations might inadvertently put money into technology that doesn't integrate well with their business or increase its value.

Healthcare data management involves storing, protecting, and analyzing data gathered from multiple sources. Providers need to be able to manage all their available data to develop comprehensive views of patients, individualize patient care, enhance communication, and improve outcomes. There are thousands of different data management systems and each organization must fit their IT needs into both the fiscal plan and the operational plan each year. Senior leaders and IT management must work together to determine which products best meet the needs of the organization. A few of the data management systems include the following:

Electronic Health Record (EHR):
Electronic Health Records (EHRs) allow physicians and other medical personnel to simplify the medical recording process by electronically recording and storing patient information. By using EHRs, hospitals and other organizations can securely access and consolidate patients' medical records. The EHR replaces the paper medical charts and contains everything from physician orders and lab work to surgical notes and medications. Each patient has a specific record with unique identifiers.

Healthcare Customer Relations Management (HCRM):
Healthcare Customer Relations Management (HCRM) systems are able to integrate, measure, analyze, and report on data from multiple sources, all inside one data hub. This technology enables organizations to consolidate consumer and patient data from EHRs and other sources, such as engagement centers

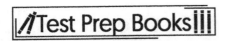

and social media. By utilizing healthcare CRM technology, organizations can gain a comprehensive view of patients that covers the patient lifecycle as well as consumer profiles, preferences, and behaviors.

Reliability Centered Maintenance (RCM)

Reliability Centered Maintenance (RCM) is typically used to create improvements such as the establishment of safe minimum levels of maintenance. Successfully implementing RCM will improve cost effectiveness, improve machine uptime, improve reliability, and give a better understanding of the risk the organization manages. RCM helps businesses create cost-effective maintenance plans that deal with the causes of equipment failure. This process finds the main function of routinely maintained equipment and determines the primary modes, causes, and consequences of failure, and then identifies the criticality level of each of those consequences. RCM focuses on addressing failures that can be solved with preventative maintenance before they ever happen. However, some functions that are less important are allowed to continue until a failure occurs, whereas highly critical functions are maintained to prevent any risk of failure. When there is a high risk associated with a function, RCM may recommend or require changing something to lower the risk. This system enables the organization increase cost-effectiveness by pre-emptively focusing on processes with the most harmful consequences of failure.

Enterprise Application Software (EAS)

Enterprise Application Software (EAS) is used to address the needs of an organization as a whole, as opposed to the needs of individuals. These organizations may include charities, education systems, businesses, or government. Because businesses frequently have overlapping divisions and processes, enterprise software is often customizable, in order to address issues that affect an entire organization rather than specific departments. The goal of EAS is to increase productivity by providing tools that utilize business logic. This software is usually hosted on servers and allows many users across a network to access its services at the same time. The services that EAS provides are usually business tools, such as the following:

- Online payment processing
- Security systems
- Human resource management
- Occupational health and safety
- Project management
- IT service management
- Customer relationship management
- Business intelligence

Data Visualization and Display Techniques

The most effective format for the dissemination and depiction of statistical data is often via a graph or chart. For those not familiar with data interpretation, visual tools such as Pareto charts, run charts, scattergrams, and control charts can easily depict the trends and correlational relationships between variables. Leadership teams will utilize appropriate tools to display data related to the organization's mission, values, and goals.

A **Pareto chart** depicts data in the form of bars placed in descending order, with a line representing the cumulative total. The 80-20 rule, otherwise known as the Pareto principle, states that for a given event, nearly 80% of effects can be attributed to 20% of causes. This rule is frequently used in business to highlight that the majority of revenue comes from roughly one fifth of its clientele. Consequently, the

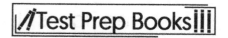

Pareto principle is used for identifying which items have the largest effect on the business and allow management to focus on the important factors in a cost-efficient manner.

Supplementary quality control tools include the run chart, control charts, histograms, scatter plot diagrams, and check sheets. Both the **run** and the **control charts** are line graphs that depict data points along a continuum; however, the control chart includes a control limit. Both charts also clearly indicate trends and patterns of specific processes and how well that process is performing. While control charts are best utilized when monitoring processes on an ongoing basis, run charts are best suited for investigating short-term process improvement activities.

Histograms graphically represent the variation of values within a group. This format depicts the center, spread, and shape of the data. The distribution will be distinctly normal, bi-modal, or skewed. One final format for depicting statistical data is the **fishbone**, or **cause and effect diagram**. Named for the shape, this diagram focuses largely on depicting the precipitating factors, or root causes, for a specific event or outcome. Those root causes can be separated into more meaningful categories. Practitioners can then engage in the brainstorming necessary to clarify potential solutions. This format for representing data is also useful when there is little quantitative data accessible for analysis.

Although every program and process evaluation project does not require the use of each tool, at least two charts are typically utilized for precision when reporting results.

Evaluate Process Improvement

An HQP is required to use a variety of statistical and analytic tools to effectively draw conclusions from the healthcare organization's data. It is important for the HQP to not only use tools that help them draw accurate conclusions but that these tools are also effective in presenting the conclusions to other staff members, members of the leadership team, or other stakeholders in the organization. The best tools for evaluating process improvement are those that efficiently communicate the HQP's conclusions to other team members.

Two useful measurement tools an HQP should include in their toolbox are **Pareto charts** and **run charts.** The use of these charts to evaluate data should be prioritized because their visual component makes it easier for the HQP to present their conclusions to other team members.

A Pareto chart is based on Vilfredo Pareto's management principle that approximately 20 percent of causes lead to 80% of effects. By focusing on the most frequent causes of failure to reach a given quality metric, the HQP can efficiently improve the quality of care. A Pareto chart is a bar chart that indicates different causes of a particular effect—for example, the different causes for incident reports in a behavioral treatment facility. In this case, the Pareto chart would be made by listing the causes of the incident report on the *x*-axis and the number of incident reports on the *y*-axis. The causes should be ordered from most frequent to least frequent.

A Pareto chart is an expedient way to visually demonstrate conclusions drawn from organizational data. It's important to remember that this method of evaluating the organization's operations is not restricted to weaknesses or failures. Successes can also be demonstrated on a Pareto chart. By evaluating both failures and successes, the HQP achieves a more holistic understanding of the organization's healthcare. This provides insight into how best to improve healthcare quality beyond a focus on one aspect—the inadequacies of current care—of the organization's performance.

A run chart is an effective tool to evaluate how a process is working over a period of time. Unlike a Pareto chart—which focuses on categorized causes—the run chart presents how the sum of a given metric changes over time. To continue from the previous example, a run chart summarizing a year's incident reports would indicate the total number of incident reports that took place in a given month and presented in chronological order.

This method of data analysis enables the HQP to determine what effect, if any, changes to the organization's operational processes are having. Continuing with the treatment facility's example, if the quantity of incident reports diminished over the months of July, August, and September following a change in the procedure for emergency restraint, that may indicate that the new procedure is effective. The HQP can also choose to increase the run chart's specificity by organizing the data with a focus on cause as well as sum quantities. In this case, the HQP would use a line graph with lines of multiple color, each indicating a particular cause for the sum of incident reports. Additional specificity with the data is an effective way to draw more accurate conclusions. However, the HQP should be sparing when presenting data this way to members of the leadership team or other members of the healthcare organization. The run chart's efficacy as a communication tool—in addition to its analytic uses—is due to the intuitive ease with which anyone can interpret the chart. By making the chart more complex, the HQP risks reducing its communicative effectiveness. This can negatively impact the organization's quality of care by increasing the difficulty of persuading leadership team members to endorse an appropriate course of action.

Describe Data and Examine Relationships with Statistics

Historically, statisticians utilize measures of central tendency when evaluating any set of data. The three most common measures of central tendency include the mean, median, and mode. The **mean** is the average of the sample and is determined by adding all of the outcomes from the sample then dividing it by the total number of events. The **median** is the middle value within the data set when all results are presented in ascending or descending order. If the midpoint consists of two numbers, then the average is to be taken of the two. The **mode** is the most common value appearing within the data set. The **range** is the difference in the span of values within the complete set, or the largest value minus the smallest value. When a normal data set is generated, the data are depicted as a bell-shaped curve; the mean, median, and mode are the same.

Variance is the sum of the squared deviations from the mean, divided by the total size of the sample. The **standard deviation** is defined as the average distance of all points of data from the mean of the data set. The **correlation**, or dependent relationship between two quantitative continuous variables, can either be positive or negative. For example, if one variable increases corresponding to the increase of another, the two variables are said to be positively correlated. Alternatively, if one variable decreases while another increases, that relationship is considered to be negatively correlated. One additional measure, a **t-test**, is used to compare the differences between the means of separate distributions. The t-test is a statistical tool that usually is done in Minitab or a similar software. It is generally thought to guide the determination of root causality between two processes.

Statistical Process Control Techniques and Tools

Statistical Process Control (SPC) is a standard method of measuring and maintaining quality that has long been used in manufacturing. Product (outcome) and process measures are collected in real time during manufacturing and used as quality data to develop **control charts** to track causes of variation. This method is similarly useful in healthcare quality control. The control chart's upper and lower limits are determined by a process's capabilities, and specification limits may be set according to regulations. Data is expected to be within the control limits, and variations inside this range are mostly due to common causes. Data that goes outside of the control limits often indicates a special cause that can be identified as the reason for the variations, and changes can then be made to prevent the issue from recurring. SPC can significantly improve outcomes and productivity, reduce variability and costs, and it allows leaders to quickly react to process changes.

SPC has been a manufacturing standard for decades but it is only within the past 20 years that it has been used in healthcare. The thinking is that an error is an error and waste is waste, whether the process is patient-related or material-related. The process is what is important to control in order to reduce costs and eliminate rework.

Common cause variation, also called **random variation**, is the process by which numerous small general factors result in a specific effect on a process. These stressors to the process are predictable and occur in every process. For example, consider the effect of staffing in a typical emergency room. If it is determined that there is a thirty-minute wait for patients to be examined by a physician once admitted to an emergency room, the management can simply act to permanently increase staffing to the ER; or reduce the possibility of variance.

Special cause variation refers to the specific rare factors that can influence a process. These are new and unexpected stressors that occur sporadically. Considering the same example, special cause variation in this instance would be a wait of three hours for a patient to be examined once admitted to the ER. Upon further examination, the evaluator may uncover a specific event of staff being preoccupied caring for numerous patients involved in a local apartment building fire. The best way to solve this problem would be to institute disaster protocols, whereby specific individuals throughout the facility can be dispatched to the ER to manage the overflow when it does occur. Both interventions would require approaching the problem at its roots, engaging in corrective or preventative actions, and mitigating as much variation as possible.

A **trend analysis** is a method based on historical data about a process. There are no fully automatic methods that can identify trends in time series, but if there is a consistent increase or decrease in the data, the trend might be obvious. If the data contains significant noise or errors, the first step to find a trend will be smoothing. **Smoothing** takes the average, or mean, of data inside a limited range so irregularities will equal out. It's also possible to use the median values instead of means to smooth data. One significant advantage to using medians it that outliers will have less effect on the data being smoothed, giving more reliable results.

The majority of patterns seen in time series data are describable by their trend and seasonality. **Trend** is defined as the general, systematic, linear or nonlinear changes in a component over time, which doesn't repeat during the time bring observed. **Seasonality**, on the other hand, is the repetitiveness in a data set. For example, over several years, a business may experience a significant overall rise in sales, but still have seasonal patterns of increasing and decreasing sales over each month, season, or year.

Establish Benchmarks

The cornerstone of data management is to ensure that the organization is reaching pre-determined goals. **Benchmarking** in healthcare is essentially the process of comparing one healthcare organization's performance against that of other organizations. A more technical definition is that benchmarking is a process in which the results of fundamental healthcare processes are continually measured and

80

compared. Typically, the ideas and practices of the best performers are compared with the host organization. The four distinct types of benchmarking for quality improvement include:

- Internal: comparing equivalent processes within the same organization
- Competitive: comparing similar processes to a competitor within the same industry
- Functional: comparing similar processes to those in different industries
- Generic: comparing the general concepts of processes in unrelated industries

Staff progress can be measured internally, and the separate business functions can be compared externally. Leadership within the organization can employ comparative analysis on a cyclical, weekly, or daily basis in an effort to respond to concerns in real time, rather than after the impact has reached the consumer.

It will be necessary to have frequent brainstorming sessions. **Brainstorming** can be referred to as a way of using a selected group of individuals to rapidly produce, clarify, and evaluate ideas or problems. Staff must be encouraged to preview the preliminary data, and leadership must allow for an open-ended and honest critique of what does and does not work. It is important to note that there are no right or wrong answers in brainstorming sessions, as the object is to generate momentum around finding solutions by coming up with as many ideas as possible. Brainstorming offers the team an opportunity to view all aspects of the problem and can often yield unexpected results. Results shared within the organization help each employee to connect with the results and recognize that they can affect change through their individual behaviors.

Internal benchmarking efforts encourage top performers to form more practical solutions to problems articulated by the data. Competitive benchmarking can help delineate how similar organizations solved similar defects. The comparative analysis can also reveal how the current processes are outpacing the competitors, which encourages the integration of what works with what does not work well enough. This approach will help the leadership team to deliver on the promise of providing exceptional care.

Data Driving Decision-Making

Once the leadership team has gathered, analyzed, and discussed the aggregated data, they will create a dialogue that will lead to the necessary changes. As the team interprets the data, they must keep in mind that a hypothesis cannot be proven true; one can only fail to reject the hypothesis. This means that no matter how much data the team collects, chance can always interfere with the results. Therefore, when interpreting the results of data, the leadership team must ask the following questions:

- Does the data answer our original question? How?
- Does the data help defend against any objections? How?
- Are there any limitations on our conclusions; any angles we haven't considered?

If the interpretation of the data can stand rigorous enough questioning, then the team has likely produced a useful conclusion. All that remains is to utilize the data analysis results to develop an action plan. As team members gain familiarity with data analysis, the process becomes faster and more accurate, and the organization will run more effectively by using well-informed decisions.

Practice Quiz

1. Which of the following elements is NOT typically included in the project charter?
   a. Problem statement
   b. Process map
   c. Stakeholder analysis
   d. Goal statement

2. Which of the following statements is true about random sampling?
   a. There is a less than equal probability of all units being selected when utilizing random sampling methods.
   b. This method requires extensive information about the population being sampled.
   c. This method can be used when little information is provided about the population being sampled.
   d. None of the above

3. Which measure for the center of a small sample set would be most affected by outliers?
   a. Mean
   b. Median
   c. Mode
   d. None of the above

4. Why should a healthcare organization adhere to the ISO's principles for quality management?
   a. Adherence to international healthcare standards ensures high-quality care.
   b. The ISO's principles are based on evidence of their effectiveness in multiple industries.
   c. Professionalism requires the use of external standards rather than internal standards.
   d. Adherence to ISO standards is mandated by CMS.

5. Which of the following is the best reason for an HQP to choose one data management system over another for their organization?
   a. The chosen system is already implemented by the organization.
   b. The chosen system has built-in data analysis tools for increased effectiveness.
   c. The chosen system is cheaper than other systems.
   d. The chosen system has a simpler user interface (UI), enabling more effective documentation.

See answers on the next page.

Answer Explanations

1. B: A process map typically isn't included in the project charter. Process maps are usually constructed later, as a tool within the project.

2. C: Random sampling entails randomly drawing an item so that every item drawn has an equal chance of being included in the sample. In other words, there is an equal probability with random sampling. Random sampling is a fairly simple and cost-effective method often used when little information can be obtained about the items in the population.

3. A: Mean. An outlier is a data value that's either far above or below the majority of values in a sample set. The mean is the average of all values in the set. In a small sample, a very high or low number could greatly change the average. The median is the middle value when arranged from lowest to highest. Outliers would have no more of an effect on the median than any other value. Mode is the value that repeats most often in a set. Assuming that the same outlier doesn't repeat, outliers would have no effect on the mode of a sample set.

4. B: The evidence published by the ISO demonstrating the effectiveness of their quality management standards indicates that healthcare organizations should use those standards to improve the quality of care. Choice *A* is incorrect because a standard's country of origin or widespread use does not guarantee its efficacy. Choice *C* is incorrect because a standard's externality does not mean the standard will necessarily improve quality of care. Choice *D* is incorrect because the ISO's standards of quality management are not mandated by a governmental agency.

5. B: Built-in data analysis tools that increase effectiveness is a concrete benefit to the organization's quality management program. Choice *A* is incorrect because retention of a current data management system should be based on that system's features, not administrative inertia. Choice *C* is incorrect because a cheaper system should be chosen only if it will not impair the quality of care. Choice *D* is incorrect because the quality of a system's UI does not correlate with the quality of the documentation made using that system.

Patient Safety

Technologies for Patient Safety

Medical records were not kept and maintained until the early 1920s, when physicians realized the importance of a patient's medical history when providing care. This practice was helpful, but patient histories were often incomplete and rarely accessible by other healthcare providers. Simply storing the numerous documents required entire rooms and often whole floors of hospitals and offices. It wasn't until the late 1960s when the first computer was created that the healthcare sector began to consider the widespread use of computers. Since the earliest computers were cumbersome and expensive, their use was common only in large hospitals and government agencies. The 1970s ushered in a need for more extensive medical record keeping. With the influx of American veterans returning home and needing significant medical and psychiatric care, paper medical files were largely traded in for computerized records. The introduction of President Obama's American Recovery and Reinvestment Act of 2009 required at least 70% of all healthcare organizations transition to electronic medical records by 2014.

The **electronic health record**, or **EHR**, is one of the primary tools utilized in the maintenance of patient safety. Within many healthcare settings, the EHR is easily accessible to physicians, pharmacists, nurses, and other ancillary providers. This allows for each individual involved in caring for a specific patient to be immediately aware of any changes in diagnoses, medications, allergies, and treatments. Medications entered hastily are flagged when contradictory information, such as other medications or allergies, is noted by the sophisticated medical software. The majority of larger medical facilities have further incorporated bedside charting for all providers so that information can be easily updated in the patient's room, and wristbands are scanned prior to medication administration to confirm that appropriate medications are dispensed.

One pitfall of the electronic medical record involves the human factor. Since a computer is only capable of providing information based on what is entered, information entered inaccurately or omitted has the potential to harm a patient. Consider a patient who enters an emergency room with an acute allergic reaction to a new medication. If the hospital is not a part of the healthcare system that the patient typically frequents, this information may not be readily available in the electronic record. This opens the door for inaccurate patient records and the possibility of harm to the patient. For these reasons, numerous companies have software specifically developed to safeguard electronic medical records. Currently, those safeguards often include extensive firewalls, applications that require rolling and random password changes, multiple tiers of medical record access, and closed network connections.

Additional technological security measures that have been instituted in healthcare organizations include those created for infants and patients managing mental health concerns. The majority of labor and delivery, nursery, and mother-baby units within hospitals are equipped with technologically enhanced abduction protocols. When admitted to the labor and delivery unit, expectant mothers receive a regular hospital wristband with a patient identification number. Once the infant is born, they also receive a similar ankle bracelet with the corresponding mother's name and their own patient identification number; this number is also connected with the medical records of the birth mother.

Infants must travel in a bassinette and are always accompanied by medical personnel from their respective units in the hospital. Once reunited with the birth mother, both arm bands are scanned, to

84

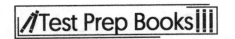

confirm that both the mother and child are related through the patient identification numbers. The ankle bracelet is also equipped with an alarm that will sound and disable all points of egress from the unit, to prevent abduction. A similar alert wristband is used for inpatient mental health units, those admitted from correctional facilities, or those at risk for suicide. Patients at risk for elopement are prevented from exiting the floor or entering elevators. Other rooms are equipped with cameras that continually monitor patients. Overall, the technological improvements and changes are necessary to guard the protected health information of all patients.

Ongoing Safety Evaluations

One of the most significant and effective practices that healthcare quality professionals can employ in risk assessment is the Lean Six Sigma method. Although initially developed in the manufacturing sector, the Lean Six Sigma method of assessing and managing risk has taken root in healthcare. Any deviation from the standard processes typically results in higher risks to the patient. The basic principles of Lean Six Sigma in relation to the management of decreasing risks to patient safety include:

- Define the expected outcome
- Measure the actual versus perceived risk
- Analyze the scope of the risk to patients
- Improve the typical versus the most-desirable outcomes
- Control the ongoing risks to patients

When improvement is required for existing processes, Lean Six Sigma helps to define, measure, analyze, improve, and control quality—or DMAIC—with staff empowered to collect the data. The **DMAIC model** allows for the methodical development of an action plan to streamline and standardize laborious processes, reduce waste, and mitigate risks to the patient population in any healthcare setting. One additional outflow in this process is to consider the Lean 5S method: sort, simplify, sweep, standardize, self-discipline. The priority for this facet of Lean Six Sigma is to teach the leadership team the importance of improving simplification. This exercise encourages managers and executives to model ways to remove all nonessential items in their work environment. The exercise informs their understanding of the adjustments required of front-line staff. All are emboldened to offer strategies that remove redundant processes, while increasing focus on what is vital.

In the initial step, Lean Six Sigma professionals partner with the leadership of healthcare organizations and their risk management team to create an assessment of current processes. The team then works to create a process map, formulate problem and goal statements, and identify the specific needs of patients and medical staff. This approach is solution focused, and unidirectional. Each interdepartmental connection is assessed for interruptions in current processes. Raw quantitative data, in the form of near-miss and sentinel events, are gathered and analyzed. Incident reports are also reviewed in an effort to backtrack and pinpoint any breakdowns in processes, areas for improving the skillset of each employee, and ways to increase the quality of care provided. Process maps are compared with actual staff activities and then restructured around the new, more practical solutions. Finally, the team will work with leadership to ensure that the new response plan is effective and discuss methods to integrate new processes throughout the organization.

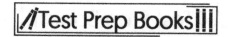
Safety Culture

Whether an administrator or a member of the leadership team, one of an HQP's duties is to encourage a culture of safety within their healthcare organization. A workplace with a **culture of safety** is an environment in which administrative and management staff, front-line staff, and people receiving services are encouraged to support a patient-centered approach to safety. This requires not just responding to safety events in the workplace—such as a medication error or a physical injury—but cultivating a proactive attitude toward safety for all employees.

A proactive approach to patient safety is one in which the organization seeks not just to have effective responses but also to establish policies and procedures intended to reduce or prevent accidents and errors from occurring. For example, a policy that all healthcare practitioners must wash their hands before each patient encounter reduces the chance that an infectious disease will spread within a clinic or hospital. The HQP ought to encourage the organization's employees to maintain a proactive perspective during their daily duties. This is one aspect of cultivating a broader safety culture in the organization. Proactive safety practices can also be encouraged through advocating for policy and procedure changes that monitor high-risk operations and require operational assessment to catch errors before patient safety is impacted.

The exact procedures that ought to be implemented will vary from one healthcare organization to another based on the needs of a particular organization. For example, it's unlikely that an outpatient provider of non-emergency psychological services will manage medications on-site. One of the HQP's job tasks as part of developing safety procedures is to determine the areas of greatest risk and devise procedures for recommendations to the leadership team, which takes a proactive approach to reducing risk.

A patient-centered approach to safety culture requires safety advocates in the healthcare organization—such as the HQP—to continually emphasize that the quality of patient outcomes is the organization's priority. Safety is a significant facet of quality of care because unsafe healthcare practices make it difficult to achieve high-quality outcomes. The essence of this perspective is that the HQP ought to ask themselves, "How does this task improve our patients' well-being?" while devising procedures, analyzing risk, or providing trainings to other employees.

These concepts can be implemented to encourage a workplace culture of safety by fostering a spirit of honest collaboration and trust within the organization. Efforts to do so should not focus on independent departments or collaboration between administration and a particular team of employees. Rather, culture-building efforts ought to take a holistic approach to the workplace milieu. Internal trust among members of a department is just as important as the camaraderie between two departments or between front-line staff and administrative staff. A universal focus on patient-centered care and safety-first principles can be a powerful way to encourage mutual *esprit de corps*.

Some techniques the HQP can use to enhance the organization's culture of safety include providing training opportunities, facilitating teamwork exercises, and actively seeking out employee feedback on the organization's current practices. In particular, trainings provide the HQP an opportunity not just to educate staff members on new policies, procedures, or safety requirements that impact their jobs but also provide an opportunity for dialogue with front-line staff about why the changes will improve patient outcomes. This dialogue increases employees' investment in the organization's operations.

However, a supportive culture about healthcare safety requires trust and sincerity from both administrative staff and front-line employees. The HQP needs to listen carefully when staff members voice safety concerns about procedures, operational requirements, or patient care. Collaboration is an active process that requires the HQP to respond to ideas and concerns raised by each individual. Providing specific details rather than broad statements encourages open communication through demonstrating administrative honesty.

Safety Concepts

Upon completion of the analysis of any near-miss or sentinel event, the findings must be integrated into the current policies and procedures. Controlling the incidence and prevalence of sentinel events involves implementing practices that also improve the quality of care provided to patients. Technological advances in medical care have dramatically impacted healthcare delivery and overall patient safety. From the EHR to abduction and elopement security systems to smart medication pumps, innovations can either enhance or endanger overall patient safety. Proponents of patient safety often speak to the benefits of utilizing technology to augment current processes. Accurate record keeping allows quality specialists to protect the interests of the organization and the patient. Tracking the incidence and prevalence of near-miss and sentinel events is vital to meeting local and governmental regulations. The leadership team is responsible for organizing, coordinating, and facilitating the development of programs that control the clinical risks associated with patient care services in healthcare organizations. The organization must periodically conduct utilization reviews to uncover documentation irregularities. Most often, safety audits begin with reviews of patient medical records; this necessitates the importance of the standardization of documentation in the legal medical records.

Patient safety has become synonymous with risk management. Unfortunately, despite the numerous safeguards, individuals evaluating the level of care that patients receive must develop practices that confront those risks. Quality control specialists require extensive knowledge in the management of patient relations and how to de-escalate conflict. Communication skills, team building, and leadership effectiveness are all integral to the maintenance of established patient safety goals.

Risk management agents work diligently to ensure that the medical treatments patients receive do not result in associated risks. They are trained to evaluate the potential for harm as well as the causes for real events. They act when near-miss or sentinel events occur and periodically review national statistics in an effort to prevent future incidents. Whenever a healthcare provider engages in activities that contradict the current policies and procedures of the organization, those actions can and often do result in actual or potential harm to the patient. Emphasis remains on how to design and alter work processes to focus on safety, quality, and improved performance standards for the hospital system. The ultimate goal of the integration of risk management and quality control in healthcare program evaluation is to streamline current processes in favor of more efficient and effective methods.

Safety Principles

Professionals that examine the principles of patient safety and quality management use qualitative and quantitative data to measure the impact of errors in healthcare delivery. **Qualitative research** in risk management yields data in the form of concepts, which gives insight and understanding to contributing factors. **Quantitative investigation** reveals raw numbers, which are then typically translated into more familiar and relatable terms. The EHR forced facilities to install costly software with no guarantee that it would meet their needs. Numerous firewalls and passwords cannot always prevent basic human error

This material is provided for exam preparation purposes only and does not indicate an endorsement of any specific scientific, political, or religious point of view. © TPB Publishing. You have been licensed one copy of this document for personal use only. Any other reproduction or redistribution is strictly prohibited. All rights reserved.

when data are entered. High-reliability organizations often flourish in adversity with above-average security measures. Proponents of systems analysis combine the deeper dive with a broad view and tie all of the factors together. Critical analysis of each element within the system facilitates improved functioning of the organization as a whole. Each form of data is combined to further the goal of increasing patient safety.

It is important to consider the ethical and financial cost of breaches in patient safety. Adverse events within healthcare organizations results in a loss of credibility for a particular organization, but also can be catastrophic to the entire healthcare industry. Hospitals may lose the confidence of patients and may even face excessive financial losses. Failures to address the root cause and the subsequent effects of near-miss and sentinel events profoundly affect the patients and medical staff, extended families, friends, and society. The more significant the event is, the higher the likelihood of the offending organization dissolving.

Using an ongoing team approach develops strategies for predicting and preventing the incidence of sentinel and near-miss events. Evidence-based practice has revealed that certain principles, when followed, improve overall patient safety. Although no specific method is significantly more valuable than any other; each has its own merit. The similarities of each technique can be found in the shared goals of enhancing the overall culture of safety, and the mitigation of risk to patients. Techniques such as systems thinking and introducing the methods associated with high-reliability organizations have produced significant advances in risk management.

Human-Factors Engineering

Human-factors engineering, also known as **ergonomics**, is a discipline that develops devices and technology based on the physical and psychological needs of those who use them. This field combines technological advances in healthcare with the specific needs of humans in mind.

As an example, the nurse manager of a thirty-bed medical surgical unit was advised of a near-miss medication error for an elderly patient receiving hypertensive medications. Although the error was caught before the patient received the medication, the director of nursing assembled a risk management team to review the case. The patient had been admitted earlier that morning, was transferred to the inpatient unit after an episode of syncope at a local skilled nursing facility, and the attending physician requested that the patient be admitted for a head computed tomography (CT) scan to determine if any head injury had occurred. The patient's diagnoses included Alzheimer's disease and hypertension. The patient was nonverbal, and no family members were available at the time of the admission. The patient was admitted with the same medication list, but the attending physician called in additional orders at the time of admission. Orders to discontinue the hypertensive medications to rule out hypotension as a cause for the fall were not transcribed or discussed during the transition of care to the next nurse. This example underscores the human factors involved in evaluating patient safety activities. Human fallibility is the cause for this near miss.

Human-factors engineering focuses on how to build technology through usability testing, forcing functions, and as a work around. Usability explains how the device is used in a real-world situation. Forcing functions prevents one step from being completed without a prior necessary step. This case presents an opportunity to enhance patient handoffs, encourage immediate order transcription, or to institute a policy adding a secondary nurse to electronically cosign medication administration at the bedside. This event also presents an opportunity for departmental leadership to offer training and discussion regarding the importance of highlighting the overall culture of quality within the department.

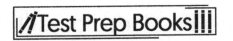

High Reliability

There are five specific factors that make operating as a high-reliability organization advantageous: reliance on practical experience, loyalty in adversity, an outcome-focused approach, an emphasis on operationalized definitions of expected outcomes, and a deeper-dive perspective when unexpected problems arise. Organizations that adopt this method of risk management achieve a high level of excellence because they focus on anticipating the best response to the worst-case scenario.

The Joint Commission has established benchmarks for quality that drive the high-reliability organization to consistently anticipate probable threats to patient safety. This model also provides transparency, accountability, and shared responsibility within the organization that reinforces problem solving. It also increases facility-wide awareness of new initiatives that reinforce patient safety. Equipped with this qualitative approach to risk management, the leadership team can prepare to follow the data points where they lead. These occurrences are not desired, but they are used as opportunities.

A sentinel event involving the death of a patient in an intensive care unit, after an anaphylactic reaction to a hastily administered blood transfusion, can be examined using the standard high-reliability approach. Facilities that utilize this approach would begin with a roundtable discussion to reveal the basic facts of the incident. Critical care nurses who routinely infuse blood, as well as emergency room nurses, would serve as the practical experts in this case. The nurse in question would not be abandoned but educated on the best practices as evidenced by the techniques of more experienced colleagues. Their collective experience can help shed light on which procedural steps were missed or how current practices may be inadequate. A more in-depth exploration of the contributing factors, and a focus on established procedures, helps to expose gaps in current processes. Once uncovered, the risk management team can begin to work quickly to find the solution.

Systems Thinking

Systems thinking involves a more holistic approach to risk management assessment. One main goal is to understand how the different parts of the whole system work together. While typical program evaluation tends to compartmentalize, this approach investigates each incident based on how the separate systems within the hospital network have influenced an outcome. This method deconstructs the incident without an expected conclusion. Systems thinking involves asking two questions. How does each separate system contribute to the problem? In what ways can each system contribute to the solution? Recognizing that each department is itself a subsystem, equally dependent on the other departments, exposes the complex relationship as it relates to the whole. It is impossible to provide excellent care to patients without the interdependency of the entire facility.

Systems thinking also enlists cognitive mapping as a way to represent physical locations. Areas where each subsystem perceives its connections to the others can help identify still more points of interaction that contributed to the sentinel event. Does each separate department have the capacity to identify and accept responsibility for their contribution to the problem? Quality experts are also assembled for the purpose of integrating departmental perspectives to identify patterns. Often, these unexpected results help to formulate a cohesive picture of how the system has broken down.

Systems thinking is also vital in building confidence throughout the organization. The ability to rely on each individual department to demand individual and collective responsibility for their own parts in the process sets the stage for interdepartmental transparency and accountability. Systems thinking challenges antiquated and inadequate processes to protect the patient population of any healthcare setting.

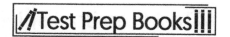

Safety and Risk Management

Safety Event/Incident Reporting

According to the US government's National Institutes of Health, a **safety event** is "any process, act of omission, or commission that results in hazardous healthcare conditions and/or unintended harm to the patient." As this broad definition indicates, it is the responsibility of all members of the healthcare organization to remain vigilant about their actions—and what actions they don't perform—to maximize patient safety and the organization's quality of care. Minimization of safety events is just one reason that continuous improvement practices are so important to a healthcare organization.

After every safety event, it is best practice for the staff who were on duty during that event to complete an **incident report.** This report documents the safety event, how staff responded to the event, and the healthcare outcomes for all patients involved. Depending on the nature of the healthcare organization, additional information may also be required. For example, it's less likely that a general practitioner's office will experience safety events that result in a staff member's injury than in a psychiatric hospital. Consequently, the incident report for the psychiatric hospital must be designed to routinely cover a broader variety of safety events than an organization that sees less diverse sources of risk.

Once the front-line staff complete the incident report, it needs to be submitted to the organization's data management system so that the HQP and other administrative personnel can complete a risk management analysis of the safety event.

The first step is to read the incident report. After that, the nurses and other staff involved must be interviewed. Did the nurse follow every step in the established protocol? Is it possible that the nurse may have been overtired or overextended with too many patients? Staffing models should be examined to determine if the nurse-to-patient ratios are adequate for each shift. In this instance, clinical quality specialists must collaborate with clinical and administrative personnel to create a workable plan of action. Once the required information has been gathered, the next step is to present the findings for the leadership of the organization to conduct a final review and root-cause analysis.

Sentinel/Unexpected Event Review

A **sentinel event** is an unforeseen occurrence that results in actual harm or death to a patient or a group of patients. In Healthcare risk management, an action or inaction that may have resulted in nonlethal injury to a patient is known as a near miss event. If there is an issue but no negative outcome occurred, and the nurse was able to resolve the issue before anything did happen, this is a near miss event. Once uncovered, a near-miss or sentinel incident highlights the policies and procedures that resulted in the error. Risk management assessments must also involve an examination of problematic behaviors within the organization that foster an unsafe environment. Simply updating obsolete policies or procedures cannot completely mitigate risk. It is often necessary to deconstruct hierarchies, review organizational management charts, leadership attitudes, and the overall culture of safety. **Adverse events** are often associated with debilitating injuries, and the risk management team can employ various techniques to analyze the actual and potential causes of the events. Formal and informal nursing practices are scrutinized, as habitual behaviors can lead to complacency. Quality and patient safety professionals then evaluate the current departmental and accreditation standards. Once it is determined which areas do not meet or exceed evidence-based standards and practices, a full risk management team is assembled to establish more effective protocols.

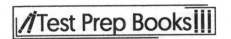
The risk management team must consist of individuals who value the organizational structure as much as they value patient safety. Medical records, incident reports, and at least one completely objective healthcare quality professional must be involved. The review panel must also include a representative from the internal ethical review board. This will ensure an accurate appraisal of the ethical implications of the incident. It will be necessary to determine which steps in the protocol led to the near-miss or sentinel event, and at which point the risk assessment team could intervene in order to prevent a recurrence of a similar incident.

Root Cause Analysis

Root-cause analysis is used to evaluate patient safety in healthcare organizations. The tool identifies the underlying causes of sentinel and near-miss events and helps develop safeguards to prevent the recurrence of the incidents. In a root-cause analysis, a healthcare quality evaluator asks a series of "why" questions regarding the incident. This process is implemented to sift through current policies and reveal causal factors within the control of the team. Patient factors are not included in this step. The team must be able to influence the root cause for the modifications to be successful. The analyst must determine a causal factor from a root cause. Although some events are identified through the detection of a near miss, a sentinel event, or an incident report, other causes may involve employees or patients requesting a resolution. This systemic approach does not insist solely upon individual accountability, but rather a consideration of areas of improvement within the organization.

Consider the following example regarding the analysis of a near-miss event, and how this event can be avoided in future interactions:

A patient being treated in an urgent care clinic was almost given a medication that would have caused an anaphylactic allergic reaction. Utilizing the "five why's," it was determined that there were multiple contributing factors. Several nurses were out sick with the flu, causing higher nurse-to-patient ratios; the nurse involved had a total of ten patients, which is more than double the allowable ratio of one-to-four ratio for the clinic. Although the nurse had received the appropriate orders from the attending physician regarding the medications, it was a verbal order, which the overextended nurse failed to transcribe. This led to a failure to add the new medication to the electronic medical record. The failure to adhere to the safeguard of scanning wristbands to retrieve the computerized medication was a significant breech in the quality of care. Interdepartmental breakdowns in staffing models, protocols for vaccinations of nursing staff (which does not replace viral control), and policies for accepting verbal orders could have all influenced this near miss. This root-cause analysis opens the dialogue to examine the best methods to verify improvement once the new processes are implemented.

An alternate form of program evaluation involves a more outcome-based method. Quality and safety professionals work to determine how any given process within the system might fail. **Failure mode and effect analysis** is not a quantitative approach but does seek to uncover ways the departments can operationalize their efforts. The purpose is to find solutions before they are needed. This form of program evaluation enlists a qualitative approach to better understand and prevent future and ongoing threats to patient safety. The actual staff must be involved, as they can help identify gaps in the practical application of the results. Both actual and perceived failures in practice are examined. Three specific questions are asked and answered:

- What is the severity of the effect on the patient?
- How often is this event likely to occur?
- How easily can the patient independently identify the problem?

91

Each category is ranked by potential effect, severity of the effect, the potential cause and probability of occurrence, and detection severity. Ranked in severity from 1 to 10 by the team, they are placed in descending order to begin the brainstorming portion of the problem-solving process. The assembled team then begins working to create solutions to the identified problems. Wherever the actual failures rank as a 5 or greater, the risk assessment team targets how to implement the most effective solutions. The process continues with the team developing an action plan and as momentum builds, more solutions become apparent. Quality analysts then examine the evidence within the incident report and compare the findings to similar events. Gaps in processes are filled and strengths leveraged within the system to prevent future recurrence of the event. The success of the intervention is determined by process improvement and evidenced by a lower incidence of comparable events.

Proactive Risk Assessment

It is essential to maintain strict guidelines regarding quality and patient safety. Patient safety specialists often need to collaborate with the risk management team, quality department, patient advocates, infection prevention, and members of the board of ethics. Quality professionals must have an intimate knowledge of healthcare organizations and accreditation standards, and they must possess the ability to apply them. **The Joint Commission of Healthcare Organizations** was officially formed in 1951 as a formalized and structured way to monitor patient safety in healthcare settings. Currently, The Joint Commission accredits, or recognizes, over 20,000 hospitals, nursing homes, and other healthcare organizations on the quality of care that they provide. The overall mission of this nonprofit association is to independently examine the policies and procedures that threaten patient safety, and it has become the gold standard of evidence-based medical care.

Risk management professionals employ multiple tactics to evaluate patient safety in healthcare organizations. The three main principles of risk management assessment are risk identification, risk analysis, and risk mitigation.

Risk identification is the initial and most important step in the process. This involves identifying any possible risks or events that could compromise patient safety. Brainstorming, performing a root cause analysis, and reviewing available records and incident reports of past adverse or near-miss events are some ways to identify possible risks. **Risk analysis** is the next step: analyzing the likelihood of these risks and their potential impact. This analysis informs the **risk evaluation**, which evaluates the acceptability of the risk and determines whether any action needs to be taken. An acceptable risk is one that is unlikely to occur, and would have minimal impact if it did; therefore, creating a mitigation plan is not a priority. Once risks are evaluated, management can begin to create mitigation plans: what specific actions, policies, and procedures would prevent this type of incident in the future? What safeguards need to be in place at various stages in related procedures to undergird current processes? Risk management teams then develop measures to increase quality of care through the adaptation of specific control measures. The following example highlights the application of this strategy:

A patient admitted for a below-the-knee amputation of the left leg reported a concern to the nursing manager. According to the patient, the physician entered the room, discussed the procedure, and marked the right leg for the procedure. When the patient protested, the physician advised him that the medical chart indicated the right leg as the limb to be removed. When the patient continued to protest and refused to sign the consent form for the incorrect limb, the physician cancelled the surgery and left the room angrily. When the nursing manager reviewed additional patient records, it was revealed that the patient had been correct; somehow, the medical record had been updated incorrectly the previous evening. The patient had developed a decubitus ulceration on the right heel, which was scheduled for

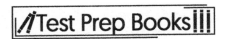

debridement. The physician that reviewed the notes assumed that the right limb, not the left, would be removed. The nurse manager consulted the physician, and the surgery was rescheduled for the correct limb. A risk management team was assembled to review this near-miss event and it became clear that there was a miscommunication during the patient handoff from the surgical resident to the attending surgeon.

Two issues were noted during the risk assessment: The policy to conduct patient report at the bedside was not followed, and the correct limb was not marked per NPS guidelines. This incident could be avoided in the future by following established procedures regarding surgery time out. To control the likelihood of this event being repeated, the quality professional proposed that the surgical team receive additional training regarding the time-out requirements and procedures regarding bedside report. Continued education credits were provided to clinical staff as part of their annual continuing education requirements. Finally, the leadership team released a facility-wide newsletter, which included a brief synopsis of the event and the NPS guidelines regarding bedside report and surgery time out. The next step is to facilitate ongoing adherence to new patient safety guidelines.

Practice Quiz

1. Which of the following is the best way to prevent the spread of infection?
   a. Keeping the mouth covered when coughing or sneezing
   b. Disinfecting shared patient equipment
   c. Practicing proper hand hygiene
   d. Avoiding contact with infectious patients

2. Which of the following is now considered synonymous with risk management?
   a. Sentinel events
   b. Systems thinking
   c. Ergonomics
   d. Patient safety

3. Which of the following tools would NOT be used to determine why goals were not achieved or why there was a discrepancy between expected outcomes and actual outcomes?
   a. Six Sigma
   b. Gap analysis
   c. Root cause analysis
   d. Cause-and-effect diagram

4. Processes should be audited regularly to ensure they are providing the same results and outcomes consistently. What method monitors a process from start to finish to ensure the same results occur every time?
   a. Transparency
   b. Validation
   c. Data collection
   d. Risk management

5. Which of the following is a proactive safety procedure?
   a. Counting medications at the end of each shift
   b. Completing incident reports within four hours of a safety event
   c. Asking the patient's name and date of birth before a surgical procedure
   d. Weekly team meetings in each department

See answers on the next page.

94

Answer Explanations

1. C: All of the answer choices are types of standard precautions, but research has shown that proper hand hygiene using soap and water or an alcohol-based hand rub (if appropriate) is the best way to prevent the spread of germs.

2. D: Patient safety has become synonymous with risk management. Prioritizing patient safety in all cases is critical in preventing injuries.

3. A: Six Sigma is a specific technique that works to improve business processes by implementing various tools and concepts to reduce errors and eliminate waste. Gap analysis, root cause analysis, and cause-and-effect diagrams; Choices *B, C,* and *D*; are incorrect because they are all tools that would be used to determine why goals were not achieved or if there was a discrepancy between the expected results and actual results.

4. B: Validation is the auditing method used to ensure that a process delivers the same outcomes each time it is used. Validation looks at each step within a process to ensure consistency and predictability. Choice *A,* transparency, is a vital component of communication that builds trust. Choice *C,* data collection, refers to the specific process of sourcing information. Choice *D,* risk management, is the process that identifies potential risks within a process.

5. C: Asking the patient's name and date of birth before a surgical procedure is proactive because it is a step prior to staff action with the intent to reduce errors in the hospital. Choices *A, B,* and *D* are incorrect. They describe practices that improve safety in a reactive way, rather than a proactive way, because they address staff action after it has been performed.

Quality Review and Accountability

Standards, Best Practices, and Other Information

Historically, **evidence-based practices (EBP)** are those that have been proven, over time, to yield the most clinically significant impact on healthcare quality and standards. Strict adherence to EBP promotes commitment and professionalism. Many different organizations contribute to the body of knowledge known as evidence-based practices. The leading agencies responsible for shaping the best-practice body of knowledge include: the Institute for Healthcare Improvement (IHI), the World Health Organization (WHO), the National Quality Forum (NQF), and the Agency for Healthcare Research and Quality (AHRQ). Combining their endorsed policies, procedures, and practices, these agencies have developed the structure for improving the quality of patient care around the world.

In 2001, the Institute of Medicine produced their "**Quality chasm**" report which detailed their major concerns about the differences in quality between current healthcare deficiencies and the ideal. The IHI later released a follow up to that report, denoting the six aims for improvement necessary to bridge the chasm: safety, effectiveness, patient-focused, timeliness, efficiency, and equitability. The goal of this report was to spark conversation around healthcare disparities and encourage momentum toward a culture of quality.

The NQF and AHRQ both endorse the utilization of quality performance measures to evaluate processes, patient experience, outcomes, and organizational structure. Both agencies also showed that repeated benchmarking (internal and external) fosters healthy competition that is needed to improve healthcare quality. The WHO implemented global efforts of quality and safety by initiating protocols on a larger scale. The WHO considers the importance of implementing healthcare interventions through a culturally sensitive approach. Since the inception of the Global Initiative for Emergency and Essential Surgical Care (GIEESC) in 2005, over 2,300 members and stakeholders from 140 countries have partnered together to improve access to quality healthcare around the world. This globalized healthcare organization has succeeded in changing the healthcare narrative to include underserved and economically-disadvantaged populations.

The **Healthcare Effectiveness Data and Information Set (HEDIS)** is a group of performance standards that the majority of health plans adhere to in an effort to standardize the overall quality of care delivered to patients. These standards include areas related to quality of care, access to care, and member satisfaction. In its entirety, HEDIS comprises a total of 92 diverse measures across six specific types of care, and it is used by over 90% of the healthcare plans in America. HEDIS is a powerful tool that is run by a private, non-profit organization called the **National Committee for Quality Assurance (NCQA)**. This data clearinghouse allows for an internal benchmark, as health plans can review their own previous results and identify upward and downward trends. With HEDIS, it is possible to measure the effectiveness and quality of healthcare plans worldwide. Healthcare leaders understand the significance of using evidence-based practice to achieve better health outcomes. When the priority is placed on improving quality outcome measures, patients and all other stakeholders reap the benefits. The **Quality Compass** is an interactive web-based tool within the NCQA arsenal that generates quality reports based on specific plans, benchmarks, and time frames.

One additional facet of the HEDIS quality standards is the **Consumer Assessment of Healthcare Providers and Systems (CAHPS)** survey, which was developed in 1995 as a method for quantifying

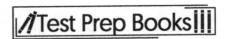

members' satisfaction regarding their overall experience with specific health plans. The general public had previously struggled to locate information regarding the standards of quality achieved and the members' subsequent satisfaction. The NCQA encourages the exchange of quality information to consumers who can view both quality adherence statistics and accreditation standards. By viewing the State of Healthcare Quality report, consumers are better equipped to monitor the report cards of healthcare plans and organizations. Completed annually, the primary goal of this quality report is focused improvement of the dissemination, implementation, and spread of evidence-based care across the country.

CMS, commercial health plans, and private physicians, as well as healthcare leaders and legislators, worked diligently to develop the Core Quality Measure Collaborative. The **Core Quality Measures** were developed to promote evidence-based care, decrease healthcare expenditures, and encourage providers to utilize bundling of services.

Internal and External Requirements

As previously mentioned, the accreditation and certification process is multifaceted and requires significant preparation and buy-in from all members of the organization. The leadership team members must be equipped with the ability to monitor the organization's rate of compliance with evidence-based standards of practice. As the experts in clinical performance, it is imperative that the leadership team develops a method of gathering the data necessary to reflect adherence to the established requirements of the governing body. It is even more important for them to establish a method for data analysis and interpretation. It is through the clarification of the data that obsolete or ineffective procedures and policies can justifiably be transformed. For healthcare organizations in the position of providing clinical bedside care, there is a particular concern regarding medication use, infection rates, service quality, practitioner performance, gaps in expected outcomes for patients, and reportable events.

Clinical Practice Guidelines, Pathways, and Outcomes

When preparing for an on-site evaluation for accreditation, the medication administration policies and procedures of any healthcare organization are crucial. The leadership team, which includes physicians and the chief nursing officer, has the responsibility of deciding which clinical practice guidelines the organization will follow. When managing the care of patients, the safe administration of those medications is of paramount importance. Each clinician bears the responsibility of adhering to the five rights of medication administration, which ensures that each encounter involves: the right drug, the right dose, via the right route, at the right time, to the right patient.

With the advent of EHR, many healthcare facilities have charting at the bedside. This step is thought to encourage the clinician to confirm that all five objectives are met with the additional act of the bedside checks. The nurse is encouraged to review the medications as shown in the EHR, ensure that the EHR and medication taken from the medication cart or Pyxis match, and confirm that the EHR matches the medication retrieved from the med cart and is placed into the correct patient's medication basin. The data are gathered through the nurse actually scanning each medication and clicking the EHR in the appropriate section. In some cases, failure to perform this added task can prevent the administration of the medication and flag the patient chart for review.

Despite advances in technology helping to reduce medication errors, adverse drug events are still a significant cause of harm to patients. The ICU presents a higher risk of medication errors due to the nature of its more complex care. Additionally, such incidents in the ICU have been shown to more frequently cause serious harm or death to patients than elsewhere. Clinical practice guidelines are used to improve medication safety by highlighting strategies and changes that can be implemented in the ICU. Following guidelines and pathways results in fewer medication errors, improves quality of care and quality of life, and reduces risk and professional liability.

There are also several guidelines for infection prevention. The CDC guidelines for preventing the spread of infections in healthcare settings is the basic guideline adopted nationwide. There are two tiers of recommended precautions:

- Standard precautions should be used in all patient care settings. They are based on the assumption that each person may have an infectious disease, so a prudent person would use protection when dealing with body fluids. Standard precautions include hand hygiene; personal protective equipment (PPE); respiratory hygiene/cough etiquette; proper placement of patients; cleaning and disinfecting equipment, instruments/devices, and the healthcare environment; careful handling of laundry and textiles; safe injection practices; and healthcare worker safety, including correct handling and disposal of needles and other sharps.

- Transmission-based precautions are used in addition to standard precautions and address the method of exposure the patient may have.

  1. Contact precautions should be used with patients who have a known or suspected infection with an increased risk for transmission via contact.

  2. Droplet precautions should be used with patients who have a known or suspected infection that is transmitted via respiratory droplets (e.g., droplets formed when a patient is talking, coughing, or sneezing).

  3. Airborne precautions should be used with patients who have a known or suspected infection that is transmitted via air from person to person (e.g., influenza, chickenpox, measles, anthrax, tuberculosis, smallpox, and SARS).

In addition to ensuring that all employees are educated about infection prevention, the leadership team must determine the best method of ensuring that the protocols are carried out. Leaders may oversee changes to infection control policies and processes and receive regular reports from infection prevention committees or teams. Administration generally also has input into who makes the determination of where patients are placed upon admission. It is not enough anymore to randomly assign beds based upon which floor has the most room. Careful attention must be made to avoid patient cross contamination.

Leadership is also responsible for ensuring that the following processes and policies are followed. These are key measures during site visits for all organizations and are often the cause of errors or sentinel events. In order to ensure patient safety each one must be regularly assessed, and policies must be reviewed and updated according to organizational policy. The healthcare organization must have policies and procedures that address the following:

- hand hygiene
- use of personal protective equipment

98

- respiratory hygiene/cough etiquette principles
- appropriate patient placement
- the proper cleaning and handling of patient equipment and instruments
- the proper handling of textiles and laundry
- safe injection practices
- safe sharps handling and disposal
- the steps needed to clean and disinfect the environment

Quality-Based Payment Programs

Leaders understand that service quality is one of the most important factors to monitor. It will always be necessary to make sure that all of the applicable quality indicators are met and that service to all patients remains at the highest level. Practitioner performance is directly related to the provider's ability to maintain a standard of excellence in clinical practice and service delivery. It is also imperative that organizational leaders work with departmental team leaders and managers to encourage their direct reports to consider options for credentialing. This is not only vital to the actual employee, but for the team, department, and organization as a whole. One of the best ways to accomplish this task is through ongoing peer reviews. Despite the fact that most managers are aware of the roles that each individual employee is supposed to play on their team, they may not be aware of how that employee interacts with other team members. It may be even more difficult for the manager to accurately assess the untapped strengths of the members of their team. Peer reviews provide colleagues with the opportunity to share constructive feedback about each other in confidence.

Value-based payment is a system originally implemented by CMS to increase accountability of healthcare providers and improve quality. Value-based payment assumes that quality is easily quantifiable, but measurement of healthcare quality is still improving. A challenge for value-based payment is that the high volume of data that needs to be recorded is time-consuming and might not always be relevant or helpful to patients. A study in 2014 reported that medical practices spend 15.1 hours per week tracking quality metrics for Medicare and other payers.

There have been efforts to implement EHRs to reduce difficulty of tracking data, but the solution isn't perfect. In many cases, using EHRs has simply changed the busy work from analog paperwork to digital data recording. One concern is that quality is largely measured by whether certain routine tasks have been accomplished. Those invested in the healthcare industry have pushed for a focus on patient health outcomes, since healthcare providers will assume greater financial responsibility under value-based repayment and other models. Additional metrics would then be necessary to reliably track such outcomes.

Documentation

Because the healthcare industry is extremely high-risk, compliance is of utmost importance. Healthcare compliance consists of obeying various rules, laws, and regulations implemented at both state and federal levels that guide the healthcare industry and its practices. Compliance impacts every area of healthcare, but its most important functions are regulating patient safety, patient privacy, and billing. Lack of compliance can lead to fines, lawsuits, and may even end with loss of licenses if a violation is serious enough.

It is vitally important for those working in the healthcare industry to maintain knowledge of compliance practices; however, this can often be a complicated process as laws and regulations change. The following is a list of some of the organizations and federal regulations that set healthcare compliance standards:

- **Social Security Act (SSA)**: Lays out the requirements for Medicare, Medicaid, and various other programs for maternal and child healthcare (e.g., CHIP) as well as supporting the administration of some of the programs.

- **Health Insurance Portability and Accountability Act (HIPAA)**: Sets national standards for patient privacy and the protection of patients' medical records and personal health information. It also includes other aspects such as the Administrative Simplification provision, which mandates that the HHS adopt standards to streamline communications between health plans and healthcare providers.

- **Health Information Technology for Economic and Clinical Health Act (HITECH Act)**: Incentivizes the use of electronic health records and other healthcare information technology.

- **False Claims Act (FCA)**: Prohibits submitting fraudulent healthcare claims to the federal government.

- **Patient Protection and Affordable Care Act (ACA)**: Regulates private insurance, expanded Medicaid, and provides subsidies to make health insurance more affordable.

- **Drug Enforcement Administration (DEA)**: Enforces laws and regulations regarding controlled substances.

- **Food and Drug Administration (FDA)**: Regulates medications, vaccines, biological products, and medical devices as well as dietary supplements.

- **Office of the Inspector General (OIG)**: Investigates fraud, waste, and abuse for programs under the Department of Health and Human Services, particularly Medicaid and Medicare.

The **Office of Inspector General (OIG)** of the **Department of Health and Human Services (HHS)** fronts efforts promoting voluntary development and implementation of compliance programs in the healthcare industry. Compliance guidelines for healthcare were issued by the OIG in 1998, which stated that comprehensive compliance programs should include at least the following seven elements:

1. The development and distribution of written standards of conduct, as well as written policies and procedures that promote the hospital's commitment to compliance, including adherence to compliance as an element in evaluating managers and employees;

2. The designation of a chief compliance officer and other appropriate bodies, charged with the responsibility of operating and monitoring the compliance program, and who report directly to the CEO and the governing body;

3. The development and implementation of regular, effective education and training programs for all affected employees;

4. The maintenance of a process, such as a hotline, to receive complaints, and the adoption of procedures to protect the anonymity of complainants and to protect whistleblowers from retaliation;

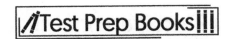
5. The development of a system to respond to allegations of improper/illegal activities and the enforcement of appropriate disciplinary action against employees who have violated internal compliance policies, applicable statutes, regulations or Federal healthcare program requirements;

6. The use of audits and/or other evaluation techniques to monitor compliance and assist in the reduction of identified problem area; and

7. The investigation and remediation of identified systemic problems and the development of policies addressing the non-employment or retention of sanctioned individuals.

The prevention of fraud, abuse, and waste in healthcare systems was improved by the development of voluntary compliance programs. Compliance programs are intended to develop a culture that prevents, detects, and resolves conduct that doesn't comply with healthcare law, healthcare program requirements, or the hospital's ethical and business practices. Ideally, a compliance program will show commitment to the compliance process and become a daily part of operations. It is important to use benchmarks that demonstrate the effectiveness and accomplishments from implementing the compliance program.

Executive leadership can, and must, lay out a framework for compliance that includes elements of transparency and ethical behavior. Ultimately, however, they can only set the tone. Compliance must be an organization-wide effort that each staff member upholds.

Most facilities use an electronic health record, which enables documentation to include time of observation, time task was performed, what was done, how it was done, and reaction to intervention. Documentation requirements are dictated by facility policy and regulatory guidelines. Two methods are commonly used: charting by exception and comprehensive charting. Charting by exception requires that only vital signs and abnormal findings are documented. This charting method is somewhat controversial since a great amount of information about the patient is usually left out. It is sometimes argued that this is the safer way to chart, as only what is deviant from normal is noted, and thus, there is less room for documentation errors. The normal is assumed, unless otherwise noted. This method also saves time, as less information needs to be documented, leaving more time for patient care.

Some facilities prefer a comprehensive method of documentation, charting everything about the patient, normal and abnormal, in a very thorough manner. This way, when the chart is reviewed, all details surrounding any event should be present in the medical record.

Practitioner Performance Evaluation

Today, peer review is acknowledged as an ideal method to create a community that promotes professionalism and trust, while maintaining physicians' agency and upholding their duty of care. Peer reviews may be performed by various committees (e.g., ethics committees, credentials committees, and utilization committees), or by other reviewing bodies. The goal of peer review is to examine the conduct of healthcare professionals, and it is the primary method of performing such an evaluation.

The **American Medical Association (AMA) Code of Medical Ethics** states that physicians are obligated not only to uphold medical ethics and professional standards themselves, but to hold each other accountable as well. **Fairness** is a necessary element to any hearing that has bearing on the reputation or livelihood of a medical practitioner. Any individuals that take part in the peer review of others must strive diligently for a fair and objective review.

101

The Joint Commission outlines both the credentialing and privileging of medical practitioners.

> **Credentialing** is the process of obtaining, verifying, and assessing the qualifications of a practitioner to provide care or services in or for a healthcare organization. Credentials are documented evidence of licensure, education, training, experience, or other qualifications.

Credentialing is used to verify that data in an organization's documents is correct. An individual responsible for credentialing physicians uses multiple resources to verify this information, including a copy of the physician's National Provider Databank (NPDB) file, a credit report, and a criminal background check. The credentialing agency will also request a copy of the physician's credentials from the organization that presented them to verify accuracy. As part of an effort to lower rates of insurance fraud and abuse, the Affordable Care Act increased the credentialing requirements for Medicare and Medicaid, requiring the implementation of a repeat credentialing and confirmation process. The Joint Commission provides a detailed description of privileging.

> **Privileging** is the process whereby a specific scope and content of a patient care services are authorized for a healthcare practitioner by a healthcare organization, based on an evaluation of the individual's credentials and performance. A privilege is defined as an advantage, right, or benefit that is not available to everyone; the rights and advantages enjoyed by a relatively small group of people, usually as a result of education and experience. Privileges are specific to services provided at a specific location. Privileges can only be granted by the organization for services that are performed in the environment or organizations' location/building.

Patient Experience

Patient satisfaction is becoming increasingly important as the cost of healthcare and health insurance increases and patients assume a larger financial responsibility in their personal healthcare. Additionally, it is clear that every provider and nurse handoff creates the potential for miscommunication and mistakes. As a result, patients wanting the best value from their healthcare services must now make more involved decisions regarding their options and their care. It is critical that healthcare organizations utilize data gleaned from sources such as patient surveys, focus groups, team meetings, grievances, and complaints to meet these needs. Recognizing this change, the Centers for Medicare and Medicaid Services (CMS) have made patient satisfaction their top priority.

The **National Quality Forum (NQF)** is a non-profit organization devoted to improving patient outcomes by standardizing measurement and reporting. In May 2005, the NQF endorsed the **Hospital Consumer Assessment of Healthcare Providers and Systems (HCAHPS)** survey, representing the interests of healthcare providers, consumers, professional associations, government agencies, and other organizations. This is the nation's first reported, standardized survey to gauge patient views on their hospital care. The HCAHPS survey features 19 questions covering the following nine topics:

- Communication with doctors
- Communication with nurses
- Responsiveness of hospital staff
- Communication about pain
- Communication about medicines
- Discharge information
- Cleanliness of the hospital environment

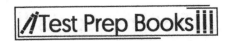

- Quietness of the hospital environment
- Transition of care

As part of the survey, there are also three screener questions to guide patients to the relevant portion of the survey, five demographic questions, and two questions for Congressionally-mandated reports, giving the survey a total of 29 official questions. Hospitals may also choose to add their own questions to the survey, but these additional survey items are not reviewed or recorded by CMS.

The purpose of the HCAHPS is to make a standardized survey and data collection method available that provides a metric of patients' views on healthcare services. Before the HCAHPS survey was implemented, there were already hospital surveys, but there was no standardization or public reporting that would allow consumers to easily compare healthcare providers. Thus, the HCAHPS was necessary to provide a standard measurement of hospital care and quality.

The survey is designed to gather data from patients that allows for relevant, objective comparisons between hospitals. Because the survey results are available to the public, hospitals are incentivized to improve the quality of their services, while increasing public accountability through the transparency of hospital care.

Reportable Events for Accreditation and Regulatory Bodies

An **adverse event** describes harm to a patient as a result of medical care or harm that occurs in a healthcare setting. A **never event** refers to a specific list of serious events or errors that should never be allowed to happen in a healthcare setting, according to the National Quality Forum. Never events include errors such as performing surgery on the wrong patient or leaving a tool or other object inside a patient after surgery. The Tax Relief and Healthcare Act of 2006 mandated that the OIG report to Congress about such events.

Patient safety event reporting systems are one of the main methods of identifying adverse events and other quality of care problems. The general term for voluntary event reporting systems is incidence reporting. It relies primarily on the healthcare providers who were involved in a patient safety incident, a near miss, or who observed unsafe conditions to give detailed reports of the event. These are passive systems, unlike provider observation, chart reviews, or electronic notifications. Additionally, they are based on each individual's definition of an incident, near miss, or unsafe conditions, which makes them less reliable than active systems.

To increase the efficacy of incidence reporting, healthcare organizations must institute reporting systems with four main components. First, they must actively support staff who report incidents and vigorously protect their privacy. Second, they must make sure that they are receiving reports from individuals at every level of the organization, not just from a narrow selection of personnel. Third, reports of any incidents must be rapidly distributed to avoid a repeat of the event. Fourth, organizations must have a system in place for reviewing incident reports and finding solutions to the issues they identify. Recent developments that can assist with these goals include web-based systems, systems that are linked to electronic medical records, and specialized systems for specific settings (e.g., the Intensive Care Unit Safety Reporting System and systems that specifically report incidents involving anesthesia).

Simply having incident reporting systems is not enough, however. Concerns have been raised that healthcare event reporting systems focus too much on gathering reports and not enough on following up with action plans to prevent further events. Without a system for finding the cause of adverse events

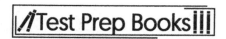
and creating solutions to avoid them, event reporting systems cannot adequately improve patient safety.

Confidentiality of Performance/Quality Improvement Records

Data management is the administrative process that acquires, validates, stores, protects, and processes data in order to maintain its accessibility, reliability, and timeliness according to the needs of the organization and consumer. Healthcare organizations analyze large data sets to guide their business decisions, discover the needs of the customer, and identify healthcare trends and opportunities to go beyond consumer expectations.

Companies develop data management solutions and platforms to handle the vast amount of data that healthcare organizations acquire. The goal with all data management solutions is to simplify the processing, validating, and handling of data, and overall become more efficient. Effective data management platforms enable healthcare organizations to manage large amounts of data from all sources to provide better communication with customers and retain customers longer. This is essential for healthcare organizations because they create and consume increasingly larger volumes of data. The best platforms provide companies a full view of their consumer base, which is necessary to gain valuable insight into consumer behavior and gain a business advantage.

In order to successfully make use of data management, organizations need to first have a goal in mind for the data they gather. A common problem for some organizations is that they may collect data well, but don't manage it properly to make it useful. Once they have a goal in mind, they can develop efficient systems to process, store, validate, and eventually analyze the data. Another problem that organizations run into is that their data might not be stored and organized in a way that can provide answers. They must focus each step of data management on their objective to make effective business decisions based on the data.

Healthcare organizations should strive to achieve the following data management best practices:

- Streamline the information flow for both traditional and emerging data
- Scrub data to ensure its accuracy and promote quality business processes
- Shape data to make it more easily understandable and usable

The **electronic health record (EHR)** is largely a collection of free-form narrative communicated by healthcare delivery. Insights, attributes of processes, prognoses, evaluations, and clinical observations are locked up in narrative. Unfortunately, narrative is not conducive to machine learning, data management, and next-generation analytics. It is only through controlled, structured, electronically-legible, and understood terminology that the value of clinical decision support, alerts, clinical rules, and analytics can be realized. Structured terminologies, also referred to as controlled medical vocabularies, provide the semantics of the concepts being conveyed in the electronic health record, and downstream in the data management foundation for analytics. Terminologies provide consistent meaning, promote shared understanding, facilitate communication, and enable comparison and integration of data. They are essential for interoperability among operational information systems, applications such as EHR sharing, and portability. Laboratory information systems also require these services as they process transactions in and out of the application. They need to translate from sending and receiving language sets.

One significant effort is underway to develop standard definitions for electronic quality measures (eMeasures). The National Quality Forum's Health Quality Measures Format recommends how health information technology (HIT) solutions should provide the data for quality measures in a standard format. The goal is to automate the measurement, feedback, and reporting of all current and future quality measures, accelerate the use of clinical decision support to improve performance on these measures, and align performance measures with the capabilities and limitations of HIT. Healthcare analytics are used to find inefficiencies in healthcare processes, identify items that can be improved, and improve implementation of resources. The lack of appropriate infrastructure, poor data integration, and privacy issues are all barriers toward adoption of analytics in healthcare.

Compliance with an organization-wide privacy policy is of paramount importance. Each individual with the potential to come into contact with protected health information must be advised of the privacy policy. The clinician must act as the gatekeeper, providing the information about any particular client's case to those specifically entitled to the information. In order to maintain the secured control of access to medical records, patients' information exists on a need-to-know basis. The **need-to-know rule** refers to individuals who must view the client's protected health information for the sole purpose of providing care. These individuals are to have access to the minimum amount of information necessary to perform the task at hand, nothing more. Only the minimum amount of information required to complete the tasks of caring for the patient should ever be released.

Signed, dated, and witnessed informed-consent forms that outline the types of information that can be released must be a mandatory facet of any treatment plan. Paper documents must be stored under lock and key with access only to the healthcare professional and necessary staff. Destruction of paper documents must occur through shredding, or by professionals proficient in document destruction. For electronic files and reports, the clinician must be diligent in the security of their desktop through the use of computer screen locks, shortened time-out locks, or black-out screens whenever the computer is left unattended. Computer access must also be limited. The clinician should consider placing the computer behind locked doors, with passwords that are changed frequently, multiple firewalls, and careful screening of incoming emails and documents to guard against computer viruses.

Whenever possible, electronic transfer of medical information, including emails and faxes, must be sent securely. The most effective process is to verbally confirm that the fax number is correct and stored in a secure location away from those without a need to know. Information to an individual should be limited to those who must have the information to perform their jobs. Any transmission of electronic medical records must contain a basic disclaimer advising the recipient on how to proceed if the documents were received in error, such as:

- This communication contains confidential information.
- If you have received this information in error, please notify the sender immediately by phone and return the original to the address listed on the form.
- Any distribution or reproduction of this transmission by anyone other than the intended party is strictly prohibited.

That verbiage, or something similar to it, should be added to all documents, emails, and other transmitted medical records. The clinician is the gatekeeper, ensuring that only the correct individuals receive the necessary information.

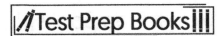

Quality Initiatives That Impact Reimbursement

Historically, physicians have received payment based on the number of patients they provide care for, defined as the **fee-for-service (FFS) method.** While the typical pay schedule generally consists of medical providers who are rarely paid incentives based on the care that they provide per qualifying health condition, recent changes to the fee-for-service model have been proposed. One of the most controversial forms of reimbursement includes the **pay for performance (P4P) method.** Although loosely based on quality indicators, the P4P model can also be seen as incentivizing physicians for efficiency, value, or reporting. It is a patient-centered quality-care model that encourages the development of a relationship between the physician and the patient. Patient perceptions of high-quality care then lead to continued collaboration with their provider. The core P4P model involves compensating providers for achieving specific quality standards or reducing healthcare costs. Quality measures typically include: patient engagement, health outcomes, care coordination, and patient satisfaction.

The current **physician value-based modifier system (PVM)** and the **value-based modifier program (VBM)** are quality-based initiatives designed to evaluate practitioners and provide payment based on adherence to specified quality indicators and cost-saving methods, rather than volume. While the P4P concept was proposed through the **Patient Protection and Affordable Care Act (PPACA)** of 2010, it was closely linked to **value-based purchasing (VBP).** The VBP operates within hospitals, as a function of CMS, providing a financial incentive for reducing the DRG payments for Medicare patients. In recent years, the shift has been toward the VBM concept, with the stipulation that sanctions will be levied against providers who fail to meet standards of practice.

Proponents of quality initiatives suggest that P4P will encourage physicians to focus on quality over quantity regarding the provision of care. Those in support of this proposal believe that physicians will take more time with each patient, which will serve to improve all of the measures simultaneously. Opponents consider the initiatives to be punitive in nature. Arguments against P4P claim that policymakers do not take into account the increasing numbers of the elderly who will require ongoing care. Increasing patient loads without a compensatory rise in the number of attending physicians will result in poor outcomes across all quality measures. Others have reported concerns regarding the logistics of implementing the reporting technology. Overall, legislators, physicians, and healthcare leaders remain divided on P4P as the primary payer system in healthcare.

Practice Quiz

1. Which is the best data collection technique to use when there's a desire to reach a large number of people while trying to minimize cost?
   a. Focus group
   b. Interviews
   c. Observation
   d. Survey

2. What does the acronym HEDIS stand for?
   a. Healthcare Effectiveness Data and Information Set
   b. Human Excellence Delivery Information Services
   c. Healthcare Episodes Data and Informative Systems
   d. Healthcare Excellence for Doctoral Interns Society

3. What is the main difference between (P4P) and (FFS)?
   a. P4P is used internationally, whereas FFS is only used in the United States.
   b. On average, FFS entails less cost for patients, whereas P4P costs more.
   c. On average, P4P entails less cost for patients, whereas FFS costs more.
   d. FFS reimburses healthcare providers based on the quantity of services performed, whereas P4P reimburses according to the quality of services performed.

4. Why is it imperative that performance and quality improvement records be kept strictly confidential?
   a. To ensure that patient privacy and anonymity is respected
   b. To ensure the anonymity of peer reviewers
   c. To ensure that practitioners' ratings are only relayed to the necessary party
   d. All of the above

5. Why are peer reviews important for the maintenance of service quality and practitioner performance?
   a. To help achieve and maintain full accreditation or certification
   b. To prevent any legal violations or citations from accrediting bodies
   c. To allow colleagues to anonymously provide the constructive feedback necessary to guide performance-improvement initiatives
   d. To provide uniformity of practice across other departments within the organization

See answers on the next page.

107

Answer Explanations

1. D: A survey is the data collection technique that's best used when there's a desire to reach a large number of people while trying to minimize cost. Focus groups are interviews with small groups of individuals (typically three to twelve) and can be time-consuming to organize. Interviews are one-on-one meetings, are usually time-consuming, and require a skilled interviewer. Finally, observation involves visiting customers and watching them as they use or misuse products or services. Observations are also time-consuming and require a skilled observer.

2. A: HEDIS, or Healthcare Effectiveness Data and Information Set, is a set of performance measures that is widely used in the healthcare industry. It is maintained by the National Committee for Quality Assurance (NCQA). Therefore, Choice *A* is correct.

3. D: Fee-for-service (FFS), as the name implies, is a healthcare model in which payment is determined by the number of services performed. Pay for performance (P4P) is a healthcare model that offers incentives to providers based on the quality of care. Therefore, Choice *D* is correct.

4. D: Performance and quality improvement records must be kept strictly confidential to maintain the anonymity and privacy of all parties involved. This includes patients, who may have sensitive information contained in one of these records, as well as peer reviewers, whose anonymity protects them from facing repercussions for their reviews. Finally, these records must also be kept confidential for the sake of the healthcare professionals themselves. Therefore, Choice *D* is correct.

5. C: It is often necessary for colleagues to provide input regarding the performance of their coworkers to highlight strengths and weaknesses not readily observed by management.

Regulatory and Accreditation

Accreditation, Certification, and Recognition Options

Once a healthcare organization achieves the status of a certified provider through CMS and OSHA, the next step is to begin developing a plan to identify appropriate accreditation, certification, and recognition options. Potential employees and patients often diligently pursue healthcare organizations with specific certifications and accreditations, as they recognize the brand as a distinction of both quality and excellence. Competitors in the healthcare arena value distinction and recognition, since the standard of care is elevated and therefore signifies advances in clinical practice. Overall, the systematic appraisal of the care provided in hospitals, nursing facilities, and other healthcare organizations serves as a safeguard for patients and ensures that national industry standards are upheld. Continued certification or accreditation over time signifies an ongoing commitment to nationally recognized benchmarks for patient care. Although the CMS and OSHA inspections and subsequent endorsements are mandatory, not every certification, recognition, or accreditation standard is required.

It is important to recognize the difference between accreditation and certification. **Accreditation** is the process of evaluation of an organization by a third party according to a set of nationally recognized standards. One example is laboratory accreditation through The Joint Commission, which ensures that laboratory services are providing superior and accurate results. **Certification** is also voluntary and is typically granted to individuals, agencies, facilities, and programs. It is also conducted by a neutral third party and signifies that the recipient has exhibited the ability to provide specialized services. Obtaining the Certification as a Professional in Healthcare Quality shows an outstanding commitment to quality and patient safety.

For the leadership teams of healthcare organizations, one of the most important objectives is to develop a vision of the organization as a whole and to ensure that accreditation is maintained. Certification and accreditation entities have the unique ability to analyze processes and goals and can assist the organization in maintaining accreditation. The accreditation and regulatory bodies provide an unbiased, comprehensive assessment of the attributes of specific clinical programs and services of healthcare organizations. Additional benefits of accreditation and certification include risk management, increased access to funding sources that recognize a specific entity, accountability, process improvement, and business networking opportunities. As a result of the successful completion of the comprehensive assessment, any deficiencies are identified, and excellence is rewarded.

The entire process of achieving recognition is a time-consuming enterprise. Effective leaders have the foresight to consider which types of distinction are crucial in the infancy stage of the development of the organization. While considering the scope of the evaluation, the organization must be prepared to complete an initial self-evaluation. This critical step can identify gaps and redundancies in established processes prior to the site visit. An internal evaluation led by the leadership team can help in the coordination of survey teams, each assigned to streamline processes to meet the rigorous standards of the chosen entity. Policy and procedure manuals must demonstrate the typical lifecycle of a patient receiving care. Process flows depicting the application of current policies and procedures will also be necessary in an effort to confirm authenticity.

There are numerous options for healthcare organizations seeking distinction as excellent service providers. The most notable include the International Organization for Standardization (ISO), National

Committee for Quality Assurance (NCQA), The Joint Commission (TJC), Accreditation Association of Ambulatory Healthcare (AAHC), Commission on Accreditation of Rehabilitation Facilities (CARF), Det Norske Veritas & Germanischer Lloyd (DNVGL), Baldrige, and Magnet. Each entity has its own distinct application and survey preparation process, evaluation procedures and duration for its award.

The following table shows certifying agencies:

Entity & Inception year	ISO 1947	NCQA 1990	TJC 1951	AAHC 2010	CARF 1966	DNVGL 2008	Baldrige 1987	Magnet 1983
Certification or Accreditation	Cert	Acc	Both	Acc	Acc	Acc includes ISO	Acc	Cert
On-Site Evaluation	Yes	No	Yes	No	Yes	Yes	No	Yes
Scope of Evaluation	Entire site	Site specific	Entire site	Site specific	Site specific	Entire site	Yes	Yes
Survey process	Yes	No	Yes	Yes	Yes	Yes	Yes	Annual
National Acceptance	Yes global	Yes	Yes	Yes	Yes	Yes global	Yes	Annual
Award Length	3 yrs	2 and 3 yrs by level	3 yrs	3 yrs	1-3	annual	annual	4 yrs

Advantages and disadvantages of accreditation

Healthcare organizations that seek to obtain and maintain accreditation recognize the advantages as well as the disadvantages of the experience. The majority of facilities are prepared to adopt stringent guidelines in favor of being added to the list of other esteemed organizations. The national brand recognition encourages competition in the healthcare marketplace and raises the standard of excellence for healthcare service delivery across the nation. State and federal laws are also built into most standards of accrediting entities.

The principles of both OSHA and CMS heavily influence the regulations developed by industry experts and provide the checks and balances necessary to sustain operational efficiency and processes. A positive review may also result in lower liability-insurance costs for the accredited organization. Since the application process includes a deep dive into procedures, policies, and risk management, unsafe practices may be uncovered that have the potential to prevent future patient harm. Once the final evaluation is published, facilities that meet or exceed industry standards are lauded for their successes.

Disadvantages are inherent in the process once violations become published. Although the offending facility is provided with a preliminary report, they cannot prevent citations from being publicized. Negative reviews impact patients' decisions to seek care at a specific organization in the future. One negative report, even if later corrected, can cause a facility to lose a once-stellar reputation and projected revenue. Employees and staff may face sanctions from a negative review as well. A failure to meet the expectations of current policies, procedures, or standard requirements could result in organizational restructuring or possible loss of employment.

Statutory and Regulatory Requirements

One of the major roles of the healthcare leadership team is to maintain awareness of all statutory and regulatory requirements and to ensure that the organization meets all of the goals. This role is detailed in the strategic quality plan, where key leaders may be listed as process owners or gatekeepers of individual requirements.

One way that the Centers for Medicare and Medicaid Services (CMS) helps consumers easily recognize whether or not an organization meets these goals is through its Overall Hospital Quality Star Ratings program, which it initiated in 2016 on its Hospital Compare website. In 2020, Hospital Compare and seven other healthcare comparison websites were rolled into a new Care Compare website and Overall Hospital Star Ratings became Overall Star Ratings. Each health organization receives an overall rating of one to five stars based on care and outcome measurements as well as a second rating of one to five stars based on patient experience. Care Compare also includes various other details about the healthcare provider such as services offered, office location, and various quality details and metrics. These ratings give consumers a clear and simple way to evaluate the quality of potential healthcare providers and compare them with other providers in their area. The ratings also impact the financial value of healthcare institutes and requires them to increase quality measurements if they want to remain competitive.

While strategic quality plans must be implemented from the top down, they will only be successful when there is an organization-wide commitment to meeting quality standards. It has become clear that the most successful healthcare organizations maintain high star ratings despite changes in quality measurements because they are committed to continuous quality improvement rather than simply checking off boxes in a strategic quality plan. Without a consistent feedback loop and a dedicated quality process, hospitals and other organizations will not have the data, analysis, or structure necessary to implement, maintain, or modify their strategic quality plans.

Hospital leaders should foster a high reliability culture that prioritizes safety, and several of its high-level corporate goals should be related to safety. When upper management has a commitment to safety transparency the programs are more likely to succeed. At hospitals where the frequency of patient handling injuries has been decreased, there are often administrators that encourage a culture of safety. Hospital administrators seeking to improve patient outcomes will need to consider how implementing safe patient handling policies, procedures, training, and equipment will all affect their bottom-line. Several case studies by the Occupational Safety and Health Administration (OSHA) have demonstrated that the initial capital investment in programs and equipment needed to safely handle patients can be regained within five years, especially when new equipment is paired with training and additional policies designed to maintain safety. Although there are significant equipment, training, and infrastructure costs are associated with implementing safe patient handling programs, hospitals that have succeeded have found that the economic costs are outweighed by the long-term benefits. Those benefits include:

- Reduced injuries
- Decreased loss of time and compensation claims
- Increased productivity
- Improved quality of work life and worker satisfaction
- Staff retention
- Better patient care and satisfaction

Management support should aim to include departments other than those involved in direct patient care, because departments such as laundry, maintenance, and engineering are also necessary to maintain patient health and safety. It's important that managers work with their employees and relevant unions prior to adding or improving on safe patient handling programs.

Because penalties for violating HIPAA are increasing, having policies and procedures in place to prevent privacy breaches is more important than ever. It is equally vital to ensure that these policies are documented and that appropriate steps are in place in the event a breach does occur. Leaders should appoint a privacy and security officer who is conversant in all HIPAA regulations and policies.

Healthcare organizations should regularly conduct HIPAA risk assessments to identify vulnerabilities. This will not only ensure that protected health information is secure, but it will also allow healthcare organizations to address any issues discovered in the course of the assessments. Organizations should be particularly wary of email usage. Emailing information is allowed under HIPAA; however, encryption is highly recommended whenever possible. Wherever encryption is not feasible, patients must be advised of the risk of a breach when sending protected health information via email.

Storage of protected health information is another key area that must be addressed during HIPAA assessments, particularly when a healthcare organization uses portable electronic devices. For example, removal of such devices from the organization's premises should be strictly controlled. Each organization should make sure that any staff who use portable electronic devices are familiar with the guidelines HHS has laid out for their use, as well as receiving and documenting HIPAA training, attending refresher courses, and receiving training in any new policies as they are implemented.

A notice of privacy practices should be correctly published and distributed to all patients. It should also be displayed on the organization's website, and the organization should obtain acknowledgement of receipt from all their patients. The notice should be updated whenever policies are revised. Healthcare leaders should ensure that they are entering into valid business agreements with all business associates and subcontractors. Any existing business associate agreements must be updated to reflect the changes to HIPAA under the final rule, such as the expansion of liability of business associates. A protocol for investigating potential breaches of protected health information is essential. The **risk of harm standard** and the **risk assessment test** can be used to determine if a breach has occurred. If a HIPAA breach has occurred, it is essential that the healthcare organization document the results of the investigation and notify the appropriate authorities. Leaders must implement privacy and security policies, and they should sanction employees who violate them.

The **Affordable Care Act** was a turning point in U.S. public health policy. The Act introduced several revisions and extensions of U.S. healthcare law that were made to reinforce the previous legal framework and create basic legal protections that had not already been established. This included a near-universal guarantee of access to affordable coverage for lifetime health insurance. The fully-implemented Act reduced the number of uninsured Americans to less than half, providing coverage for nearly 94% of the national population. This reduced the number of uninsured individuals by 31 million and increased enrollment in Medicaid by 15 million people.

The Affordable Care had three main goals that it strove it accomplish. The first goal was to change the private insurance market by requiring companies to have competitive, reasonable prices, that would ultimately help individuals and small groups. The second goal was to expand Medicaid to cover US. citizens and legal residents whose family income was less than 133% of the federal poverty level. The final goal was to change how decisions were made concerning the medical industry.

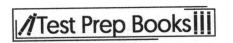

To achieve these goals, the Affordable Care Act instituted the **Health Insurance Marketplace**, which uses **Exchanges** in each state to help families, individuals, and small businesses compare and enroll in medical insurance plans. The Exchanges dramatically simplify the process of selecting a health insurance plan by including side-by-side information on various types of plans, the cost and benefits of each, and the federal tax subsidies available to the consumer. Once a consumer selects a plan, enrollment through the Exchange is a simple process and there is frequent and clear communication regarding any additional documentation needed to complete enrollment (e.g., income verification for federal subsidies).

Additionally, the Affordable Care Act mandates that all qualified health insurance plans, even those sold outside the Exchanges, must meet certain federal standards. These standards include coverage of ten essential benefits: preventative and wellness services, outpatient services, hospitalization, emergency services, laboratory services, maternity and newborn care, mental health and substance use disorder services, prescription drug coverage, rehabilitation services and devices, and dental and vision coverage for children. Qualified plans must also meet other federally mandated quality and care standards. These provisions ensure that consumers will have at least a minimum level of coverage regardless of the plan they choose.

In addition to streamlining the purchase of insurance and setting basic standards for qualified plans, through changes to Medicare and Medicaid the Affordable Care Act gave the U.S. Department of Health and Human Services (HHS) and state Medicaid programs new authority to measure the effectiveness of new payment methods and new ways to deliver healthcare services to consumers. These changes are designed to increase the effectiveness and quality of healthcare services, make them more flexible to meet the diverse needs of consumers, lower the number of hospital admissions and readmissions due to chronic health conditions, and increase information transparency. If these programs work, it is hoped that they will become standards for the healthcare system as a whole.

The Affordable Care Act also instituted the **National Quality Strategy**, a set of goals, priorities, and levers that provide a roadmap of methodologies designed to improve healthcare quality and lower costs. It also created the **Patient Centered Outcomes Research Institute**, which is an independent, non-profit organization designed to provide information to patients about their health and the choices of healthcare available to them. One of its overarching goals is to make clinical research and, ultimately, healthcare more patient centered.

Another goal under the Affordable Care Act is establishing the Prevention and Public Health Trust Fund, a $15 billion initiative designed to support investments by communities that will improve public health. Such prevention initiatives include health centers in schools, activities to support oral healthcare, programs that encourage pregnant women enrolled in Medicaid to stop smoking, and adding Medicare personalized prevention planning. The Act has also focused on improving the quality of Indian healthcare programs.

Organizational, State, and Federal Requirements

Every healthcare organization in the United States is required to follow state and federal regulations. These regulations are developed and maintained by the Department of Health and Human Services and its internal agencies (such as CMS). In addition, many successful healthcare organizations choose to become accredited by one or several nongovernmental agencies as a guarantee of that organization's high quality of care. One important role of the HQP is to develop procedures and practices for the

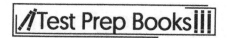
workplace that ensure the organization's operations are in compliance with all regulatory and accreditation guidelines.

Accreditation is important to the healthcare organization because it benefits its quality of care as well as its business objectives. The certification process ensures that the organization's healthcare is held to rigorous industry standards, provided the accreditation program is from a nationally recognized agency. Some nonprofit agencies that have received national acclaim for their accreditation programs include the **Joint Commission**, the **Healthcare Facilities Accreditation Program,** and the **Council on Accreditation.** Although high-quality programs can be more difficult to receive accreditation from, it's important to recognize that this same difficulty is why the agency is so well regarded.

The HQP has a responsibility to remain up to date on legal regulations and guidelines published by their organization's accreditation agencies. New guidance is published in accordance with each agency's own internal standards. Quarterly revision (once every three months) is the most common standard, with an update to rules and guidelines at the end of each fiscal period. The HQP should check each agency's website quarterly to confirm whether its guidelines for the HQP's organization have been revised. Some other ways to remain updated include subscribing to agency newsletters and signing up for mailing lists. In addition, social media sites are increasingly being used to announce and distribute information and should also be considered by the HQP.

Maintaining compliance with these standards is an aspect of the quality improvement process. Compliance is supported by both **internal** and **external audits** of the healthcare organization's operations. Internal audits are generally the responsibility of the HQP, whereas external audits are performed by a regulatory or accrediting agency. Each agency has its own standard for how frequently an external audit is completed. For example, the Joint Commission performs an on-site audit of its Gold Seal agencies as part of the initial accreditation process and then every three years afterward. The HQP should audit their organization's operations at a minimum frequency of once per year.

More frequent audits of specific guidelines or areas of operation may be necessary to optimize quality improvement. For example, an HQP discovers during their yearly audit that incident reports are, on average, filed twelve hours after the documented safety event. This indicates unacceptable violations of the organization's standard that incident reports must be filed before the end of the employee's shift during which the safety event took place. The HQP reports this information to supervisory personnel and decides to audit the time lapse between the safety event and filing of the incident report on a monthly basis. At the end of the next quarter, the HQP will reevaluate whether these monthly audits remain necessary based on if the data improves.

Communication with Accrediting and Regulatory Bodies

Communication with the accrediting and regulatory entities does not end with the initial evaluation. Maintaining an excellent standard of clinical practice is ongoing and never ending. At each level within the organization, there must be an expectation that the entire organization works toward individual and collective success. Once a specific recognition has been obtained, the organization must remain diligent in maintaining continued compliance. Leaders must be alert for changes in the standards and practices of the governing bodies and accrediting agencies they work with.

When attempting recertification, senior leaders must have current copies of all manuals that dictate the standards associated with specific accrediting bodies. It is also essential to review the previous assessment in order to ensure that all areas where the organization met or exceeded expectations will

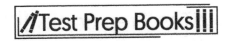

continue to do so. Areas of deficiency must be reviewed. In areas that were previously deficient, have enough improvements been made? Next, it will be necessary to observe changes in state and federal laws and amendments for necessary policy or procedural changes. Benchmarking must be done to determine if the organization compares well to competitors. This is important when reviewing the scorecard for the individual facility and for patient outcomes. The scorecard is a way for the public to monitor the status of any healthcare facility. If the competitors are equally accredited and have scored higher on quality indicators, leaders can utilize this information to gauge areas for improvement. It will then be necessary to prepare the organization to repeat the self-assessment, pretraining, and mock-interview process before the recertification process begins.

For the majority of organizations that provide direct patient care, The Joint Commission is the initial choice for accreditation. Once the accreditation is obtained, it is imperative that any failure to adhere to the agreed-upon standards is reported along with corrective measures. For example, any sentinel events involving the universal protocol, National Patient Safety Goals, or the speak-up initiative must be reported directly to The Joint Commission. It is important to note that although voluntary error reporting is a demonstration of best practice, it does not often yield actionable results.

When a sentinel or near-miss event arises within the organization, it must be reported as both an act of good faith and as a standard of evidence-based practice guidelines with The Joint Commission. Concerns can be filed anonymously online, faxed, or sent via US mail. It is vital that as much information as possible is provided so that The Joint Commission can conduct an investigation of the event. Once received, the incident will be cross-checked for other reported infractions within the organization in question. The investigation may begin with written notification to the agency or a site visit if the incident is deemed necessary. The personal information of the individual who files the concern can be shared without fear of reprisal, as the information will not be shared with the offending facility. Any resolution will be communicated to the reporting individual but, if there is no jurisdiction on the part of The Joint Commission, the issue may need to be referred to the state's department of health or legal authorities.

CVO Credentialing

The most efficient method for verifying a new practitioner's reported education and work history when hiring for the healthcare organization is to outsource this task to an accredited **Credentials Verification Organization (CVO)**. Accreditation of this organization is important to guarantee quality of service and accuracy of results. Some nonprofit organizations that might accredit the CVO's operations include the National Committee on Quality Assurance or the Utilization Review Accreditation Commission. The HQP should only choose to work with an accredited CVO and should confirm the CVO's accreditation with its accrediting organization before establishing a business relationship.

The CVO's relationship to an HQP's healthcare organization is to confirm that all new hires have the experience and credibility they are claiming. The CVO will take received information and confirm that it is true based on public records and records requests at appropriate institutions. For example, the CVO will confirm that the new practitioner's medical license was approved by their state licensing board (and is current), that their education credentials are valid, and that the practitioner does not have any sanctions, disciplinary action, and so forth, that might preclude them from employment with the healthcare organization.

This process is important to the HQP because an uncredentialed healthcare practitioner presents a significant risk of harm to the people served by the organization. A healthcare organization should never hire a new practitioner with invalid, out-of-date, or unclear credentials. Outsourcing confirmation of a new employee's right to practice medicine to a CVO is more efficient than the HQP spending work hours researching this topic. In addition, confirmation by a CVO increases the quality of care through increased professionalism. Verification by a third party reduces the likelihood of bias or nepotism in the healthcare organization's hiring practices. Using a CVO increases the quality of the employees in the HQP's organization.

To remain in compliance with CMS regulations regarding healthcare practitioners, the HQP must ensure that their organization engages in both **focused professional practice evaluations (FPPEs)** and **ongoing professional practice evaluations (OPPEs)**. The purpose of these evaluations is to determine if the organization's healthcare practitioners are performing their job in a safe and effective manner. The frequency of evaluation is up to the healthcare organization provided that every practitioner is evaluated at least every twelve months.

The difference between an FPPE and an OPPE is that the focused evaluation ought to draw upon more data about the practitioner's performance. The FPPE is conducted when performance metrics indicate possible deficits in the employee's performance—for example, an increase in infection rates compared to prior years. An FPPE ought to also be conducted for a new practitioner's first evaluation with the healthcare organization. This thorough study of their performance ensures that the new practitioner is meeting the healthcare organization's quality of care requirements.

Survey and Accreditation Readiness

Excellence in leadership requires a distinct level of expertise in vigilant surveillance. Once the leadership team has established which statutory and regulatory requirements are applicable to the organization, it is essential that the team members thoroughly understand the various standards of the accrediting bodies. Each organization will need to determine which entities provide the types of recognition that they seek and which will be the most valuable to their organization. Conversely, the leadership team must also consider the importance of accreditation in order to remain competitive in the healthcare marketplace. At each stage of growth, different forms of accreditation or certification become necessary. For example, it is mandatory for facilities that receive Medicare and Medicaid funds to obtain TJC accreditation to become eligible to care for those patients, but Magnet status is only established after several years of practice.

The leadership team must also take steps to prepare the facility and staff for the pending evaluation. Developing a culture of safety, customer-focused service, and clinical excellence is imperative. Discussing the purpose of the accreditation that the organization is seeking and how it will not only impact the company but also each department and individual employee, will bolster participation and commitment to succeed. Staff must also be made aware of the random nature of the on-site visit and the expectation that each individual employee be prepared to participate in any aspect of the investigation. It is ideal if the organization begins the preparation for the assessment within a reasonable time frame, in order to allow time to adjust to any changes in established processes and integrate them into the daily tasks of employees. Daily, weekly, and monthly reminders of accreditation standards and principles during staff meetings, in email correspondence, and on the organizational bulletins and screensavers encourages familiarity with site visit objectives. A simple motto to encourage employees to remember the rationale behind the site visit and to guide their preparation is essential.

The next logical step in preparing for an accreditation site visit is to obtain a copy of the applicable standards, associated fees, and an in-depth self-assessment. Each entity typically utilizes an online application process along with supporting software and web-based evaluation tools to guide those

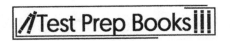

preparing for the assessment. The leadership team oversees the accreditation process, so they must carefully research the standards in each domain and compare the requirements to the current policies and procedures of the organization. Organizations seeking accreditation from The Joint Commission must be prepared to review and demonstrate compliance with the National Patient Safety Goals. Top-performing individuals and departments can be recognized for their adherence to established guidelines listed in site-visit materials.

The methodical review of the accreditation standards and comparison to the existing organizational structure must be followed by a mock review. This step moves beyond self-assessment and presents the leadership and employees with intensive, periodic, and impromptu question-and-answer sessions. This type of preparation provides an advantage to the staff and reinforces their understanding of significant principles. Each simulated interview session can build upon its predecessor, increasing the overall score until the leadership team is satisfied with the results. If not required during the initial application process, the next step is to request a date for the actual site visit.

During the on-site assessment, leaders must remain impartial and have a working knowledge of the organizational structure, policies, procedures, and scope of the accreditation standards. After the opening conference, introduction to the leadership team, and discussion, the site surveyors will begin the actual interviews. In the case of a TJC evaluation, the assessors will conduct both individual and systemic tracer sessions. These roundtable discussions are a hallmark of The Joint Commission survey and include the use of an actual patient's journey through the organization from initial contact to exit.

Systemic tracer consultations are related to the review of the metrics associated with staff-to-patient ratios, medication administration, appropriate documentation, and National Patient Safety Goals. The assessment then enters the final phase, and the surveyors tour the facility and complete the exit interview with the leadership team. At that time, the surveyors will present their preliminary findings. Soon after the survey is completed, the final conclusions are disclosed to the management team of the organization. Organizations that do not receive any **requirements for improvement (RFI)** are notified of findings just prior to their public release. If any RFI are received, the facility will need to provide evidence that the citations have been addressed and corrected through the submission of an evidence of standards compliance report.

Developing and Providing Survey Preparation Training

The leadership team will devote considerable time to the development and provision of the preparatory survey required for initial and ongoing accreditation. As previously mentioned, one of the most important tasks is to determine which accrediting bodies are vital and which are optional. The leadership team will begin by assembling the department leaders, top performers, risk-management staff, and medical governing board. The group must engage in roundtable discussions regarding their impressions of how each department has succeeded in their adherence to the organization's mission, values, and strategic goals. Wherever possible, established data from competing organizations is utilized and compared to current processes.

This strategy will help to answer the following questions: Where are we in reference to our articulated organizational mission, core values, and goals? Have current processes led to success or failure toward the realization of the articulated mission, core values, and goals? Which processes need to be changed, eliminated, or added to achieve our business goals? Where do we go from here strategically? How can we get to where we want to go? How can we operationalize our business objectives as a healthcare organization? Do our proposed safety goals and activities align with established industry standards? The

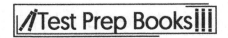
answers to these questions will guide the quality assurance team to prepare for the self-assessment required for accreditation.

Initially, the teams gather the basic timelines and presurvey guidelines from each accrediting body. For the majority of governing bodies, the suggested preparatory schedule allows for at least one year of current-process analysis, followed by status updates every three months. The correct standards and manuals must be obtained from each governing body and reviewed for new regulations as well as updates to prior standards. Previous surveys from the organization must also be scrutinized in order to ensure that any deficiencies or areas where policies or procedures failed to meet industry standards can be highlighted. Next, the committee will sift through the data to determine if any new areas within the organization need to obtain accreditation.

The team must initiate the actual self-assessment, with each individual staff member advised of performance expectations and measurement tools. This communicates individual and collective accountability for the survey results. This culture of expected excellence compels clinical staff to raise their performance to meet or exceed the projected outcome. The fundamental objective in these phases is to compare the organization's specified goals and activities to those proposed by the accrediting body.

Effective governance over survey preparation in the third interval prior to the on-site survey, or within approximately four months, involves documentation. Once the mock survey has been conducted, any gaps in services, policies, or processes will be uncovered. Process flows and policies must be updated and deemed legally appropriate. A separate but easily accessible electronic clearinghouse for the legally verified process and procedural documents must be created. There must also be evidence of strict policies regarding the method of approval regarding requests to update or revise documented processes and procedures.

Lead informatics managers must be named, along with their specific areas of expertise within the organization. Those identified leaders must be prepared to answer the questions of the review personnel and locate all documents associated with their respective departments. Actual staff must also be shadowed to prepare for their interactions with review personnel. Finally, within the month preceding the actual on-site survey, it is highly recommended that the organization conduct a second full-scale mock survey.

Practice Quiz

1. How often should an HQP complete an internal audit of their organization's operations to ensure compliance with federal regulations?
   a. Monthly
   b. Quarterly
   c. Biannually
   d. Annually

2. What is the purpose of an HQP's internal audit?
   a. To improve the organization's quality of care
   b. To improve the organization's efficiency
   c. To ensure the organization's compliance to regulations
   d. To ensure the organization will pass its next external audit

3. What is the main difference between performance measurements and quality measurements?
   a. There is no difference; these terms are interchangeable.
   b. Quality measurements focus solely on the outcome measurements of care, whereas performance measurements are more concerned with the improvement of clinical processes.
   c. Performance measurements focus solely on the outcome measurements of care, whereas quality measurements are more concerned with the improvement of clinical processes.
   d. Performance measurements are used to assess whole healthcare facilities, whereas quality measurements are used to assess specialized areas of care within larger facilities.

4. The Occupational Health and Safety Administration (OSHA) sets standards for employee safety in the workplace. Which of the following areas is NOT addressed by OSHA standards?
   a. Workplace violence
   b. Patient transfer ergonomics
   c. Potential for infectious contamination
   d. Workers' Compensation claims

5. Which of the following is NOT a requirement for HIPAA compliance?
   a. Following the HIPAA Privacy Rule standards
   b. Following the HIPAA Security Rule standards
   c. Following the HIPAA Breach Notification Rule standards
   d. Following the HIPAA Administration Rule standards

See answers on the next page.

Answer Explanations

1. D: The HQP should perform a complete internal audit once per year. More frequent audits should only be performed to evaluate known problem areas until compliance has been achieved. Choices *A*, *B*, and *C* are incorrect because frequent complete audits consume inappropriate amounts of the HQP's time.

2. A: The most important reason for the HQP to perform an internal audit annually is acquiring data about current operations to seek continuous improvement of the quality of care. Although Choices *B*, *C*, and *D* are all potential goals, they are incorrect because they are not the most important reason.

3. C: Performance measurements are primarily used to identify methods of improving patient care; therefore, they are largely derived from measurements of care outcomes. Quality measurements are more generally concerned with measuring and analyzing all healthcare processes, including factors that are not outcome based. Therefore, Choice *C* is correct.

4. D: Workers' Compensation insurance does provide financial support for injured employees; however, the Occupational Safety and Health Administration (OSHA) is not associated with any aspect of the compensation plan. The OSHA standards address the safety issues related to the care of potentially violent patients, which means that Choice *A* is incorrect. Healthcare workers sustain injuries at three times the national average for other industries. Most of these injuries are musculoskeletal injuries that can be avoided with the use of mechanical aids to transfer patients. The financial investment in mechanical lift systems is returned by decreased employee injuries, increased patient safety related to falls and skin injuries, and increased patient satisfaction. This means that Choice *B* is incorrect. There are OSHA standards aimed at decreasing the risk of contamination such as the use of personal protective equipment (PPE), which means that Choice *C* is incorrect.

5. D: HIPAA has four primary rules that are necessary for compliance. These include the Privacy Rule, the Security Rule, the Breach Notification Rule, and the Omnibus Rule. Therefore, Choice *D* is correct.

120

CPHQ Practice Test #1

1. When preliminary denial of accreditation by TJC requires the organization to provide additional detail, when must the organization provide the information?
   a. Within one month
   b. Within ten working days
   c. Before the end of the current survey
   d. Before the end of the current month

2. Which statement best describes the Lean Six Sigma approach to process improvement?
   a. The Lean Six Sigma approach can be defined as the continual and collaborative discipline of measuring and comparing the results of key work processes.
   b. A plan to eliminate or lower the likelihood of an error, or to make the occurrence of an error so obvious that any possibility of that error impacting the consumer is practically impossible.
   c. The primary goal is to produce more effective processes, policies, and procedures that reduce variation and significantly lower the chances of negative outcomes.
   d. A specific methodology that calculates the true costs of a potential solution compared to the actual benefits.

3. What is the best definition for critical to quality measures (CTQs)?
   a. The correlation, or dependent relationship, between two quantitative continuous variables, whether positive or negative
   b. The necessary countermeasures to solve any problems before they actually occur
   c. The measurable data that will further indicate whether the goals and objectives are attainable
   d. The aspects of a business process or product that must be met in order to satisfy the consumer

4. What is the basis for The Joint Commission's adoption of the National Patient Safety Goals?
   a. To force healthcare organizations to prevent mistakes during surgical procedures
   b. To institute inflexible patient-safety measures to provide high-quality care
   c. To encourage healthcare organizations to institute high quality standards for patient safety
   d. To capitalize on the fees paid to The Joint Commission or accreditation

5. What is the most necessary step in evaluating the success of process improvement?
   a. Teamwork
   b. Executing the pilot study
   c. Informing administration of the plans
   d. An action plan

6. Which statement best describes the purpose of the project charter?
   a. The primary goal is to determine the ability of a specific process to deliver value as required by the customer.
   b. This written agreement usually includes the primary reason for the project, the goal and scope of the project, the expected budget, and the roles of each team member.
   c. The written agreement acts as measurable data to indicate if the goals and objectives of the project are attainable.
   d. The primary goal is to produce more effective processes, policies, and procedures that reduce variation and significantly lower the chances of negative outcomes.

121

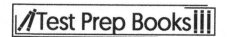

7. During strategic planning, what is the main task of the leadership team?
   a. To lead teams
   b. To act as clinical advisors
   c. To develop strategies
   d. To maintain records

8. Before sending out a meeting invite, what is the most important thing the facilitator must do?
   a. Decide who to have on the team
   b. Get approval from administration
   c. Define the objective of the meeting
   d. Set goals

9. Which is the best description for the acronym SIPOC?
   a. Supplier, inputs, process, outputs, customer
   b. Supporter, inputs, process, outcomes, consumer
   c. Supplier, improvement, product, outputs, consumer
   d. Supporters, inputs, products, outcomes, consumer

10. How does a healthcare risk management assessment typically begin?
    a. Interviewing the patient to get their reaction.
    b. Meeting with attorneys to discuss possible causes of the incident.
    c. Reviewing the incident report.
    d. Interviewing the leadership of the organization.

11. What is meant by fiduciary duty to care?
    a. Assurance that the board members of a healthcare organization are prudent, acting in good faith, and making decisions in the best interest of the organization
    b. A measure of the fiscal responsibility of the stakeholders within any healthcare organization
    c. Assurance that the board members of a healthcare organization are applying the specific, measurable, accurate, reliable, and timely (SMART) method of goal setting for the organization
    d. A measure of the ability of the CPHQ professional to control the costs of obtaining and maintaining accreditation and/or certification

12. What is the major advantage of using scorecards and dashboards during a process and performance improvement?
    a. Both are designed as a visual representation of the current processes, in an effort to find areas of redundancy and lacking in value to the customer.
    b. Using scorecards and dashboards during a performance review can help highlight areas where additional training around related processes and procedures is needed.
    c. The election and introduction of team members based on the areas of expertise helps to achieve optimal results.
    d. Both individual and collective contributions of employees are recognized, reinforcing the establishment of the newly developed skills.

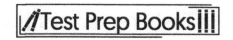

13. How are credentialing and privileging different?
    a.   Credentialing involves the oversight of licensing to medical professionals under their scope of practice; privileging refers to the evaluation of a practitioner's actual performance and qualifications.
    b.   Credentialing is typically based on payment for the number of individuals a physician provides care for, whereas privileging is typically based on the quality of care provided.
    c.   Privileging involves the oversight of licensing to medical professionals under their scope of practice; credentialing refers to the evaluation of a practitioner's actual performance and qualifications.
    d.   Credentialing is the passive and unplanned span of new practices; privileging is the rate at which the new practices are adopted and implemented.

14. What is the major difference between scorecards and dashboards?
    a.   Scorecards involve comparing equivalent processes within the same organization; dashboards can be comparing similar processes to a competitor within the same industry.
    b.   Scorecards are a single payment made to cover the costs of the treatment provided; dashboards are written agreements that act as measurable data to indicate if the goals and objectives of the project are attainable.
    c.   Scorecards can be defined as a written account that compares and measures the performance of specific individuals against the projected goals of the organization; dashboards are quality measurement tools that actually allow the management team to compare and contrast different reports or access diverse datasets in one place.
    d.   Scorecards can be defined as the passive and unplanned spread of new practices; dashboards are defined as the active spread of those new practices to a target audience utilizing planned methodologies.

15. What does the Administrative Simplification provision of HIPAA do?
    a.   It mandates that the HHS adopt standards to help improve and simplify communications between healthcare providers and health plans.
    b.   It mandates that healthcare providers limit the number of administrative workers to save time and resources.
    c.   It mandates that all communications to clients/patients be written in language that is as plain as possible.
    d.   It mandates that the HHS assist and facilitate healthcare providers with internal organization and strategic planning initiatives.

16. Which of the following is true regarding data management?
    a.   It is only done by IT personnel with education in data management.
    b.   It is always done on local servers within a hospital.
    c.   It is done via cloud based systems in a healthcare environment.
    d.   It involves acquiring, validating, storing, protecting, and processing data.

17. Why should processes be evaluated frequently?
    a.   To eliminate waste and reduce risk
    b.   Because it is mandated by The Joint Commission
    c.   To reinforce employee trainings
    d.   To determine if they still work

18. What is the leadership team's first action when preparing for a survey by an accreditation agency?
    a. To assemble all of the policy and procedure books
    b. To inform all the staff of the impending survey by email
    c. To engage staff in discussions regarding how each department has succeeded
    d. To begin writing an action plan

19. Which of the following statements is true regarding the policies and procedures for healthcare settings?
    a. They ensure patient safety and typically include factors that meet The Joint Commission National Patient Safety goals.
    b. Many focus on developing devices and technology based on the physical and psychological needs of those who use them.
    c. The purpose is to evaluate patient safety in healthcare organizations and identify the underlying causes of sentinel and near-miss events, and then develop safeguards to prevent the recurrence of the incidents.
    d. They use a quality approach to better understand and prevent future and ongoing threats to patient safety.

20. Which of the following best describes what occurs during the norming phase of Tuckman's model for team development?
    a. When the projects comes to a close and the team moves on, appreciating and reflecting on their growth as a team
    b. Selecting the team members based on the areas of expertise necessary to achieve optimal results
    c. Diffusing or quieting the naturally-occurring conflicts between different team members' communication style
    d. When team members are encouraged to assume responsibility for their assigned roles

21. In order to secure electronic files and reports, the clinician must do which of the following?
    a. Use computer screen locks and shortened time-out locks
    b. Use black-out screens whenever the computer is left unattended
    c. Limit access to computers
    d. All of the above

22. Root-cause analysis is used to do which of the following?
    a. Identify the cause of sentinel and near miss events
    b. Evaluate patient safety
    c. Answer the "why" questions
    d. All of the above

23. What is the purpose of the dashboard in performance improvement?
    a. Dashboards are tools that enable the management team to visually analyze the KPIs (key performance indicators) of each individual on the healthcare team.
    b. Dashboards depict the precipitating factors or root cause for an event or outcome
    c. Dashboards contain measurable data that indicates whether the goals and objectives are attainable.
    d. Dashboards are a written account that compares and measures the performance of individuals against the projected goals of the organization.

124

24. What are the two major stipulations of the Health Insurance Portability and Accountability Act of 1996?
    a. To protect the rights of healthcare organizations to deny medical care to indigent patients, and to prevent unnecessary malpractice suits
    b. To protect physicians' rights to provide medical care, and to hold healthcare organizations accountable for how patients' protected health information is utilized
    c. To protect patients against retaliation when reporting malpractice, and to hold healthcare organizations accountable for how patients' protected health information is utilized
    d. To protect patients' rights to maintain health-insurance coverage in the event of job loss, and to hold healthcare organizations accountable for how patients' protected health information is utilized

25. How frequently are scorecards used internally for performance improvement?
    a. Quarterly
    b. Quarterly and annually
    c. Annually
    d. Monthly and quarterly

26. What does the acronym NPS refer to?
    a. New Patient Safety
    b. National Patient Safety
    c. Net Promoter Score
    d. National Population Safety

27. The IHI Simple Data Collection Plan begins data collection planning by first doing which of the following?
    a. Asking why this data is being collected
    b. Deciding the tools to use
    c. Deciding on team members
    d. Setting goals

28. Which statement about near-miss and sentinel events is true?
    a. Both are ways to define an accident in a healthcare setting.
    b. Both events always prove that the provider was negligent in caring for the patient.
    c. A near-miss event does not result in death, while a sentinel event may result in death.
    d. The responsible party should always contact the police immediately.

29. What is the purpose of the cost-benefit analysis in process improvement?
    a. To determine the true costs of a potential solution compared to the actual benefits
    b. To ensure that the outcome actually solves the problem
    c. To confirm the passive and unplanned spread of new practices
    d. To find solutions before they become necessary

30. The Institute for Healthcare Improvement reported the six aims necessary to improve the current quality of healthcare as:
    a. safe, effective, problem-focused, timely, efficient, equitable
    b. secure, effective, patient-focused, timely, efficient, equitable
    c. satisfaction, expectancy, problem-focused, timeliness, efficiency, and eagerness
    d. safe, effective, patient-focused, timely, efficient, equitable

31. What do process measures show?
    a. If the team met their goals
    b. How the steps in the system perform
    c. If the measures improved care
    d. All of the above

32. Which of the following is true about FMEA?
    a. It is a program evaluation method that is primarily process based.
    b. It is a program evaluation method that is primarily outcome based.
    c. It is a program evaluation method that is primarily observation based
    d. It is a program evaluation method that is mandated by OSHA.

33. What is the advantage of identifying process champions for process and performance improvement projects?
    a. Process champions provide a visual representation of the current processes, in an effort to find areas of redundancy and lacking in value to the customer.
    b. Process champions consider the importance of adding to, rather than detracting from, the value delivered to customers.
    c. Process champions can identify potential pitfalls during the brainstorming phase of process improvement.
    d. Process champions ensure that the VOC is heard and confirm that there is a precisely defined focus on the correct processes.

34. Internal benchmarking can be described as which of the following?
    a. Comparing similar processes to a competitor within the same industry
    b. Comparing equivalent processes within the same organization
    c. Comparing the general concepts of processes in unrelated industries
    d. Comparing similar processes to those in different industries

35. What is a process champion?
    a. An administrative team member
    b. Someone that has authority over the involved process
    c. A member of the process improvement team
    d. All of the above

36. What do control charts tell the team?
    a. The control limit of the process
    b. What processes are out of control
    c. If they met their goals
    d. How a process changes over time

37. The need for more extensive medical record keeping increased during what time period?
    a. 1950s
    b. 1960s
    c. 1970s
    d. 1980s

38. The core portions of the SIPOC method include which of the following?
    a. Suppliers, inputs, processes, outputs, customers
    b. Scorecards, inputs, processes, outputs, customers
    c. Sponsors, investors, products, outputs, customers
    d. Suppliers, inputs, processes, opportunities, consumers

39. Innovation in healthcare can best be described as which of the following?
    a. Passively spreading a new process or spreading it in an unplanned fashion
    b. A form of predictive technology that will enhance physicians' ability to provide medical care
    c. Developing a new process, policy, or standard that improves upon the quality outcomes of previous processes
    d. Providing a format to create uniformity of practice across other departments within the organization

40. What does a trend analysis help the team do best?
    a. Decide which trend to follow
    b. Understand historical data about a process
    c. Identify the mean, median, and mode
    d. Prove a hypothesis

41. Which of the following is true of telemedicine?
    a. It is a form of medical care provided remotely by credentialed and licensed healthcare professionals.
    b. It is prohibited by the Health Insurance Portability and Accountability Act of 1996.
    c. The primary role of the CPHQ professional.
    d. It is required by the Health Insurance Portability and Accountability Act of 1996.

42. What is the goal of the improve phase of the DMAIC model?
    a. To enable the management team to visually analyze the KPIs (key performance indicators) of each individual on the healthcare team
    b. To assimilate all the ideas into a strategic plan that prioritizes opportunities for improvement and amends all processes associated with changes, including any process flows and job aids
    c. During the improve phase of the DMAIC model, the CPHQ professional will need to implement strategies to determine the sustainability and benefits of the newly defined processes.
    d. During this phase, the manager enables team members to do it themselves.

43. What is the best description of a correlation?
    a. A correlation is a dependent relationship between two quantitative continuous variables and can either be positive or negative.
    b. A correlation is a way of using a selected group of individuals to rapidly produce, clarify, and evaluate ideas or problems.
    c. A correlation is an independent relationship between two quantitative continuous variables and can either be positive or negative.
    d. A correlation is defined as the continual and collaborative discipline of measuring and comparing the results of key work processes.

127

44. What is the VOB?
    a. The reputation of the business
    b. The needs of the business
    c. The organization's goals
    d. All of the above

45. Which of the following is true of competitive benchmarking?
    a. It is not advised by TJC.
    b. It can be done by reviewing a competitor's public summary.
    c. It helps improve internal quality processes.
    d. It is not necessary for accreditation.

46. The most problematic issues of the EHR are caused by which of the following?
    a. Security measures
    b. Cyber crimes
    c. Human errors
    d. Passwords

47. Broken down into each individual function, what does the acronym DMAIC stands for?
    a. Define, measure, analyze, improve, control
    b. Define, measure, adjust, improve, complete
    c. Define, measure, amend, institute, control
    d. Depict, measure, analyze, improve, control

48. Which quality control tool is best suited to use when investigating short-term process improvement activities?
    a. Run charts
    b. T-tests
    c. Control charts
    d. Pareto charts

49. The HCAHPS initiative's goal is to provide a standardized survey instrument and data collection methodology for measuring which of the following?
    a. The quality of care in hospitals
    b. Patient satisfaction
    c. Employee satisfaction
    d. Patient perceptions of care

50. Extra safety and security measures are important for which specialized hospital area?
    a. ICU
    b. ED
    c. Surgery
    d. Nursery

51. What does the project charter typically include?
   a. The sponsor or the project, a champion or resource allocation manager, subject matter expert, process owner, process operator
   b. The primary reason for the project, the goal, the scope of the project, the budget and roles of each team member
   c. Yellow belt, green belt, black belt, master black belt, process champion, executives.
   d. Suppliers of inputs, materials to input, processes that convert inputs to outputs, outputs to provide to customers, customers

52. What is the suggested preparatory schedule for accreditation?
   a. Six months of current-process analysis in advance of survey
   b. One year of current-process analysis prior to survey
   c. At least one year of current-process analysis followed by status updates every three months
   d. Preparation for the next survey should begin immediately after this one ends.

53. What does the acronym DMAIC refer to in the Lean Six Sigma project management model?
   a. Describe, manage, accountability, interpret, and compare
   b. Define, manage, analyze, interpret, and control
   c. Describe, measure, analyze, improve, and compare
   d. Define, measure, analyze, improve, and control

54. Any deviation from the standard process typically results in higher risk, according to which methodology?
   a. 5 S
   b. Six Sigma
   c. Lean
   d. National Safety Standards

55. Why is it important to review scorecards and dashboards during performance improvement projects?
   a. The professional accountability and adherence to ongoing performance and process improvement measures afford the chosen organization the opportunity to remain competitive in the healthcare marketplace.
   b. Managers must always remain diligent and keenly aware that the responses of the process innovators, early adopters, and the early majority will most likely determine the success of the newly developed process and performance expectation.
   c. The results from the aggregated quality and performance data equip the management team to develop specific, measurable, achievable, relevant, and timely (SMART) metrics for gauging the staff's effectiveness and efficiency.
   d. When employees feel that their contribution is linked to the mission, values, and goals of the host organization, they are more likely to accept responsibility for their results.

56. When meetings have dysfunctions, they impact which of the following?
   a. The quality agenda
   b. The cost and team confidence
   c. The cost, schedule, quality, and project manager's credibility
   d. The schedule and cost

129

57. A facilitator needs to consider all EXCEPT which of the following?
    a. The time available for meetings
    b. The structure of the meeting
    c. Which goals to set
    d. The number of team members

58. Which statement best describes the purpose of bundled payments?
    a. This initiative was established to encourage payers to employ a set of core measures to utilize during reporting.
    b. The primary goal is to produce more effective processes, policies, and procedures that reduce variation and significantly lower the chances of negative outcomes.
    c. This initiative depicts the active spread of those new practices to a target audience, utilizing planned methodologies.
    d. This initiative can best be defined as measurable data that will further indicate if the goals and objectives of the project are attainable.

59. What do Pareto charts allow the leadership team to do?
    a. Focus on the value of the services provided
    b. Focus on the just-in-time process timeline
    c. View statistics on their dashboard
    d. All of the above

60. Loyalty in adversity and an outcome-focused approach are two of the five factors of which of the following?
    a. Human factors engineering
    b. Standard operating procedures
    c. Lean Six Sigma
    d. A high reliability organization

61. Why is it crucial to consider the voice of the customer (VOC) during process improvement?
    a. The customer's voice is the outward image of the business, and the reputation that the business has earned among consumers.
    b. The voice of the customer uses a selected group of individuals to rapidly produce, clarify, and evaluate ideas or problems.
    c. The customer's voice enables the leadership team to understand the passive and unplanned spread of new practices.
    d. During this phase, the manager can begin to take a less direct role and delegate activities to team members.

62. According to the Lean Six Sigma framework, which two quality tools are typically utilized in the analyze phase?
    a. Run charts and Pareto charts
    b. Process capability assessments and critical to quality trees
    c. Project charter and process mapping
    d. Brainstorming and benchmarking

130

63. Functions of the leadership team include which of the following?
    a. To ensure cohesion, define vision and values, ensure alignment, and deliver results
    b. To engage stakeholders, develop talent, and manage performance
    c. To build accountability, ensure succession, allocate resources and craft the culture
    d. All of the above

64. Why should correlations be reviewed with caution during process and performance improvement projects?
    a. At this stage, it is crucial to create linkages between the mission, goals, and objectives of the host organization to the actual performance metrics, skills, and quality standards of the supportive team members.
    b. The CPHQ professional will need to implement strategies to determine the sustainability and benefits of the newly defined processes.
    c. When considering what may go wrong, the team professional must determine whether the individual actions in the newly developed processes are logical.
    d. The team must remain aware that the data may only represent the relationship between variables, not the actual causes and effects of current processes.

65. Which of the following is true regarding the benefits of using a CVO?
    a. A CVO can help align internal best practices.
    b. Certification by a CVO can help improve revenue and secure new contracts.
    c. A CVO can improve the likelihood of an organization's operations aligning with state requirements.
    d. All of the above

66. What is values-based leadership?
    a. An attitude about people, philosophy, and process
    b. Leading by example rather than manipulation
    c. Integrity, listening, and respect for followers
    d. Clear thinking, inclusion, and respect

67. Which of the following is necessary for a team meeting to be considered successful?
    a. Actions have follow-up.
    b. There are clear activities.
    c. Process owners are present.
    d. All of the above

68. What is the best description of positive correlation depicted in a scattergram?
    a. One variable decreases while another increases; the points on the scatter plot will be close together and trend up to the left in the form of a line.
    b. The correlation would yield a value of zero, with the data on the scatter plot appearing to have no clear shape or direction within the middle of the axes.
    c. One variable increases while another increases; the points on the scatter plot will be close together and trend up to the right in the form of a line.
    d. One variable increases while another increases, up to a certain point; the data points will resemble a checkmark.

69. What is the best definition of verification?
    a. The active spread of those new practices to a target audience utilizing planned methodologies
    b. A process that ensures that the outcome actually solves the problem.
    c. The testing that the proposed solution produces the desired outcome.
    d. Measurable data that will further indicate whether the goals and objectives are attainable.

70. What are organic organizations?

    I. Those that have a loose structure with more innovation and less specialization
    II. Those that have expertise and knowledge rather than authority of position
    III. Those that have loosely-defined responsibilities rather than rigid job definitions
    IV. Those with fewer constraints on the activity of members, enabling and encouraging the expression of individual behavior by leaders and potential followers

    a. Choices I and IV
    b. Choices III and IV
    c. Choices I, III, and IV
    d. All of the above

71. Which of the following best describes the Healthcare Effectiveness Data and Information Set (HEDIS)?
    a. The continual and collaborative discipline of measuring and comparing the results of key work processes
    b. A group of performance standards that the majority of health plans adhered to in an effort to standardize the overall quality of care delivered to patients
    c. The written agreement acts as measurable data to indicate if the goals and objectives of the project are attainable.
    d. The primary goal is to produce more effective processes, policies, and procedures that reduce variation and significantly lower the chances of negative outcomes.

72. Which of the following is true regarding critical to quality measures?
    a. They are defined by the leadership team.
    b. They are set by CMS.
    c. They must be met to satisfy the customer.
    d. They are always key processes.

73. Systems thinking uses which of the following?
    a. A centrist approach
    b. Cognitive mapping
    c. Scorecards
    d. Technology to drive ideas

74. What are the two phases of the strategic quality planning process?
    a. Planning and implementing
    b. Research and implementing
    c. Strategy and implementing
    d. Research and strategy

75. What happens when the needs of the business do not meet the needs of the customer?
    a. Resources are exhausted.
    b. Processes have succeeded.
    c. The voice of the customer is needed.
    d. Certification is not possible.

76. Which Lean Six Sigma format targets current processes?
    a. Define, measure, analyze, improve, and control
    b. Define, maintain, analyze, improve, and control
    c. Define, measure, analyze, design, and verify
    d. Define, measure, analyze, investigate, and contain

77. What is the best description of statistical process control?
    a. The continual and collaborative discipline of measuring and comparing the results of key work processes
    b. The process by which numerous small general factors result in a specific effect on a process
    c. The specific rare factors that can influence a process
    d. A strategy for instituting ongoing process improvement

78. A patient suspected of having TB would be placed under what type of infection control?
    a. Universal precautions
    b. Droplet precautions
    c. Airborne precautions
    d. Contact precautions

79. What is the order of the Lean Six Sigma certification belts according to rising expertise level?
    a. White, yellow, green, black, master black
    b. Black, white, yellow, green, master black
    c. Master black, green, yellow, black, white
    d. White, green, yellow, black, master black

80. What factors are the primary focus of human factors engineering?
    a. Devices and technologies based on the physical and psychological needs of those who use them
    b. How to build technology through asking a series of "why" questions
    c. Reliance on practical experience, loyalty in adversity, and an outcome-focused approach
    d. Building technology through measurement, analysis, and improving current technology

81. Which agency mandated that hospitals designate a chief compliance officer to have the responsibility of operating and monitoring the compliance program, and who reports directly to the CEO and the governing body?
    a. TJC
    b. Medicare
    c. CMS
    d. OIG

133

82. What is the best description of critical to quality measures?
    a.   This quality control tool helps to emphasize the frequency of the most impactful problems in order to allocate the appropriate amount of resources to rectify the problem.
    b.   Critical to quality measures graphically represent the variation of values within a group; this format depicts the center, spread, and shape of the data.
    c.   Critical to quality measures can be defined as the specific measurable facets of a process whose performance standards must be met to satisfy the customer.
    d.   This tool helps the CPHQ professional to determine the purpose, roles, scope, and budget of the investigation.

83. An action plan should include which of the following?
    a.   Missing capacities
    b.   Signatures of all team members
    c.   Who, what, when, where, why, and how
    d.   A list of primary problem areas

84. What are key performance indicators (KPI)?
    a.   Goals for change
    b.   What employee evaluations are measured against
    c.   Measurable data about organizational goals
    d.   Attainable goals

85. Output is:
    a.   Tangible results
    b.   Goods and services
    c.   Under team control
    d.   All of the above

86. In healthcare risk management, an action or inaction that could have resulted in a nonlethal injury to a patient is known as which of the following?
    a.   A sentinel event
    b.   An incident
    c.   A near-miss event
    d.   A human factor

87. Which of the following best describes a whistleblower?
    a.   An individual protected from retaliation under the law
    b.   An identified person who has information of importance
    c.   Someone who was recently fired from the organization
    d.   All of the above

88. Indicators are:
    a.   Linked to objectives
    b.   Measurable
    c.   Linked to quality
    d.   All of the above

89. What is the best method of noting quantitative or qualitative data?
    a. Scorecards
    b. Check sheets
    c. Fishbone diagrams
    d. KPI

90. When does implementation occur?
    a. When the board members sign off on the project
    b. When everyone on the team agrees on the process
    c. When practices are adopted and integrated
    d. When the team finishes its work

91. Organizations that adopt which of the following methods of risk management achieve a high level of excellence because they focus on anticipating the best response to the worst-case scenario?
    a. High reliability
    b. Six Sigma
    c. Systems thinking
    d. Human factors engineering

92. Which statistical quality tool would be the best choice to depict the center, spread, and shape of data?
    a. Histograms
    b. A run chart
    c. Control charts
    d. A fishbone diagram

93. What are the primary goals of the OSHA inspection?
    a. To provide a reference for surveyors to specify deficiencies within the organization being evaluated
    b. To protect the safety of patients and/or residents in healthcare organizations
    c. To provide healthcare to individuals that cannot afford health insurance
    d. To protect the safety of the employees of healthcare organizations

94. Which of the following is included in the PLAN stage of PDSA?
    a. Complete the action plan
    b. Develop the calendar
    c. Test the validity of the plan
    d. Identify possible interventions

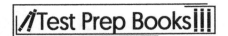

95. What is the difference between common cause variation and special cause variation?
    a.   Common cause variation is the process by which numerous small general factors result in a specific effect on a process; special cause variation refers to the specific rare factors that can influence a process.
    b.   Common cause variation is the process of comparing equivalent processes within the same organization; special cause variation refers to comparing similar processes to a competitor within the same industry.
    c.   Common cause variation can be defined as the passive and unplanned spread of new practices; special cause variation is defined as the active spread of those new practices to target audiences utilizing planned methodologies.
    d.   Common cause variation is the process by which a single payment is made to cover the costs of the treatment provided for any given treatment; special cause variation refers to measurable data that will further indicate if the goals and objectives are attainable.

96. What is the difference between accreditation and certification?
    a.   Accreditation and certification are the same; both are typically granted to individuals, organizations, and facilities.
    b.   Accreditation is typically granted to organizations and facilities, whereas certification is typically granted to individuals.
    c.   Accreditation is typically based on the total billed for the number individuals a physician provides care for, whereas certification is typically based on the quality of care provided.
    d.   Accreditation is typically granted to individuals, whereas certification is typically granted to organizations and facilities.

97. What is the best definition of validation?
    a.   The rate at which newly disseminated innovations are adopted and implemented
    b.   Developing the necessary countermeasures to solve any problems before they actually occur
    c.   A dependent relationship between two quantitative continuous variables
    d.   A process that ensures that the outcome actually solves the problem

98. Outcome measures tell the organization how the system impacts which of the following?
    a.   The organizational goals and values
    b.   HEDIS measures
    c.   Accreditation measures
    d.   Values of patients and others

99. Lean Six Sigma drives customer satisfaction and the bottom line by doing which of the following?
    a.   Analyzing PDSA steps closely
    b.   Using Pareto charts to track improvement
    c.   Using competitive benchmarking
    d.   Reducing variation and waste

100. Cognitive mapping is important in the systems thinking approach because it is a way to do which of the following?
    a.   Visualize what happened during the incident
    b.   Visualize otherwise unnoticeable connections
    c.   Visualize what the patient was thinking
    d.   Visualize what to do next

101. What is the industry-standard methodology for measuring and controlling quality during the manufacturing process in real time with pre-determined control limits called?
    a. Lean manufacturing
    b. Statistical Process Control (SPC)
    c. Variability Index
    d. Quality Control (QC)

102. Protected health information (PHI) includes which of the following?
    a. The patient's EHR
    b. Physician orders
    c. Medical bills
    d. All of the above

103. What is the best definition for key performance indicators (KPIs)?
    a. The provider of inputs into a business process
    b. Measurable data that indicates whether the goals and objectives are attainable
    c. Materials and resources needed to complete a business process
    d. The products or services resulting from inputs during the implementation of a process

104. What is the purpose of the "five whys" in a root-cause analysis?
    a. To sift through current policies and reveal causal factors within the control of the team
    b. To make sure patients understand what happened
    c. To prepare an incident report
    d. To communicate the cause to the leadership of the organization

105. Public reporting of the survey results is designed to do what?
    a. Create incentives for hospitals to improve their quality of care
    b. Enhance public accountability in healthcare
    c. Increase the transparency of the quality of hospital care
    d. All of the above

106. What are the two steps where data mistakes happen most often?
    a. Entering and collating
    b. Saving and editing
    c. Downloading and importing
    d. All of the above

107. What is the best definition for mistake-proofing?
    a. The ways to determine whether there is a dependent relationship between two quantitative continuous variables, which is either positive or negative
    b. Using a selected group of individuals to rapidly produce, clarify, and evaluate ideas or problems
    c. Developing the necessary countermeasures to solve any problems before they actually occur
    d. The election and introduction of team members based on the areas of expertise necessary to achieve optimal results

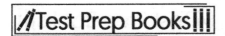
108. Why is it crucial for the leadership team to prepare the entire organization for the on-site survey portion of the accreditation process?
   a. To actively observe any gaps in processes, procedures, and policies prior to the actual survey
   b. To provide a uniformity of practice across other departments within the organization
   c. To assure that the leadership team is prudent and acting in the best interests of the organization and in good faith
   d. To encourage competition across other departments within the organization

109. What is the best definition of cost-benefit analysis?
   a. Testing that the proposed solution produces the desired outcome
   b. Quality measurement tools that actually enable the management team to visually analyze the KPIs (key performance indicators) of each individual on the healthcare team
   c. The action or process of developing a new idea, methodology or action, that improves on its predecessor
   d. An activity used in the Lean Six Sigma methodology as a way to determine the true costs of a potential solution compared to the actual benefits

110. Which of the following is true about non-probability sampling?
   a. It is based on human choice.
   b. It uses volunteer samples.
   c. It contains sources of bias.
   d. All of the above

111. Which of the following are true regarding the Hospital Compare site?

   I. It is free on the internet for everyone.
   II. It communicates the CMS scores for every hospital in the U.S.
   III. It posts the scores for healthcare quality measures.

   a. Choices I and II
   b. Choices I and III
   c. Choices II and III
   d. All of the above

112. What is the best definition of norming?
   a. Norming is when people begin to resolve their differences and come to accept their coworkers' strengths.
   b. Norming is a process that ensures that the outcome actually solves the problem.
   c. Norming is the passive and unplanned spread of new practices.
   d. Norming is measurable data that will further indicate whether the goals and objectives are attainable.

113. Which of the following is NOT a standard of ACMA's transition of care guidelines?
   a. Identify patients at risk for poor transitions.
   b. Establish a dynamic care management plan.
   c. Coordinate with the family/friends of patients.
   d. Complete a comprehensive transition assessment.

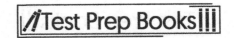

114. Which of these statements about Failure Mode and Effects Analysis is NOT true?
    a. Failure mode analysis is an outcome-based method of program evaluation.
    b. Failures are ranked in severity from one to five and managed in order of severity of three or greater.
    c. Analysts ask about the severity, probable cause, potential for harm, and patient detection.
    d. Failure mode analysts interview the patients involved in the incident.

115. What is the term for the tendency of a statistic to overestimate or underestimate a parameter?
    a. Central tendency
    b. Bias
    c. Smoothing
    d. Common cause variation

116. Why is it important to identify and report errors to regulatory and accrediting bodies?
    a. To create an atmosphere of patient-centered care within the organization
    b. To maintain ongoing accreditation
    c. To prevent any sanctions or violations for the organization
    d. To identify the appropriate employees to be held accountable

117. Which of the following best describes the purpose of storming?
    a. To develop countermeasures to solve any problems before they actually occur
    b. To explain the stages of the process and confirm that each team member is aware of their expected contribution
    c. To adopt and integrate practices in the proposed setting
    d. To visually analyze the KPIs (key performance indicators) of each individual on the healthcare team

118. What is a sentinel event?
    a. A method showing how 80% of the process efforts occur as a result of 20% of the causes
    b. An unforeseen occurrence that results in harm or death to a patient or group of patients
    c. All of the medical services for one individual patient for a specific medical condition
    d. An action or inaction that nearly resulted in a nonlethal injury to a patient

119. Which of the following is true regarding informed consent forms?
    a. They must be completed at admission.
    b. They must be signed, dated, and witnessed.
    c. They must be maintained under lock and key.
    d. All of the above

120. With Tuckman's model (forming, storming, norming, performing) what is the primary goal of the forming stage?
    a. To encourage discussion among colleagues
    b. To form a strong team
    c. To meet the goals of the organization
    d. For the team to follow the facilitator's plan

121. What are the four types of benchmarking?
    a. Investigative, internal, external, and generic
    b. Internal, cooperative, external, and competitive
    c. Internal, competitive, functional, and generic
    d. Intensive, competitive, functional, and generic

122. Root-cause analysis is used to do which of the following?
    a. Analyze healthcare systems
    b. Prevent incidents from happening again
    c. Respond to OSHA complaints
    d. Investigate patients

123. What is diffusion?
    a. A method of brainstorming
    b. A way to control a team that is off course
    c. The passive spread of a new process
    d. Prohibited by most organizations

124. What is the best description of brainstorming?
    a. Brainstorming is defined as the continual and collaborative discipline of measuring and comparing the results of key work processes.
    b. Brainstorming can be referred to as a written account that compares and measures the performance of specific individuals against the projected goals of the organization.
    c. Brainstorming can best be defined as the rate at which newly disseminated ideas or innovations are adopted and implemented.
    d. Brainstorming can be referred to as a way of using a selected group of individuals to rapidly produce, clarify, and evaluate ideas or problems.

125. Every quality management initiative must be tied to what?
    a. The key business processes
    b. The mission and values
    c. How the competitors are doing
    d. Patient care

126. A public health official is looking to obtain data regarding a population's treatment outcomes. Which of the following would be the best resource to use?
    a. Census data
    b. Environmental data provided by the Environmental Protection Agency
    c. Death certificates
    d. Electronic health records (EHRs)

127. A public health official is reviewing the mortality and morbidity rates within a community. Which of the following is a potential benefit of tracking these rates?
    a. Treatment options can be improved based on the data.
    b. Water contamination can be prevented.
    c. Hospitalizations can decrease over time.
    d. Life expectancy can be increased.

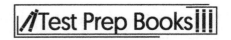

128. A patient is seeking educational resources available in the community to help manage their chronic illness. Which resource would be most beneficial?
    a. A local cooking class
    b. A local wellness program that promotes healthy eating
    c. A community health fair about disease prevention
    d. A community health fair about smoking cessation

129. Which healthcare improvement initiative best assists with managing a chronic illness?
    a. Providing patients with medication management education
    b. Holding an immunization campaign
    c. Providing patients with screening questionnaires
    d. Providing patients with mental health support

130. A healthcare worker is educating a patient on the importance of implementing healthy behaviors. Which of the following examples best illustrates this?
    a. "It is important to be up to date on all vaccines."
    b. "You should attend a local seminar about ways to prevent diabetes."
    c. "You should focus on eating twenty servings of fruits and vegetables during the day."
    d. "You should take a walk after lunch to reach your physical activity goal."

131. A healthcare provider is working to improve healthcare access for a patient. Which intervention would be most appropriate for a patient in a marginalized population?
    a. Refer the patient to a private physical therapy office.
    b. Educate the patient on when to return to the hospital.
    c. Educate the patient on correct medication administration techniques.
    d. Provide locations for free or low-cost vaccine clinics and local food pantries.

132. A patient is preparing to move from the hospital to a long-term care facility. Which course of action would be the most appropriate?
    a. Provide the patient and their family with clear discharge instructions.
    b. Request that the patient attend a discharge seminar.
    c. Request that the patient ask all their questions to the next healthcare provider.
    d. Provide the patient with all hospital records needed at the long-term care facility.

133. Adverse effects may occur while a patient is transitioning care due to several factors, including miscommunication. What is the best option for improving communication during the transition process?
    a. Update the next healthcare provider with potential problems that may arise during the patient's discharge.
    b. Use the facility-wide handoff checklist.
    c. Provide the patient with updated discharge teaching.
    d. Inform the patient's family members of the discharge plan.

134. A healthcare provider is working on a patient's discharge plan. What should the provider focus on to help avoid readmission?
    a. Review medications given to the patient during their hospital stay.
    b. Evaluate the patient's understanding of the procedures done in the hospital.
    c. Evaluate the patient's understanding of medication care instructions upon discharge.
    d. Review the patient's prior admissions to determine their likelihood of compliance.

141

135. A healthcare provider uses a screening tool upon admission to assess the patient's social determinants of health. Which question best depicts such a screening?
    a. "What is the layout of your house?"
    b. "What level of education have you received?"
    c. "Can you tell me about your current medical diagnoses?"
    d. "Have you ever applied for government funding?"

136. Which of the following is NOT a tool associated with Six Sigma?
    a. Value stream mapping
    b. 5S
    c. TQM
    d. Seven wastes

137. Which of the following correctly describes a Pareto chart?
    a. A bar chart in which contributing factors of an effect are arranged according to magnitude
    b. A pie chart in which types of administrative waste are categorized and compared
    c. A line graph showing changes in patient health outcomes for a specific healthcare facility
    d. A density map of a healthcare facility that shows the location and severity of sentinel events

138. A nurse notices that a fall-risk patient is not wearing the correct kind of non-skid socks, so he gets her the correct pair. Which of the following is this an example of?
    a. Sentinel event
    b. Actual event
    c. Root cause
    d. Near miss event

139. Ideally, when should Failure Mode and Effects Analysis (FMEA) first be implemented into a system?
    a. After a failure has occurred in the system; otherwise, there is no data for FMEA to process
    b. From the beginning; even in the conceptual stages, FMEA has a role to play
    c. After a system has begun its normal functioning and the outcome data can be analyzed
    d. Once a system has stopped functioning; it is impossible to gather accurate data while the system is ongoing

140. Which of the following correctly lists the steps of Lewin's change model?
    a. Unfreezing, changing, refreezing
    b. Acknowledgement, adaptation, advancement
    c. Pausing, reforming, overhauling
    d. Accident, investigation, conclusion

Answer Explanations #1

1. B: If the answers regarding the issues addressed in a preliminary denial are provided by the organization to the TJC within 10 working days, the TJC will grant the accreditation so long as the answers are acceptable.

2. C: The primary goal of Lean Six Sigma is to produce more effective processes, policies, and procedures that reduce variation and significantly lower the chances of negative outcomes.

3. D: Critical to quality measures (CTQs) are the aspects of a business process or product that must be met in order to satisfy the consumer. This leads to a discovery of the voice of the customer (VOC), which is also crucial to improving processes.

4. C: The primary goal of The Joint Commission's adoption of the NPSGs is to encourage healthcare organizations to institute high quality standards for patient safety. The Joint Commission does not force organizations to comply with regulatory standards; federal regulations require adherence for reimbursement of healthcare services.

5. B: The most necessary step in evaluating the success of process improvement is executing the pilot study. The other choices do not evaluate the success of a PIP.

6. B: The project charter is a written agreement that usually includes the primary reason for the project, the goal and scope of the project, and the expected budget and roles of each member of the team.

7. C: During strategic planning, leadership's main task is to help the team understand the existing strategies and work to develop new ones that align with and support corporate goals.

8. C: Before sending out a meeting invite, the most important thing is that the facilitator must define the objectives of the meeting. They should also establish the tangible outcomes or outputs that the team aims to achieve. Doing so sets expectations and will ensure that people know precisely what is expected.

9. A: Choice *A* is correct; SIPOC stands for suppliers, inputs, processes, outputs, customers.

10. C: The incident report is reviewed first in most healthcare risk management assessments. Recall that the three main principles of risk management assessment are risk identification, risk analysis, and risk evaluation. In the most critical step, risk identification, what happened and why is considered. The analyst will need access to all available records, participants, policies, and procedures associated with the event. Methodical and purposeful deconstruction of every step should be mapped, and any discrepancies in processes, hardware, human factors, and organizational culture scrutinized. Similar incidents and associated resolutions within other healthcare settings should be compared and analyzed for probability of success.

11. A: The fiduciary duty-to-care regulation involves assurances that the board members are acting in good faith, in a prudent and reasonable fashion, and making decisions that are in the best interests of the organization. This rule essentially provides the board time to prepare a prompt response or adjust any detected errors or concerns.

12. B: Using scorecards and dashboards during a performance review can help highlight areas where additional training around related processes and procedures is needed. Choice *A* is incorrect because it describes the purpose of process mapping. Choice *C* is incorrect because it describes the forming step of Tuckman's model. Choice *D* is an aspect of effective team communication, so it is incorrect.

13. A: Credentialing involves the oversight of licensing to medical professionals under their scope of practice, which means assessing their education, certifications, and training. Privileging refers to the evaluation of a practitioner's actual performance and qualifications, and includes granting practitioners benefits based on their abilities.

14. C: Scorecards can be defined as a written account that compares and measures the performance of specific individuals against the projected goals of the organization; dashboards are quality measurement tools that actually allow the management team to compare and contrast different reports or access diverse datasets in one place. They visually present summaries, key trends, comparisons, and exceptions.

15. A: The Administrative Simplification provision of HIPAA mandates that the HHS adopt standards to help improve and simplify communications between healthcare providers and health plans.

16. D: Data management involves acquiring, validating, storing, protecting, and processing data. The other choices are incorrect because data management procedures are a responsibility of personnel at all levels, and are not restricted only to local servers or cloud services.

17. A: Processes should be evaluated frequently to eliminate waste and reduce risk. Choice *B* is incorrect; The Joint Commission does not explicitly mandate frequent evaluations, but rather they should be done to meet accreditation requirements. Choices *C* and *D* are incorrect because, although they might reinforce employee training and reevaluate their effectiveness, the main purpose is reducing waste, redundancy, and risk.

18. C: Engaging department leaders, top performers, risk-management staff, and the medical governing board in discussions regarding how each department has succeeded in its adherence to the organization's mission, values, and strategic goals is one of the best ways to prepare for a survey.

19. A: The majority of policies and procedures enacted by healthcare organizations to ensure patient safety include factors that meet The Joint Commission's requirements and National Patient Safety goals.

20. D: Tuckman's model of team building includes five steps: forming, storming, norming, performing, and adjourning. Norming occurs after storming. In this stage, members are encouraged to assume responsibility for their assigned roles, and they come to recognize each other's strengths and resolve their differences. Managers play the pivotal role of acts as scaffolding, keeping the team members on task and fostering more collaboration. Choice *A* describes adjourning. Choice *B* describes forming. Choice *C* describes storming.

21. D: In order to secure electronic files and reports, the clinician must use computer screen locks and shortened time-out locks, use black-out screens whenever the computer is left unattended, and limit access to computers.

22. D: All of the above. The root-cause analysis is used to evaluate patient safety in healthcare environments. It identifies the cause of sentinel and near-miss events by asking "why" questions regarding the incident with the goal of process improvement.

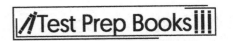

23. A: Dashboards are quality measurement tools that enable the management team to visually analyze the KPIs (key performance indicators) of each individual on the healthcare team. Choice *B* is incorrect since it describes the role of a fishbone diagram. Choice *C* is related, since it describes the purpose of KPIs, but the question asks for the purpose of dashboards, so it is incorrect. Choice *D* describes the role of scorecards.

24. D: The two major stipulations of the Health Insurance Portability and Accountability Act of 1996 are to protect patients' rights to maintain health-insurance coverage in the event of job loss, and to hold healthcare organizations accountable for how patients' protected health information is utilized.

25. B: Scorecards are used internally during quarterly and annual employee evaluations. The other choices represent intervals that are too often or too infrequent.

26. B: NPS is the acronym for National Patient Safety. The Joint Commission established the NPS goals in 2002 and implemented them in 2003. This nationwide effort instituted a set of uniform, realistic, and specific goals that could be consistently applied and measured in every healthcare setting. National Patient Safety goals are set annually and have established the standard for excellence.

27. A: The IHI Simple Data Collection Plan begins data collection planning by first asking why data is being collected. Additional questions to consider include things like what type of data will be necessary, what data analysis tools will be used to display that obtained data, and where and how the data can be obtained.

28. C: A near-miss event does not result in death, while a sentinel event may result in death. Choice *A* is incorrect because a near-miss event is an avoided incident. Choice *B* is incorrect because a near-miss event is not necessarily a result of negligence, and may be the result of unforeseeable circumstances. Choice *D* is incorrect because such events are instead reported to The Joint Commission.

29. A: The cost-benefit analysis is an activity used in the Lean Six Sigma methodology as a way to determine the true costs of a potential solution compared to the actual benefits.

30. D: The IHI aims to make healthcare safe, effective, patient-focused, timely, efficient, and equitable.

31. B: Process measures show the steps in the system perform. They are used to indicate to consumers what a healthcare provider will do to maintain or improve health.

32. B: Failure Mode and Effects Analysis (FMEA) is a program evaluation method that is primarily outcome based. It seeks to uncover ways that business leaders can most effectively operationalize the efforts of frontline staff.

33. C: Process champions can identify potential pitfalls during the brainstorming phase of process improvement. These individuals are team members with the administrative authority to allocate time and resources for a project.

34. B: Internal benchmarking involves examining processes in different departments and teams within the same company or organization to determine best practices for the organization as a whole.

35. D: A process champion is an administrative leader who is a team member with the authority to allocate the time and resources needed to plan and launch the program. The process champion should also have authority over the areas that will be affected by changes to clinical and administrative systems and practices; and coordinate communication internally to senior leadership, Board of Directors, staff, etc. They provide positive action-oriented leadership to ensure that process improvement projects get across the goal line.

36. D: Control charts show a process changes over time. As line graphs, they clearly indicate trends and patterns of specific processes, and how well that process is performing.

37. C: The 1970s ushered in a need for more extensive medical record keeping. With the influx of American veterans returning home needing significant medical and psychiatric care, paper medical files were largely traded in for computerized records.

38. A: SIPOC stands for suppliers, inputs, processes, outputs, and customers. It is a process improvement tool used to define each step of a process before it's implemented.

39. C: Innovation involves developing a new process, policy, or standard that improves upon the quality outcomes of previous processes. Choice *A* refers to diffusion. Choice *B* refers to patient analytics and medical informatics. Choice *D* refers to internal benchmarking.

40. B: A trend analysis helps the team understand historical data about a process. Choice *A* is incorrect because the analysis observes past trends to understand why they occurred. Choice *C is* wrong because identifying the mean, median, and mode of a data set is only one aspect of identifying trends. While trend analysis may be useful in disproving a hypothesis, one cannot prove a hypothesis true, so Choice *D* is incorrect.

41. A: Telemedicine is a form of medical care provided remotely by credentialed and licensed healthcare professionals. It has reformed healthcare delivery across the country. Providers can now conduct patient assessments, prescribe medications, and collaborate with other medical professionals remotely, via Skype, telephone, email, and secure chatrooms. This type of distance healthcare eliminates the constraints of geography and mobility, which allows providers access to increasing numbers of previously underserved populations.

42. B: The goal of the improve phase is to assimilate all the ideas into a strategic plan that prioritizes opportunities for improvement and amends all processes associated with changes, including any process flows and job aids.

43. A: A correlation is a dependent relationship between two quantitative continuous variables and can either be positive or negative. Choice *B* is incorrect because it describes brainstorming. Choice *C* is incorrect because a correlation is found between dependent, not independent, variables. Choice *D* describes benchmarking, so it is also incorrect.

44. B: The voice of the business (VOB) includes the implicit and explicit needs and requirements of the business, such as profit, competitive edge, and growth. It is an important process measure for meeting the business's goals.

45. B: Competitive benchmarking can help reveal how similar organizations solved defects similar to what a given healthcare organization is facing. The comparative analysis can also illuminate how the current processes are outpacing the competitors, which encourages the integration of what works with what does not work well enough. This approach will help the leadership team to deliver on the promise of providing exceptional care. Quality information for all hospitals is available for the public to view.

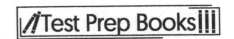

46. C: One pitfall of the electronic medical record involves the human factor. Since a computer is only capable of providing information based on what is entered, information entered inaccurately or omitted has the potential to harm a patient.

47. A: The DMAIC acronym stands for define, measure, analyze, improve, control. This is an important tool in the Six Sigma model of process improvement.

48. A: Run charts are best suited to investigate short-term process improvement activities. Like control charts, they are line graphs that indicate trends and patterns of specific processes, and how well that process is performing.

49. D: The Hospital Consumer Assessment of Healthcare Providers and Systems (HCAHPS) initiative's goal is to provide a standardized survey instrument and data collection methodology for measuring patient perceptions of care. This allows patients to compare hospitals' quality of care (in multiple areas) based on the survey scores from other patients.

50. D: Nursery. Due to the possibility of an abduction, there are special safeguards in place.

51. B: The project charter includes the primary reason for the project, the goal, the scope of the project, the budget, and the roles of each team member. The project charter is not a list of individuals involved in the project, so Choices A and C are incorrect. Choice D is incorrect because it describes the steps of SIPOC, not the purpose of a project charter.

52. C: The suggested preparatory schedule for accreditation typically involves a year of planning along with close monitoring. The other choices represent incorrect timelines for planning.

53. D: DMAIC stands for define, measure, analyze, improve, and control. The DMAIC model helps improve existing processes and allows for the methodical development of an action plan to streamline and standardize laborious processes, reduce waste, and mitigate risks to the patient population in any healthcare setting.

54. B: According to Six Sigma, any deviation from the standard process typically results in higher risk. Choice A, the 5 S method, is incorrect because it is an organization tool used in Lean. Choice C, Lean, is incorrect because it focuses specifically on reducing waste, not variety. The National Safety Standards are not a methodology in process improvement, so Choice D is incorrect.

55. C: The results from the aggregated quality and performance data equip the management team to develop specific, measurable, achievable, relevant, and timely (SMART) metrics for gauging the staff's effectiveness and efficiency.

56. C: Meeting dysfunctions have significant negative impacts on the progress of the project. Dysfunctional meetings not only impact the cost, schedule, and quality of the project, but they also reduce the project manager's credibility within the team.

57. C: Goals are set by the team during the meeting, not solely by the facilitator. The allowed time, meeting structure, and members in the meeting are all responsibilities of the facilitator.

58. A: Bundled payments were established to encourage payers to employ a set of core measures to utilize during reporting. Choice B is incorrect because it describes the purpose of Lean Six Sigma. Choice C is incorrect because it describes dissemination. Choice D describes the key performance indicators, not bundled payments, so it is incorrect.

59. A: Pareto charts track key operations over time, allowing leadership to identify the most significant issues affecting quality. Pareto charts are not related to the just-in-time training process and are only one component of quality statistics.

60. D: Loyalty in adversity and an outcome-focused approach are two of the five factors in any high reliability organization. The other three are reliance on practical experience, an emphasis on operationalized definitions of expected outcomes, and a deeper perspective when unexpected problems arise. Organizations that adopt this method of risk management achieve a high level of excellence because they focus on anticipating the best response to the worst-case scenario.

61. A: The customer's voice is the outward image of the business, and the reputation that the business has earned among consumers. Understanding the VOC is critical for developing processes and products that are customer-focused.

62. A: The run and Pareto charts are most frequently used in the analyze stage. Choice *B* is incorrect because the terms describe measurements used to determine a process's success and are not a key component of the DMAIC analyze phase. Choice *C* is incorrect because a project charter is used to outline the stages of a project, while process mapping involves diagramming the steps of a process. The tools in Choice *D* are used to improve processes through new ideas.

63. D: Leadership teams have many roles. They should strive to do all of the things listed here.

64. D: The team must remain aware that the data may only represent the relationship between variables, not the actual causes and effects of current processes. The other choices do not represent reasons for caution when reviewing correlations.

65. D: A CVO (Credentials Verification Organization) helps establish a healthcare provider's credentials. CVOs help align internal best practices, secure contracts and revenue, and increase the likelihood of compliance with state regulations. Therefore, Choice *D* is correct.

66. A: Values-based leadership is based on an attitude of the value of people, processes and philosophy. The other choices represent parts of values-based leadership, but do not describe it as a whole.

67. D: For a team meeting to be successful, actions must have follow-up, there must be clear activities, and process owners must be present. A beneficial meeting is one that generates follow-up, and in order to best generate that follow-up, the meeting must define the process owners, review dates, and have clear actions to take.

68. C: A positive correlation occurs when one variable increases while another increases; the points on the scatterplot will be close together and trend up to the right in the form of a line. The other choices represent different types of correlations. A negative correlation would show one variable decreasing while the other increases and trend up to the left. No correlation corresponds to data points that don't fit close on a line, while a curvilinear correlation corresponds to data points that fit best to a non-linear shape, such as a checkmark or parabola.

69. C: Verification refers to testing that the proposed solution produces the desired outcome. Choice *A* is incorrect because it describes diffusion. Choice *B* describes validation, so it is incorrect. Choice *D* is incorrect because it describes KPIs.

70. D: Organic organizations are relatively flexible and adaptive and have a loose structure that is appropriate for changing conditions. They emphasize lateral communication and exchanging information rather than the vertical handing down of instructions. Organic organizations tend to be more innovative and less specialized. They utilize experts and knowledge rather than position authority. They offer loose responsibilities rather than rigid job descriptions. Their decentralized decision-making processes, are less standardized and the division of labor is less structured. Additionally, they impose fewer constraints on the activity of members and they encourage the expression of individual behavior.

71. B: The Healthcare Effectiveness Data and Information Set (HEDIS) is a group of performance standards that the majority of health plans adhere to in an effort to standardize the overall quality of care delivered to patients. The other choices are incorrect; Choice *A* describes benchmarking, Choice *C* describes key performance indicators, and Choice *D* describes the main goal of Lean Six Sigma.

72. C: Critical to quality measures are the aspects of a business process or product that must be met in order to satisfy the consumer. These are used to help split up customer demands into distinct, prioritizable items to improve on.

73. B: Systems thinking uses cognitive mapping, Choice *B*, to represent physical locations. Reviewing areas where each department connects to others can help identify more points of interaction that contribute to incidents. A centrist approach, scorecards, and technology to drive ideas, Choices *A*, *C*, and *D*, are not central to systems thinking.

74. D: The strategic quality planning process consists of research and strategy. The research phase serves a preparatory phase, which involves everything necessary to collect and analyze data before the strategic quality planning starts. The strategy phase incorporates the steps needed to develop the actual plan. Every initiative must be tied to the key business processes and their performance indicators or there would be no real impact on the balance sheet.

75. A: When the needs of the business do not meet the needs of the customer, resources will be exhausted. This necessitates the use of a needs assessment to find which organizational goals aren't being met.

76. A: The Lean Six Sigma format that targets current processes is DMAIC, which stands for define, measure, analyze, improve, and control.

77. D: Statistical process control is a strategy for instituting ongoing process improvement. It is the industry-standard methodology for measuring and controlling quality during the manufacturing process in real time with pre-determined control limits.

78. C: Airborne precautions are used with patients suspected of having TB.

79. A: The correct level-by-level categorization of Lean Six Sigma certification is white, yellow, green, black, and master black. Each successive level of certification demands a higher level of proficiency in Six Sigma methodology.

80. A: Human factors engineering, also known as ergonomics, is the discipline that develops devices and technology based on the physical and psychological needs of those who use them. This field combines technological advances in healthcare with the specific needs of humans in mind. Choice *B* is incorrect because a series of "why" questions are used for determining root cause. Choice *C* describes the

149

benefits of the high reliability approach to risk management. Improving current technology is not the primary goal of human factors engineering, so Choice *D* is incorrect.

81. D: The OIG mandated that hospitals designate a chief compliance officer to have the responsibility of operating and monitoring the compliance program, and who reports directly to the CEO and the governing body.

82. C: Critical to quality (CTQ) measures can be defined as the specific measurable facets of a process whose performance standards must be met to satisfy the customer. It is necessary to know CTQs in order to best identify problems.

83. C: Action plans should always include the who, what, when, where, why, and how. An action plan includes a list of existing capacities in order to identify missing capacities, so Choice *A* is incorrect. Choice *B* is incorrect because responsible parties, not member signatures, are an aspect of action plans. Problem areas are not included in an action plan, so Choice *D* is incorrect.

84. C: Key performance indicators (KPIs) are measurable data about organizational goals. KPIs are not goals, but rather the data that indicates whether goals can be met, so Choices *A* and *D* are incorrect. While KPIs may be used in evaluating employee productivity, KPIs represent data on the organization level, and are not always used to evaluate employees, thus Choice *B* is incorrect.

85. D: The outcome and outputs for each objective of an action plan have to be identified. While the outcome is the development outcome at the end of the NSDS implementation, or, more specifically, the expected benefits to the target groups, the outputs are the direct and tangible results (goods and services) that will be delivered. Outputs are largely under project management's control.

86. C: In healthcare risk management, an action or inaction that could have resulted in a nonlethal injury to a patient is known as a near-miss event. These must be reduced and eliminated as much as possible to promote safe, high-quality healthcare.

87. A: A whistleblower is protected under law. While the other choices may actually be true of whistleblowers in some situations, they are not always the case (nor are they ideal), leaving Choice *A* as the best choice.

88. D: Indicators are measurable items that are linked to objectives and quality. They are an aspect of action plan frameworks and measure how the objectives, purpose, results, and activities will be achieved.

89. B: Check sheets are best for notating data for collection when data can be collected by the same person at the same time.

90. C: Implementation occurs when practices are adopted and integrated. This is one of the four aspects of starting a new process or method in an organization.

91. A: Organizations that adopt the high reliability methods of risk management achieve a high level of excellence because they focus on anticipating the best response to the worst-case scenario. This model provides transparency, accountability, and shared responsibility within the organization that reinforces problem solving.

92. A: Histograms are the best format to depict the center, spread, and shape of aggregated data. Run and control charts focus on trends of process performance, while control charts additionally show

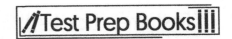

control limits to visualize how close data is to the average or to being an outlier. Fishbone diagrams instead are used to illustrate root causes of an outcome.

93. D: This answer is correct because it refers to the primary goal of an OSHA inspection.

94. D: The PLAN stage of the PDSA involves identifying a goal or purpose, formulating an intervention or theory for change, defining success metrics and putting a plan into action. When using PDSA to improve a process, the first step is to identify possible goals and strategies to implement. After the goal is set, it's necessary to identify possible interventions and select one that seems promising.

95. A: Common cause variation is the process by which numerous small general factors result in a specific effect on a process; special cause variation refers to the specific rare factors that can influence a process. Both types of cause variation represent events that contribute to waste and errors.

96. B: Accreditation is typically granted to organizations and facilities, whereas certification is typically granted to individuals.

97. D: Validation is a process that ensures that the outcome actually solves the problem. This occurs after the verification stage of process evaluation. Choice *A* is incorrect; the rate at which newly disseminated innovations are adopted and implemented is the definition of spread. Choice *B* is incorrect because it refers to mistake-proofing, and Choice *D* is incorrect because it describes correlation.

98. D: Outcome measures tell the organization how the system impacts the values of patients and others. They reflect the impact of the healthcare service or intervention on the health status of patients served. While they may seem to represent the gold standard in measuring quality, an outcome is the result of numerous factors, many beyond providers' control.

99. D: Lean Six Sigma drives customer satisfaction and the bottom line by reducing variables and waste. The term comes from a combination of two methodologies. The Six Sigma methodology focuses on the standardization and reduction of variation, while Lean focuses on waste reduction.

100. B: Cognitive mapping in systems thinking is used to represent physical locations. Areas where each subsystem perceives its connections to others can help identify more points of interaction that contribute to incidents.

101. B: Statistical Process Control is the industry-standard methodology for measuring and controlling quality during the manufacturing process in real time with pre-determined control limits.

102. D: PHI includes all health information that might identify the patient. Everything in the patient's EHR, including physician orders and medical bills, is part of PHI.

103. B: Key performance indicators (KPIs) are the measurable data that indicate whether the goals and objectives are attainable. These are often developed from trends of past data.

104. A: The "five whys" help sift through current policies and reveal causal factors within the control of the team. This process takes a problem and asks why the problem occurred, why the problem's most direct cause occurred, and so on, in order to determine the initial, or root, cause.

105. D: Transparency is the goal of public reporting of survey results because it can enhance public accountability in healthcare. Public reporting of the survey results also creates incentives for hospitals to improve their quality of care.

106. C: Downloading and importing are the two areas where most data mistakes occur. These steps should always be double checked to reduce errors.

107. C: Mistake-proofing develops countermeasures to solve problems before they occur. Once potential issues are identified, steps can be taken to prevent them. Choice A is irrelevant to mistake-proofing. Choice B describes brainstorming, so it is incorrect. Choice D is part of the forming step of the Tuckman model.

108. A: Preparatory training is the best way to get a close look at all areas of the organization before the survey.

109. D: The cost-benefit analysis is an activity used in the Lean Six Sigma methodology as a way to determine the true costs of a potential solution compared to the actual benefits. It is frequently necessary to conduct a cost-benefit analysis at the start of the project charter, during the define phase, and throughout implementation of the project.

110. D: Non-probability sampling should be avoided because it involves volunteer samples and haphazard (convenience) samples, which are based on human choice rather than random selection. Statistical theory cannot explain how the samples might behave and potential sources of bias are rampant.

111. D: In 2016 CMS unveiled the Overall Hospital Quality Star Ratings on its Hospital Compare website. The rating system combines 64 public measures into a single, one-to-five star rating. CMS rated more than 3,000 hospitals on the star scale. This website is free to the public.

112. A: Norming is when people begin to resolve their differences and come to accept their coworkers' strengths. This is the third stage in Tuckman's team-building model. Members are encouraged to assume responsibility for their assigned roles. The manager acts as scaffolding, keeping the team members on task and fostering more collaboration.

113. C: ACMA has five standards for their transition of care guidelines: identify patients at risk for poor transitions; complete a comprehensive assessment; perform a medication reconciliation; establish a dynamic care management plan; and communicate essential care transition information. Therefore, Choices A, B, and D are incorrect, and Choice C is correct.

114. B: It is not true that failures are ranked in severity from 1-5, and managed in order of severity over the rank of 3. They are ranked for 1-10, put in descending order, and those ranked at greater than 5 are managed in order of severity.

115. B: Bias is the tendency of a statistic to overestimate or underestimate a parameter. It can occur from sampling or measurement errors, or by using unrepresentative samples. If the statistic is unbiased, the average of all statistics from all samples will average the true population parameter.

116. A: Choice A is the best answer and clearly articulates why error reporting is significant. Choice B is incorrect because this is not the most important reason. Choice C is incorrect because sanctions are not automatically levied against an organization that reports errors. Choice D is incorrect because individual employees are protected against organizational retaliation when reporting errors; reporters remain anonymous.

117. B: The goal of storming is to explain the stages of the process and confirm that each team member is aware of their expected contribution. Storming is the second stage of Tuckman's model. In this step, mutual trust in the team is built as each team member begins to recognize their separate and collective strengths.

118. B: A sentinel event is an unforeseen occurrence that results in harm or death to a patient or group of patients. These events require immediate attention. Choice *A* is incorrect as it describes the 80-20 rule. Choice *C* describes an episode of care, so it is also incorrect. Choice *D* is incorrect because it describes a near-miss event, in which no injury actually occurs but might have, if not for intervention or fortune.

119. D: All of the choices are accurate statements regarding informed consent. Informed consent forms must be completed at admission. Additionally, they must be signed, dated, and witnessed, as well as maintained under lock and key (in the case of hard copies).

120. A: The goal of the forming stage of Tuckman's model is to encourage discussion among colleagues. Forming is the first step in Tuckman's model. During this stage, the team manager will choose members based on the areas of expertise necessary to achieve optimal results.

121. C: The four types of benchmarking are internal, competitive, functional, and generic. They allow the organization to measure and compare key work processes.

122. B: Root-cause analysis is a tool used to evaluate patient safety in healthcare organizations. The process identifies the underlying causes of sentinel and near-miss events and helps develop safeguards to prevent the recurrence of the incidents.

123. C: Diffusion is the passive and unplanned spread of new practices. Diffusion is said to occur through a five-step decision-making process culminating in the choice of whether or not to use a new idea.

124. D: Brainstorming can be referred to as a way of using a selected group of individuals to rapidly produce, clarify, and evaluate ideas or problems. Staff must be encouraged to preview the preliminary data, and leadership must allow for an open-ended and honest critique of what does and does not work.

125. B: Quality management initiatives should be tied to the mission and values of the organization to achieve sustainable change. Most organizational change is not maintained because it is not tied into the current culture or it is so different than the culture that employees do not embrace it. Issues that may negatively impact the sustainability of a project should be identified at both the planning and implementation stages.

126. D: Choices *A* and *C* are incorrect because they are used for collecting vital statistics data. Choice *B* is incorrect because it is a resource for obtaining environmental data. Choice *D* is the correct answer because EHRs can provide treatment outcomes for a population.

127. A: Choice *B* is incorrect since it is related to environmental data and is also not a realistic benefit. Choice *C* is associated with quality of life and health outcomes, so it is incorrect. Choice *D* is incorrect because there is no intervention listed that leads to increased life expectancy. A potential benefit of tracking morbidity and mortality rates is the ability to alter interventions (such as treatment options) and improve population health. Therefore, Choice *A* is the correct answer.

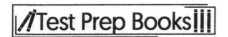

128. B: Choice *A* is incorrect since it doesn't specifically help manage a chronic illness. Choices *C* and *D* are incorrect, as they relate more to overall disease prevention rather than chronic illness management. Choice *B* is the correct answer because healthy eating is one way to manage a chronic illness.

129. A: Choices *B* and *C* are incorrect because they assist with preventing illnesses rather than managing a chronic disease. Choice *D* is helpful and could be encouraged, but it is not the best option to help a patient directly manage their illness. Therefore, Choice *A* is the correct answer since it provides education regarding medication adherence, which greatly impacts a person's ability to cope with a chronic illness.

130. D: Choice *A* should be encouraged, but it is not a direct way to implement healthy behaviors and is therefore incorrect. Choice *B* is also helpful but incorrect since it is not a healthy behavior that can be implemented. Choice *C* is incorrect since it is not a realistic healthy behavior. Choice *D* is the correct answer since it provides a specific and attainable way for the patient to implement a healthy behavior.

131. D: Choice *A* is incorrect because it is not the best fit for a patient in a marginalized population. Choice *B* may be helpful, but it is very broad and not a direct intervention; therefore, it is incorrect. Choice *C* may also be helpful but is incorrect since it is an intervention that should apply to all populations. Choice *D* is correct since it provides specific interventions for marginalized populations.

132. A: Choice *B* may be helpful, but it is not the most direct way to provide the patient with discharge information. Choice *C* delays any necessary information that the patient may need and is incorrect. Choice *D* can cause a disruption of information needed by the long-term care facility. Hospital records should be transferred between facilities, not given through the patient. Choice *A* allows for the smoothest transition of care; therefore, it is the correct answer.

133. B: Choice *A* does not improve communications; it only alerts the provider to potential problems. Choices *C* and *D* are helpful and should be done for the patient, but they do not help facilitate the transition process between facilities. Choice *B* allows for the most consistent communication, and it is the correct answer.

134. C: Choice *A* is incorrect since medications given during the hospital stay may differ from discharge medications. Choice *B* is incorrect because understanding procedures completed in the hospital will not help with readmission factors. Choice *D* is incorrect and unhelpful because it only provides speculation. Choice *C* helps enforce medication adherence, which contributes to a successful discharge.

135. B: Choice *A* is incorrect because the layout of someone's house is not a social determinants of health (SDOH) factor; these include where someone was born, where they grew up, where they currently live/work, and their age. Choice *C* is incorrect because it does not relate to any factors of SDOH. Choice *D* asks if they've ever applied for funding, but it doesn't ask about their current financial status. Choice *B* allows the healthcare provider to understand more of a patient's social standing; therefore, it is the correct answer.

136. C: TQM (Total Quality Management) is an entirely different management approach than Six Sigma. While Six Sigma focuses on reducing the probability of errors, TQM holds the principle that all employees or members of an organization must commit to helping improve procedures or operations. Therefore, Choice *C* is correct.

137. A: Pareto charts are based on the "Pareto principle," which states that a relatively small number of factors will account for the majority of a common effect. Therefore, Choice *A* is correct.

138. D: No negative outcome occurred, and the nurse was able to resolve the issue before anything did happen. This is called a near miss event. Therefore, Choice *D* is correct.

139. B: FMEA is an incremental process designed to identify all possible failures in a process. Therefore, it is essential that FMEA be implemented as early as possible. This means Choice *B* is correct.

140. A: Lewin's model of change—which proposes a way for organizations to conceptualize and approach the creation and management of organizational change—has three steps: unfreezing, changing, and refreezing. Therefore, Choice *A* is correct.

CPHQ Practice Test #2

1. Which of the following choices is consistent with the definition of the strategic quality planning process?
    a. The strategy phase includes the analysis of data related to the proposed project.
    b. The research phase is associated with changes in the balance sheet.
    c. The overall strategic quality plan must be based on key performance indicators (KPIs).
    d. The process consists of three phases: research, strategy, and cost containment.

2. Which of the following activities is consistent with the process of data cleansing?
    a. Review the content of all datasets for unexpected findings.
    b. Merge datasets to capture novel data.
    c. Eliminate all visible documentation errors.
    d. Collect data from multiple sources.

3. According to the Eisenhower matrix, which of the following items is urgent and important?
    a. Planning an in-service activity for next year
    b. Moderating today's panel discussion for a colleague who is ill
    c. Reading an Instagram invitation to submit an abstract for a conference
    d. Re-organizing the email inbox

4. Which of the following describes the general characteristics of mechanistic organizations?
    a. Social change
    b. Centralized management
    c. Lateral communication
    d. Individual expression

5. What is the primary expected outcome when portions of the agenda are assigned to different individuals?
    a. Effective time management
    b. Presentation experience for additional team members
    c. Decreased workload for the facilitator
    d. Positive participant engagement

6. Which of the following choices is consistent with the data analysis e-measures developed by the NQF?
    a. The NQF reviews hospital use of e-measures every three years.
    b. Hospitals are required to use NQF e-measures for data reporting.
    c. CMS requires reporting on all 113 NQF measures.
    d. Hospitals can use the Measure Authoring Tool for measure development.

7. How does benchmarking affect the strategic quality planning process?
    a. It adds the voice of the customer.
    b. The resulting information dictates the new organizational strategy.
    c. It controls vendor pricing.
    d. Strategic planners learn from the experience of other organizations.

8. The facilitator is planning to use multivoting on a new list of possible solutions generated during a previous meeting. Which of the following techniques would be most helpful in this situation?
   a. The Eisenhower matrix
   b. Small-group discussion
   c. An affinity diagram
   d. A brainstorming session

9. How can the HQP best encourage the development of a supportive workplace culture among the organization's employees?
   a. Engage in dialogue with front-line staff by explaining leadership decisions.
   b. Ensure that yearly performance evaluations are completed on time.
   c. Audit the frequency of training opportunities.
   d. Incentivize employee participation in ongoing education beyond regulatory requirements.

10. The Agency for Healthcare Research and Quality (AHRQ) has published a survey to assess an agency's culture of safety. Which of the following areas would NOT be included in this assessment?
    a. Cost per patient admission
    b. Environmental service plan
    c. Patient portal usage
    d. Temporary staffing rates

11. Which of the following definitions is consistent with goal-setting in the strategic quality planning process?
    a. Short-term goals are more appropriate in healthcare organizations.
    b. Organizational planners decide on the specific goals for the institution.
    c. Long-term goals are usually met successfully.
    d. Goals are set according to present circumstances.

12. Once a scribe has been assigned to assist with meeting details, the facilitator remains responsible for which of the following activities?
    a. Room accommodations
    b. Availability of appropriate IT resources
    c. Plans for follow-through of actions taken
    d. Attendance documentation as required for individual participants

13. Which of the following choices is NOT one of the four basic principles that guide institutional goal-setting?
    a. Eliminate all inequalities.
    b. Strengthen information technology structures.
    c. Decrease provider workload.
    d. Encourage local improvement solutions.

14. The team leaders are assessing the time policy for ER-to-nursing-unit transfers. According to the IHI plan, which of the following sampling methods is most appropriate?
    a. Convenience sampling
    b. Block sampling
    c. Self-selection sampling
    d. Systematic sampling

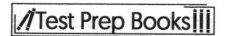

15. Which of the following choices describes the function of key performance indicators (KPIs)?
    a. Annual employee performance appraisal
    b. Long-range planning models for larger healthcare systems
    c. Measurement of growth potential for individual primary providers
    d. Measurable standards of performance that can reveal areas of weakness

16. Team leaders are estimating RN staffing requirements for the next fiscal year. Which of the following would be an appropriate outcome measure?
    a. Daily bed turnover rate
    b. Medication reconciliation
    c. Fall assessment
    d. Skin assessment

17. A team is reviewing institutional Critical to Quality measures (CTQs). What is the relationship between these measures and institutional process improvement?
    a. CTQs are customer-based priorities.
    b. CTQs are imposed by CMS.
    c. CTQs are directly related to financial profit.
    d. CTQs can replace KPIs (key performance indicators) in the planning process.

18. Which of the following activities is an example of mistake-proofing?
    a. Surgical "time out"
    b. Quiet environment rules
    c. Valet patient parking
    d. Patient portal appointment scheduling

19. According to recent research, the EHR (electronic health record) improves patient safety. Which of the following choices has been identified as a significant safety issue associated with its use?
    a. Inventory charges are not recorded.
    b. Computer access time is increased.
    c. Providers demonstrate alarm fatigue.
    d. Additional IT support is required.

20. Which of the following choices is consistent with the definition of diffusion?
    a. In-service educational modules for all certified nursing assistants
    b. Person-to-person discussion of possible changes
    c. Use of the new CAUTI (catheter-associated urinary tract infection) bundle
    d. Community vaccination information sessions

21. Which of the following choices is consistent with the stratified sampling method?
    a. The sampling for the patient satisfaction survey sample included males and females.
    b. The HbA1C level was measured for every sixth patient in the diabetic clinic population.
    c. Annual prostate exam rates were compared for two random groups of Medicare patients.
    d. Blood pressure readings were measured for volunteer employees.

158

22. When is a "time out" required?
    a. When AM medications are given
    b. Prior to lab testing for an infection
    c. Before the start of a colonoscopy
    d. When a chest x-ray is done

23. Which of the following choices would be an output for an action plan objective?
    a. Central line infection rates will be zero this quarter.
    b. RNs will complete a dressing change module.
    c. Nursing staff will demonstrate safe practice.
    d. Patient pain satisfaction scores will increase.

24. Which of the following choices is consistent with the Meaningful Measures initiative of the Centers for Medicare & Medicaid Services (CMS)?
    a. Promotion of patient involvement in care planning
    b. Elimination of racial bias in program planning
    c. Attention to issues with potential for improvement
    d. Improvement of data systems

25. How does the Pareto principle relate to outcome analyses in a healthcare institution?
    a. It is predicted that 80% of the cost centers will exceed their budgeted total by 20 percent.
    b. The areas with the largest number of employees tend to have the greatest variations in performance measures.
    c. Up to 80% of the variations in performance measures are due to only 20 percent of areas that are measured.
    d. The areas with the largest number of employees tend to have the smallest variations in performance measures.

26. Which of the following should alert nursing staff to the possibility of an infant abduction attempt?
    a. A nurse is carrying the infant in the hallway.
    b. The mother has removed the blanket with the security tag.
    c. The CMA says that the infant's name bracelet came off during a diaper change.
    d. The father forgot his name badge.

27. The hospital would be penalized for the 30-day readmission of which of the following diagnoses?
    a. Abdominal surgery for colon cancer
    b. Right total knee arthroplasty
    c. Sepsis due to multiple trauma
    d. End-stage renal disease

28. The AHRQ (Agency for Healthcare Research and Quality) has published quality standards that define the safety culture of a healthcare system. Which of the following standards is viewed as the most controversial?
    a. Strive for safety in an admittedly high-risk environment.
    b. Involve individuals at all levels of the agency hierarchy.
    c. Commit sufficient resources to achieve safety goals.
    d. Maintain a blame-free framework for error reporting.

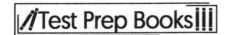

29. A manager is addressing the Lean criteria for performance improvement. Which of the following strategies would address the People mode?
   a. Requiring managers to communicate process change requirements to all employees
   b. Including employees in the process evaluation decisions
   c. Contracting with the vendor with the lowest price
   d. Limiting stakeholders' evaluation of process changes

30. What is the HQP's role in the reporting process for a safety event?
   a. Writing the incident report
   b. Completing risk analysis
   c. Debriefing front-line staff
   d. Reporting the safety event to regulatory agencies

31. Which of the following choices identifies the most critical outcome of patient-care documentation?
   a. Use of the EHR makes it easier for nursing supervisors to monitor staff compliance.
   b. Utilization of specialized equipment is documented.
   c. Supply levels depend on documentation of usage for adequate replacement.
   d. Value-based reimbursement plans depend on accurate documentation.

32. Which of the following quality improvement goals has the greatest impact on patient outcomes?
   a. Reducing the duration of an average inpatient stay by two days
   b. Completing employee performance evaluations before their annual due date 95 percent of the time
   c. Reducing patient mortality in the emergency department
   d. Revising documentation guidelines for surgical procedures within thirty days for compliance with new regulatory directions

33. The team is identifying goals to address the improvement of a specific process. Which of the following goals is stated correctly?
   a. Hospital readmission rates will decrease over the next quarter.
   b. CAUTI infections will be zero for the second quarter.
   c. Patient reports of adequate pain control will increase 10 percent in the next quarter.
   d. Community feedback will be positive.

34. Which of the following choices would be an appropriate outcome for an organizational safety goal aimed at harm reduction?
   a. Improved access to healthcare information
   b. Empowerment of the workforce
   c. Reduction of duplicate services
   d. Improved rate of medication errors

35. The project team is planning the implementation of the patient-portal online access for a healthcare system. The team will use a Gantt chart to organize the project. What is the first step in the development of this chart?
   a. Identify all managers with responsibility for the project.
   b. Acquire all materials required for each level of the project.
   c. Construct outcome measures for each stage of the project.
   d. Create a work breakdown structure.

160

36. Which of the following data management systems consolidates patient-care information from multiple sources?
    a. Healthcare customer relations management (HCRM) system
    b. Enterprise application software
    c. Electronic health record (EHR)
    d. Reliability-centered maintenance system

37. Which of the following safety interventions has demonstrated the least positive effect on error rates?
    a. SBAR communication
    b. Greater resources for training
    c. Safety teams in individual nursing units
    d. Senior management unit visits

38. The acronyms PDCA (Plan, Do, Check, Act) and PDSA (Plan, Do, Study, Act) are often used interchangeably. How is the PDSA model different than the PDCA model?
    a. The PDSA model is used more effectively in human services industries.
    b. The PDSA model was originally designed as a continuous improvement model.
    c. The PDSA model provides more reliable estimates of project outcomes.
    d. The PDSA model compares results to expected outcomes.

39. What is the main function of program champions?
    a. Management of cost-reduction initiatives
    b. Maintenance of stakeholder relationships
    c. Management of nursing staff contract negotiations
    d. Monitoring of root cause analysis for fall injuries

40. What is the most basic requirement for any data management system?
    a. Standardized data collection methods
    b. Elimination of human error in data entry
    c. Use of the system that competitors are using
    d. Estimation of CMS incentive payments

41. According to the American Hospital Association's Triple Aim, what is the intended outcome of an alliance among an acute-care hospital system, primary care providers, and specialty providers?
    a. Shared financial risk to reduce the per capita costs
    b. Decreased emergency room visits
    c. Improved revenue stream for all participants
    d. Improved employee retention

42. In the Six Sigma process improvement model, the role of process champion also may be used to label which of the following team roles?
    a. Facilitator
    b. Sponsor
    c. Team leader
    d. Scribe

161

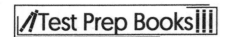

43. A large healthcare system in the Northeast was recently fined more than $18 million for a HIPAA violation related to the security of the system websites. Which of the following choices is consistent with that error?
   a. Data sharing between providers was blocked.
   b. Patient data was accessible to third parties.
   c. Excessive time elapsed between testing and posting of results.
   d. Inaccurate data was not corrected in a timely manner.

44. Which of the following elements is most critical to effective organizational priority-setting?
   a. Stakeholder interests
   b. Objectives
   c. Timing
   d. Resources

45. Who is responsible for the development of a hospital's emergency preparedness plans?
   a. The Centers for Medicare & Medicaid Services (CMS)
   b. The Centers for Disease Control and Prevention (CDC)
   c. The American Hospital Association (AHA)
   d. The individual hospital

46. A fishbone diagram is most closely associated with which of the following processes?
   a. Process champion identification
   b. Root cause analysis
   c. Benchmarking
   d. Systems thinking

47. Which of the following statements is consistent with the development of an organizational action plan?
   a. There needs to be a separate action plan for each major element of the organizational structure.
   b. Development of employee action plans is focused on contractual issues rather than project planning.
   c. In large organizations, the action plan is only used to identify those responsible for each element of the plan.
   d. Action plans for individual groups in an organization are considered stand-alone plans that address specific problems for that group.

48. Which of the following choices is consistent with the project charter for a quality improvement program?
   a. It is an outline of the entire quality improvement plan.
   b. The document is legally binding.
   c. It requires unique performance measures.
   d. It is developed by and for senior managers.

49. Which of the following choices is consistent with the purpose of the 2016 National Strategy for Healthcare initiative?
   a. Improve end-of-life care.
   b. Promote lifelong learning for all providers.
   c. Promote active participation of patients and families.
   d. Improve IT infrastructure.

50. The acronym CIA—confidentiality, integrity, and accessibility—refers to the priorities of information security in a healthcare institution. Which of the following choices is an example of a breach of confidentiality?
    a. Data entry errors in the EHR
    b. Restricted interdepartmental data sharing
    c. Unsecured mobile nursing computers
    d. Complicated app and device syncing

51. Which of the following choices is an example of a balancing measure as used in a quality improvement project?
    a. Number of defective items per 1000 pieces delivered last quarter
    b. Percentage of orders completed on deadline
    c. Customer satisfaction rating for a new product
    d. Comparison of actual cost to estimated cost per unit

52. Which of the following statements is consistent with the process of credentialing?
    a. The leadership team evaluates the clinical performance of all licensed providers.
    b. State boards determine the scope of practice for licensed providers.
    c. Credentialing requires that all providers must be licensed and certified in their specialty.
    d. All applicants who are properly licensed must be accepted by the leadership team.

53. Leaders are assessing the KPIs for a newly opened trauma unit. The average patient stay in the trauma unit is 48 hours greater than in the clinical pathway model. Which of the following choices is a potential special cause variation for this example?
    a. The Level 1 trauma center's transfer policy
    b. The RN staffing levels on all shifts
    c. The availability of surgical suites
    d. An average patient age range of 25 to 76 years

54. All personnel wear name tags. What additional safety strategy can be used to increase the efficiency of the staff identification methods?
    a. Color-coding is changed according to a random schedule.
    b. Embedded door codes are randomly reassigned.
    c. Require agency-provided scrubs.
    d. All of the above are correct.

55. The group is developing an action plan for improving compliance with eye health guidelines for patients with diabetes. Which of the following choices would be an appropriate indicator for this plan?
    a. Patients with diabetes will have decreased progression of retinopathy.
    b. The patient compliance with twice-yearly eye checks will improve.
    c. Reminder messages will be sent to all patients with diabetes.
    d. The number of ophthalmology visits will be tracked in the patient portals.

56. What is the principal market condition that has prompted the expansion of the scope of the risk management process for healthcare organizations?
    a. Value-based care models
    b. Diagnosis-related groups (DRGs)
    c. Fee-for-service services
    d. Escalating legal costs

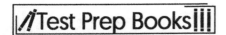

57. Which of the following activities would be appropriate to introduce a QI initiative?
    a. Implement the change based on an executive consensus.
    b. Broadcast an email message to announce policy changes.
    c. Add the new performance criteria to the employee handbook.
    d. Conduct an information session for interested employees.

58. Which of the following choices is NOT an intended function of the control chart?
    a. Identify areas for possible improvement.
    b. Conduct root cause analysis of process failure.
    c. Evaluate the effectiveness of new initiatives.
    d. Monitor sustainability of improved processes.

59. Which of the following statements is consistent with the structure and/or function of the Agency for Healthcare Research and Quality (AHRQ)?
    a. The agency has statutory power to enforce practice guidelines.
    b. The agency is funded by private-sector donors.
    c. The agency provides toolkits for quality improvement.
    d. The agency's database use is restricted to funded researchers.

60. The government has published a security risk assessment tool (SRA) to be used for agency risk assessment efforts. Which of the following choices is NOT correct?
    a. The assessment is required by the HIPAA Security Rule.
    b. This instrument is best for larger systems.
    c. The SRA identifies potential areas of risk.
    d. The data is used to devise a mitigation plan.

61. There has been criticism of the Six Sigma approach to performance improvement. Which of the following issues is modifiable?
    a. The protocol is expensive in terms of time and resources.
    b. The initiatives often fail.
    c. The program is difficult to learn.
    d. Customer satisfaction is difficult to predict.

62. Healthcare managers have adopted the fishbone diagram from the Toyota business model. The fishbone diagram provides a framework for root cause analysis. Which of the following choices is consistent with this diagram?
    a. Team members must be quality improvement experts.
    b. Human error is always identified as one of the "causes" by the model.
    c. The analysis is commonly used for staff evaluation and punitive action.
    d. The success of the model depends on an accurate problem statement.

63. Which of the following describes the Science of Improvement as defined by the Institute for Healthcare Improvement (IHI)?
    a. The improvement process is focused on root cause error analysis.
    b. The process uses the plan, do, study, act (PDSA) sequence to identify areas of improvement.
    c. The successful implementation of the improvement plan can be tied to CMS reimbursement.
    d. The process is more appropriate for inpatient care settings than primary care settings.

64. Pareto analysis can generate a prioritized action plan. Which dimension of other action plans is NOT part of the Pareto analysis?
   a. Estimation of costs associated with the implementation of the plan
   b. Identification of interested stakeholders and employees
   c. Prioritization of the problem list
   d. Comparison of group performance

65. Which of the following choices is consistent with the characteristics of a high-reliability healthcare organization?
   a. The organization has no reported system failures for extended periods.
   b. Work processes are reduced to the simplest form possible.
   c. Senior management is responsible for risk assessment and quality improvement.
   d. Success is measured in terms of near-misses.

66. Which of the following is consistent with the mission of the National Quality Forum (NQF)?
   a. The forum is funded by the United States government.
   b. The NQF develops communication plans aimed at improved safety.
   c. Only specialty providers can approve the use of new NQF measures.
   d. NQF measures are used to evaluate patient care in multiple settings.

67. The group is conducting a root cause analysis of a discrepancy in the reporting of the controlled substance counts on a specific nursing unit. Which of the following choices would be an organizational cause for this error?
   a. The count was signed by a single RN instead of two licensed personnel.
   b. The count could not be completed because the computers were down.
   c. There was no agency protocol for controlled substance reconciliation.
   d. The RN signed for a dose that wasn't used or discarded.

68. Which of the following choices is consistent with risk-adjustment methods?
   a. They were developed to accommodate the Affordable Care Act.
   b. They are only used to adjust the effect of age on outcome measures.
   c. They project costs based on factors beyond the provider's control.
   d. They are used only by third-party payers.

69. Which of the following would NOT be considered a sentinel event?
   a. An older patient falls on their way to the bathroom while in the hospital.
   b. A younger patient commits suicide shortly after being discharged.
   c. A surgical guide wire is left inside a patient after surgery completion.
   d. A patient suffering from late-stage heart failure suffers a massive stroke and passes away.

70. What is the role of the World Health Organization (WHO) concerning safe care?
   a. The WHO stresses the need for the application of research results to improve health.
   b. The WHO issues pandemic regulations that require one hundred percent compliance by member nations.
   c. The WHO case-manages all active tuberculosis infections.
   d. The WHO conducts vaccine development for newly identified infections.

71. A provider wants to develop a visual representation of the ages of diabetic patients and the number of clinic visits in the past year. Which of the following tools could display that information?
    a. Scatter diagram
    b. Fishbone diagram
    c. Control chart
    d. Pareto chart

72. What is the definition of a process control?
    a. Any assessment measure that avoids errors at the customer level
    b. A measure that identifies links among specific causes
    c. A process that evaluates employee performance outcomes
    d. A time and motion study of a new manufacturing procedure

73. What is the most significant risk associated with canceled patient appointments that are not rescheduled?
    a. Lost agency revenue
    b. Staffing issues
    c. Patient outcomes
    d. CMS evaluation

74. Which of the following choices is consistent with the Healthcare Effectiveness Data and Information Set (HEDIS) databases that are developed by the National Committee for Quality Assurance (NCQA)?
    a. HEDIS data tracks the incidence of communicable diseases in a population.
    b. HEDIS measures hospital compliance with environmental standards.
    c. HEDIS data is used to evaluate the effectiveness of healthcare plans.
    d. HEDIS data does not currently track electronic health record (EHR) usage in Special Needs Plans (SNPs).

75. Process champions must be skilled in many different areas of organizational management. When assessing the performance of a process champion in a healthcare system, which of the following qualities may be difficult to measure objectively?
    a. Establishing the patient connection
    b. Mentoring new team members
    c. Maintaining the connection between team members and senior management
    d. Separating personal vision from institutional priorities

76. What is the key element that distinguishes enterprise risk management (ERM) from earlier healthcare risk management models?
    a. Cybersecurity is now included in the risk assessment.
    b. Patient outcomes are the driving force.
    c. Strategic planning assessment is included.
    d. All of the above are correct.

77. The team leaders of the 20/20 Eye Care center are discussing marketing strategies. Which of the following choices is a structural measure associated with this process?
    a. Percentage of patients over forty-five who were screened for glaucoma
    b. Number of full-time and part-time board-certified providers
    c. Hospital admissions from the ambulatory surgical center
    d. Annual rate of post-operative infections

166

78. Which of the following statements is consistent with the effect of change theory on quality improvement?
    a. When the purpose of a proposed quality innovation is well articulated, diffusion is rapid.
    b. Early adopters of quality improvement innovations are often group leaders.
    c. Late majority adopters quickly recognize the potential of the proposed changes.
    d. Diffusion cannot occur without prior formal dissemination of information.

79. Which of the following choices is a business value-added activity?
    a. Accommodating government-mandated safety requirements
    b. Completing client-specific product configurations
    c. Updating risk management protocols
    d. Revising a defective prototype

80. The I-PASS mnemonic was developed to improve quality of communication in the patient handoff, which has been identified as an area of significant risk. According to the model, which of the following handoff statements is consistent with "situation awareness"?
    a. "The patient is scheduled for a CT of the head at 9 AM."
    b. "The patient is stable and was admitted with an upper GI bleed yesterday."
    c. "The patient is a 59-year-old male with acute MI, stable vital signs, and no pain, and is resting."
    d. "Based on my assessment, he needs a chest x-ray to check for pneumonia today."

81. Which of the following patients would qualify for the disease management model of case management?
    a. A 75-year-old female patient with right knee arthroplasty
    b. A 62-year-old male patient with a right-sided hemorrhagic stroke
    c. A 49-year-old male patient with a posterior wall myocardial infarction
    d. A 45-year-old female patient with tumor lysis syndrome

82. Which of the following choices is consistent with the Pareto chart?
    a. The chart is used to identify common cause and special cause variation.
    b. The chart can only be used effectively in the problem identification phase of quality improvement.
    c. The Pareto chart requires interval-level variables.
    d. The results of the Pareto chart identify areas for improvement.

83. Which of the following choices is a common cause variation according to SPC (statistical process control) measurement?
    a. Environmental variations
    b. Human error
    c. Machine malfunctions
    d. Variations in materials

84. Communication errors in patient hand-off situations are estimated to be the root cause for as many as seventy-five percent of all sentinel events. Using the I-PASS reporting format, if a patient were experiencing chest pain, where would that information be reported?
    a. I
    b. P
    c. A
    d. S

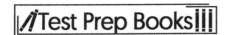

85. The end product of the 5 Whys technique is the identification of a countermeasure. How is a countermeasure different than a solution?
    a. Countermeasures assess blame.
    b. Countermeasures address the root cause.
    c. Countermeasures are less difficult to implement.
    d. Countermeasures must be evaluated by managers.

86. According to the I-PASS model, which of the following choices is consistent with "illness severity"?
    a. The 79-year-old male is being treated with warfarin for A-fib, and he is a watcher.
    b. The patient is scheduled for a CT scan: to provide detailed views of the heart and lungs today.
    c. The patient will need skilled nurses' visits when discharged.
    d. The patient will need new IV orders if the infusion is to be continued.

87. Which of the following is consistent with the purpose of registries for healthcare data management?
    a. Allowing data sharing among multiple healthcare systems
    b. Collecting data about specific patient conditions for quality care innovation
    c. Capturing care costs for reimbursement
    d. Tracking of provider reimbursement schedules

88. What is the primary focus of the CMS Meaningful Measures 2022 initiative?
    a. Identification of potential areas for quality improvement
    b. Fee schedules for patients covered by CMS services
    c. Primary care preventive medicine best practices
    d. Surgical readmission rates

89. Scorecards and dashboards are used to measure organizational effectiveness. Which of the following choices is consistent with these reports?
    a. Scorecards can identify root cause.
    b. Dashboards address structural outcomes.
    c. Both measures provide actionable data.
    d. Both measures have "drill-down" capability.

90. The team leader is tracking the number of conversions for several social media websites. Which of the following choices is the best engagement metric for that question?
    a. Likes
    b. Follows
    c. Direct messages
    d. Social shares

91. Concerning HIPAA reporting, which technical safeguards address access to protected health information (PHI)?
    a. Integrity controls
    b. Audit controls
    c. Transmission security
    d. All of the above

92. Which of the following would be tracked on a scorecard?
    a. Telemetry unit census
    b. Current ER wait time
    c. 30-day readmissions
    d. L&D nurse-to-patient ratio

93. The IHI identified six patient-care qualities to serve as benchmarks for addressing healthcare disparities. Which of the following is NOT included in that list?
    a. Timeliness
    b. Effectiveness
    c. Efficiency
    d. Cost control

94. ISO (the International Organization for Standardization) is a nongovernmental agency that publishes standards for more than one thousand goods and services. The ISO 9000 list also includes the principles of quality management. Which of the following is NOT one of the characteristics of this model?
    a. Relationships with employees
    b. Product quality
    c. Customer-first attitude
    d. Organizational QI mindset

95. Which of the following statements about sampling is correct?
    a. Probability samples are more prone to bias.
    b. Convenience sampling is a non-probability sampling method.
    c. Voluntary sampling is a form of probability sampling.
    d. Random data is required for non-probability sampling.

96. Electronic clinical quality measures (eCQMs) include abstracted data from the hospital's EHR system that are submitted to CMS to demonstrate patient-care effectiveness. These measures are submitted in addition to mandatory quality measures, and the hospital can voluntarily decide which eCQMs to report. Which of the following choices is an example of a voluntary eCQM?
    a. Infants who are bottle-fed exclusively from birth to discharge
    b. ICU patients who are diagnosed with new pressure ulcers
    c. Time in minutes from ER admission decision to patient transfer to the nursing unit
    d. Patients who are discharged with one or more new opioid medications

97. When comparing Lean with Six Sigma, which one of the following statements is consistent with Lean?
    a. Lean philosophy is focused on waste control.
    b. Lean uses more advanced analytic procedures.
    c. Lean assesses data for variation or outliers.
    d. Lean is best employed after Six Sigma analysis.

98. Which of the following is consistent with the hospital's use of outside sources for data analysis?
    a. Outside performance data may be biased.
    b. Generating the data in-house is less expensive.
    c. Creating tables helps to identify importing errors.
    d. Formatting issues affect data quality.

169

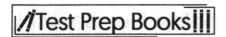

99. Why was the PDCA model refined into the PDSA model?
   a. To measure and analyze system outcomes rather than customer outcomes
   b. To emphasize the importance of bottom-up strategies rather than top-down ones
   c. To emphasize the importance of reflecting on the choice of metrics used
   d. To create an IT-friendly version of the PDCA model

100. Which of the following statements regarding the current state of cyber security in many healthcare systems is consistent with industry cyber security expert assessments?
   a. HIPAA technical standards are insufficient for the current threat level.
   b. Access controls are adequate to the threat.
   c. EHR platforms from leading vendors are secure.
   d. Two-factor authentication is not required for associate partners of the system.

101. Which of the following statements is true about benchmarking?
   a. All stakeholders are included in the evaluation process.
   b. All benchmarks are chosen by senior managers.
   c. JCAHO sets all agency benchmarks.
   d. Benchmarking only applies to acute-care facilities.

102. Which of the following Health Insurance Portability and Accountability Act of 1996 (HIPAA) violations could result in a ten-year prison sentence?
   a. Hospital clerical staff sells Social Security numbers.
   b. Hospital staff accesses the EHR record of a "celebrity" patient.
   c. A newly hired nursing assistant takes home worksheets with identifiable patient information.
   d. Patient pages are left open on the computer when the nurse is called to an emergency in the next room.

103. The team is using the SWOT (Strengths, Weaknesses, Opportunities, and Threats) model to consider adding additional services to their product line. Which of the following choices would be considered an "external-helpful" factor?
   a. Existing organizational resources
   b. Knowledge gained from past failures
   c. Federal pandemic relief funds
   d. Loss of customers due to supply chain issues

104. The PETT instrument (people, environment, tools, task) is used in human systems engineering to identify the entire scope of a process, including the interactions among patients, staff, and families. The model also identifies facilitators and barriers to successful outcomes. Which of the following barriers is an environmental issue?
   a. Language barrier
   b. Insufficient staff
   c. Complex device instructions
   d. Departmental conflicts

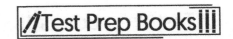

105. Which of the following choices would NOT satisfy provider compliance with any of the Meaningful Use criteria?
    a. E-prescribing of medications
    b. Reimbursement schedules
    c. Interagency EHR connectivity
    d. A1C results for diabetic patients

106. Which of the following choices is NOT one of the most common "ribs" of the fishbone diagram?
    a. Materials
    b. Methods
    c. Costs
    d. Environment

107. Which of the following accurately describes the difference between quality improvement (QI) and performance improvement (PI)?
    a. QI focuses on a healthcare facility as a whole, whereas PI is concerned with an individual member's performance.
    b. QI focuses on improving processes, whereas PI is concerned with improving human performance.
    c. QI focuses on a healthcare facility's performance in relation to its peer facilities, whereas PI is concerned with an individual healthcare facility's maintenance of internal best practices.
    d. QI focuses on an individual member's performance, whereas PI is concerned with the healthcare facility as a whole.

108. Which of the following issues related to the interstate regulation of telemedicine is state-specific?
    a. Technology availability
    b. Software licensing
    c. Medicare payments
    d. Licensing restrictions for MDs and RNs

109. Which of the following accurately describes the difference between Lean and Six Sigma?
    a. Lean is focused on the elimination of waste from a system, while Six Sigma is more concerned with reducing variation by minimizing defects in a system.
    b. Six Sigma is focused on the elimination of waste from a system, while Lean is more concerned with reducing variation by minimizing defects in a system.
    c. Lean is focused on identifying individual process champions, whereas Six Sigma is more concerned with the maintenance and improvement of internal best practices.
    d. Six Sigma is focused on identifying individual process champions, whereas Lean is more concerned with the maintenance and improvement of internal best practices.

110. What is the most significant advantage of multi-stage sampling for data management?
    a. Large groups are sampled more efficiently.
    b. It works best with homogenous populations.
    c. The method eliminates population bias.
    d. The method requires a predetermined sample size.

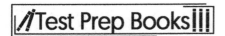
111. Which of the following choices is consistent with Kotter's change theory?
    a. Creating a vision and strategy for change requires first removing the obstacles.
    b. The members of the coalition should be senior managers.
    c. Rewarding small behavioral changes leads to greater success.
    d. Communicating the vision is the final step of the process.

112. What is the first step of process improvement in healthcare?
    a. Identify a new key performance indicator.
    b. Establish target goals for the process.
    c. Review current guidelines and procedures.
    d. Measure performance based on existing key performance indicators.

113. Which of the following describes the benefit(s) of using a Gantt chart?
    a. Gantt charts provide a high-level overview of a project and its timeline, making it easier to decide where to allocate time and resources.
    b. Gantt charts allow all members of a team to see overlaps and dependencies.
    c. Gantt charts make it easier to set realistic expectations and deadlines for a project.
    d. All of the above

114. Which of the following choices is consistent with the concept of resiliency in high-reliability healthcare organizations?
    a. Respect for individual work product
    b. Effective mitigation strategies
    c. Prompt feedback for all employee concerns
    d. Comprehensive educational resources

115. Which of the following functions is the most common reason for using a virtual private network (VPN) in place of a conventional network?
    a. It is a private email network for senior managers.
    b. The system accommodates remote staff positions.
    c. It protects against unauthorized system access.
    d. It is used to stream patient teaching modules.

116. Which of the following choices is consistent with the Physician Value-Based Modifier (PVM) program?
    a. Provider groups accept all financial risk.
    b. Providers are reimbursed for the quality rather than the number of patient-care encounters.
    c. Hospitals are rewarded for timely discharge of preterm infants covered by Medicaid.
    d. Hospitals can opt out of the program.

117. The team decides to create a process map to monitor the progress of a project. The team is particularly interested in tracking the availability of all necessary resources and the identification of waste that may be occurring at any point in the process. Which of the following process maps is the best choice for the team?
    a. Value stream map
    b. Basic flow chart
    c. Value chain map
    d. Cross functional map

118. Value-based care models are associated with varying degrees of financial risk. Which of the following choices is consistent with the definitions of upside risk and downside risk?
   a. Upside risk is associated with penalties for failure to meet metrics.
   b. CMS can limit participation in downside risk models.
   c. Plans that assume downside risk must be well coordinated to be successful.
   d. Downside risk models are not penalized for failure to meet CMS benchmarks.

119. Which of the following choices explains how stratified sampling decreases variability?
   a. Simple random selection
   b. Homogenous strata
   c. Self-enrolled strata
   d. Restricted sample size

120. Which of the following choices is consistent with BPM (business process management)?
   a. BPM is an informal annual review of all customer satisfaction data for senior managers.
   b. The business process champion is responsible for only a retrospective review of processes.
   c. Six Sigma expertise for team members is not required or encouraged.
   d. The continuous review process assumes that people store plans in their heads.

121. Which of the following choices is consistent with the use of control charts?
   a. The chart tracks structural measures.
   b. Stable processes are not tracked.
   c. Special cause variations cannot be identified.
   d. Control charts identify areas for improvement.

122. Which of the following choices identifies the CMS benchmark for the transition of care from the hospital to the home environment?
   a. Preventing early readmission
   b. Verifying the medication list
   c. Self-regulating chronic diseases
   d. Providing timely follow-up care

123. A team is using the VMOSA framework (Vision, Mission, Objectives, Strategies, and Action Plans) to develop an organizational action plan for a company that sells widgets. Which of the following choices is a mission statement?
   a. The company will market products that increase leisure time for the entire family.
   b. The company will provide quality products that meet customers' expectations through continuous process improvement.
   c. There will be a thirty percent increase in customer satisfaction at the end of the next quarter.
   d. The team will use the eighty-twenty rule to focus the action plan.

124. Which data management system could be used to track OSHA compliance?
   a. Reliability-centered maintenance (RCM) system
   b. Enterprise application software
   c. Electronic healthcare record (EHR)
   d. Healthcare customer relations management (HCRM) software

125. Healthcare economists predict that Medicare costs will continue to increase because existing care plans do not successfully integrate social services. Which of the following choices is suggested as a solution to this deficiency?
    a.   Increasing Medicare payments for using social determinants of health as benchmarks
    b.   Using EHR data to identify individual patient needs
    c.   Mandatory reporting of patients' employment and housing status
    d.   Actively enrolling all Medicaid patients in qualifying programs

126. A healthcare provider is reviewing available resources to assist in obtaining vital statistics data. Which resource is most appropriate?
    a.   Electronic health records
    b.   Data from the state health department
    c.   Data provided by the Environmental Protection Agency
    d.   Health outcomes from national surveys

127. A teenage patient is newly diagnosed with type I diabetes. Which resource would be most appropriate for the healthcare provider to recommend?
    a.   A booklet with tips for managing chronic conditions
    b.   A smartphone app to help manage type I diabetes
    c.   An upcoming public health campaign about diabetes
    d.   A local wellness program for healthy eating

128. A healthcare provider is planning to host a health fair in the local community to raise awareness of health risks. Education on which topic should be promoted during the health fair?
    a.   Proper hand hygiene
    b.   Healthy cooking techniques
    c.   Medication management strategies
    d.   Signs of a heart attack or stroke

129. A community health official is looking to promote disease prevention within the community. Which strategy would be most appropriate?
    a.   Provide educational pamphlets at the local library.
    b.   Provide a screening questionnaire that anyone can use to detect potential diseases.
    c.   Ask local clinics to promote physical activity.
    d.   Hold a question-and-answer session about common chronic illnesses.

130. A healthcare administrator is reviewing ways to reduce costs without compromising patient care and safety. Which of the following is the best solution?
    a.   Provide optional health screenings for patients and family members.
    b.   Review hospital readmission rates.
    c.   Partner with community organizations to provide patients with local health programs.
    d.   Review medication lists and choose the lower-cost options.

131. Various forms of data are available to monitor improvement efforts within healthcare organizations. Which is an example of analyzing clinical data?
    a.   Reviewing electronic health records
    b.   Reviewing patient demographics
    c.   Reviewing care given to marginalized populations
    d.   Reviewing a patient's housing situation

132. A healthcare provider is preparing to give a standardized shift handoff. What is the purpose of a shift handoff?
    a. To provide accurate information to another provider located at the next facility
    b. To update the physician on the patient's status
    c. To provide information that ensures a smooth transition between healthcare providers
    d. To inform the other healthcare provider of any family member needs

133. A healthcare provider is cross-training a fellow employee. How does cross-training improve the care team and flow of work?
    a. It improves employee retention rates.
    b. It improves workplace morale.
    c. It allows care team members to interact with a variety of patients.
    d. It allows for more flexibility in the event of an unexpected situation.

134. Which question would allow a provider to better understand their patient's health behavior?
    a. "How frequently do you exercise?"
    b. "What kinds of medications do you take?"
    c. "How often do you go grocery shopping?"
    d. "When was the last time you were in the hospital?"

135. A healthcare provider is preparing to discharge a patient home. Which resource best allows the patient to receive continuity of care outside of a healthcare facility?
    a. A local emergency department closest to the patient's residence
    b. A local physician's office
    c. A local organization with programs for smoking cessation
    d. A nearby pharmacy

136. _____ is a term that refers to the ability of an individual or group to obtain the necessary services to achieve proper health.
    a. Equity
    b. Access
    c. Amenities
    d. Patient preference responsiveness

137. Which of the following is considered a primary purpose of implementing cultural competency trainings within a healthcare organization?
    a. To lower the cost of healthcare services
    b. To promote health equity and address health disparities
    c. To streamline the administrative process
    d. To improve patient satisfaction scores

138. To what does the acronym ISO refer?
    a. International Service Organization
    b. Institute for the Study of Organisms
    c. International Organization for Standardization
    d. International Systems Organization

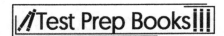

139. What is the difference between FPPE and OPPE?
    a. OPPE evaluates performance over a much shorter timespan than FPPE.
    b. FPPE evaluates performance over a much shorter timespan than OPPE.
    c. OPPE is only used in situations where medical error or malpractice is suspected, whereas FPPE is used to evaluate all medical professionals.
    d. FPPE is only used in situations where medical error or malpractice is suspected, whereas OPPE is used to evaluate all medical professionals.

140. Which of the following is NOT true regarding healthcare compliance?
    a. Healthcare compliance is designed to prevent fraud, waste, and abuse.
    b. Responsibility for healthcare compliance lies with the administrative heads of an organization.
    c. Healthcare compliance helps to promote a culture in which individuals feel empowered to speak out and help correct instances of fraud, waste, and abuse.
    d. The ACA mandates that providers establish a compliance plan.

Answer Explanations #2

1. C: Institutional quality is measured by key performance indicators (KPIs), which means that any effort aimed at improving or maintaining quality must be tied to a specific KPI. The strategy phase of the strategic quality planning process identifies all of the project's specific steps, and the research phase includes the analysis of the data that forms the basis for the project. This means that Choices *A* and *B* are incorrect. Choice *D* is incorrect because the strategic quality planning process has two phases: the research phase and the strategy phase.

2. C: Effective data analysis requires the preparation of the raw data. One of the preparatory steps is the data cleansing process, which includes the correction of readily apparent documentation errors. Data exploration includes searching individual databases for unanticipated findings, which means that Choice *A* is incorrect. Data blending is the process of merging datasets to identify novel information that results from the combined sources. This means that Choice *B* is incorrect. Data aggregation from multiple sources follows an extract, transfer, and load sequence. Therefore, Choice *D* is incorrect.

3. B: Activities that are both urgent and important are commonly associated with a specific deadline or element of time. Stepping in to moderate a panel discussion in place of a colleague who is suddenly taken ill would be important because there are possible consequences if the discussion were not moderated, and it would be urgent because of the immediacy of the event. Choice *A* is incorrect because although the project is important, there is no immediate need to complete the planning of the project. Choice *C* is incorrect because the Instagram invitation may or may not be important, and it does not require an immediate response. Choice *D* is neither urgent nor important because according to the model, the time could be better spent answering and sending messages.

4. B: Mechanistic organizations take a rigid approach to problem-solving that often results in a less effective response to the changing organizational demands, and employees who are not encouraged to reach their potential. This rigid approach is the result of centralized leadership that depends on rigid protocols and top-down communication, which serves to discourage or eliminate employee involvement in planning and problem-solving. The remaining choices describe leadership styles that depend on empowering each individual in the organization. Values-based leadership involves supporting individual equality and liberty that can result in social change, which means that Choice *A* is incorrect. Choice *C* is incorrect because organic organizations, which are viewed as the opposite of mechanistic organizations, depend on lateral communication to encourage input from individual employees. As noted, values-based leadership and transformational leadership encourage the active participation of the individual employee, which is common to the organic organization rather than the mechanistic organization; therefore, Choice *D* is incorrect.

5. A: The facilitator assigns portions of the agenda to individuals with the appropriate expertise to expedite the discussion. The alternate speaker presents the content and answers questions from the group. This strategy also encourages group participation. While team members do gain experience, the intended outcome for this strategy is to provide expert content expeditiously; therefore, Choice *B* is incorrect. The facilitator needs to be knowledgeable about the content, choose the right person to present the information, and clear all scheduling constraints. This means that Choice *C* is incorrect, because delegating this portion of the agenda potentially adds work for the facilitator. Although the facilitator should strive to maintain the attention of the group, the purpose of delegating a portion of the agenda is to improve time management; therefore, Choice *D* is incorrect.

6. D: The National Quality Forum (NQF) developed the e-measures to transition data analysis results from paper and pencil to electronic reporting. The NQF published 113 measures; however, a guide for developing new e-measures (the Measure Authoring Tool, or MAT) was also published for IT team leaders. This authoring tool guides the development of additional tools by measurement specialists. The NQF reviews the e-measures and posts updates every three years, but it does not monitor the usage of the e-measures, which means that Choice A is incorrect. Hospitals are free to use the MAT to develop hospital-specific e-measures, which means that Choice B is incorrect. CMS originally adopted 44 of the available measures, which means that Choice C is incorrect.

7. D: Benchmarking is the process of assessing the strategic planning activities of a competing organization. This information is used to weigh different options rather than as a planning blueprint. Choice A is incorrect because the voice of the customer is a separate form of evaluation that differs from benchmarking. The voice of the customer is measured in satisfaction surveys or other face-to-face situations, and the resulting information impacts the quality planning process in a different way than benchmarking. Because no two organizations are identical, the information acquired through benchmarking is viewed only as a general view of what was successful or unsuccessful for a similar organization. This means that Choice B is incorrect. Price controls would not be identified in the benchmarking process, which means that Choice C is incorrect.

8. C: The affinity diagram would be a useful first step for this meeting because the diagram identifies common themes among the solutions, which provide a starting point for the multivoting process; therefore, Choice C is the correct answer. The Eisenhower matrix is used by the individual to prioritize tasks and would not be useful in the stated scenario, so Choice A is incorrect. Multivoting provides individuals the ability to make personal decisions about the identified solutions as part of the larger group. Small-group discussion would limit the possible decisions about any single issue; therefore, Choice B is incorrect. Brainstorming sessions are often used before multivoting to identify the possible solutions or ideas that are to be addressed in the multivoting process, so Choice D is incorrect.

9. A: Although all the options provide positive contributions to the workplace, open and honest dialogue is the best way for an HQP to encourage employees to continue providing safety suggestions and to help them feel that leadership members are listening to their concerns. Communication has a stronger impact on workplace culture than performance evaluations and training. Therefore, Choices B, C, and D are incorrect.

10. A: Choice A is correct because the AHRQ assessment of a healthcare agency's safety culture addresses many aspects of the delivery of patient care; however, the financial costs are not directly assessed. The survey does assess the opinions of the personnel as well as the safe practices of environmental services and the information technology department, which means that Choices B and C are incorrect. Choice D is incorrect because the rate of temporary staffing is closely related to patient safety, and the issue is addressed in the survey.

11. A: Strategic planners are responsible for planning for the current and future needs of the organization. In healthcare, this means that long-term goals can become quickly outdated in the rapidly changing environment, so well-defined short-term goals can be more reliable in measuring the quality of care. Choice B is incorrect because the planners are also responsible for including goals set for the organization by other authorities such as the Centers for Medicare and Medicaid Services (CMS). Choice C is incorrect because there is no evidence that long-term goals are more successful than short-term goals; however, as noted above, there is evidence that long-term goals often become obsolete. Choice D

178

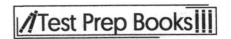

is incorrect because successful healthcare strategists look beyond current circumstances when setting goals and priorities because the future needs most often do not resemble current circumstances.

12. C: The facilitator is responsible for providing a plan for follow-through of actions taken. This action should not be delegated to the scribe; therefore, Choice C is correct. The remaining activities are consistent with the role of the scribe, which means that Choices A, B, and D are incorrect.

13. C: CMS has set six national goals for healthcare improvement, which are based on four broad principles. Choice C is not one of the four broad principles; it is one of the Meaningful Measures established by CMS to improve healthcare delivery while decreasing provider burden. Choices A, B, and D correctly identify three of the four principles.

14. B: Block sampling is the appropriate sampling method for processes that relate to timing or sequencing, and the ER-to-nursing-unit transfer-time policy includes the assessment of both elements. Convenience sampling means that the sample can be chosen from any available source, without regard to the specific sampling requirements for the assessment of transfer times. This means that Choice A is incorrect. Self-selection sampling may or may not fulfill the sampling requirement for any inquiry, which means that Choice C is incorrect. Systematic sampling is used with large populations for processes that are not sequenced or time-dependent. For example, systematic sampling would be appropriate for assessing documentation of COVID-19 vaccination data for patients over 65 who were admitted in the first quarter. This means that Choice D is incorrect.

15. D: The key performance indicators (KPIs) are measurable standards that are consistent with the mission and goals of a healthcare organization. These measures vary from one institution to another; however, assessments of financial issues such as bed occupancy rates and patient care issues such as safety are common. Trended data from these assessments can be used to identify areas of weakness in the organization; therefore, Choice D is correct. There are performance measures for specific groups in healthcare, such as nurses or doctors who practice as primary care providers; however, the institutional KPIs address system-wide issues rather than individual performance. Therefore, Choices A and C are incorrect. The use of KPIs for performance assessment is not exclusive to large healthcare systems, so Choice B is incorrect.

16. A: Daily bed turnover rate as compared to national standards is an outcome of the quality of patient care. The remaining choices are incorrect because they are process measures or procedures that meet standards for preventing harm.

17. A: CTQs are institutional processes or products that determine customer satisfaction, which is essential to process improvement; therefore, Choice A is correct. CMS does not directly affect the identification of the CTQs by the individual institutions, so Choice B is incorrect. Institutional profit is assessed through the voice of business (VOB) elements rather than the CTQs; therefore, Choice C is incorrect. The research indicates that consideration of both measures is required for optimal process planning, so Choice D is incorrect.

18. A: Mistake-proofing is the process of identifying specific prevention measures for high-risk patient situations. For instance, the surgical "time out" protocol was developed to prevent surgical errors such as procedures on the wrong patient, the wrong limb, etc. Mistake-proofing measures consider every possible element of an adverse event to develop a prevention plan. Choice A is the correct answer because the "time out" is specific to the prevention of adverse events. Choice B is incorrect because the quiet environment rules are aimed at patient satisfaction rather than error prevention. Similarly, Choice

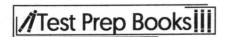

C is incorrect because the primary purpose for convenient parking options is patient satisfaction rather than error prevention. Scheduling access in a patient portal enhances patient satisfaction and also substantially decreases staffing time spent on scheduling. This means that Choice *D* is incorrect.

19. C: The EHR generates clinical decision support (CDS) alerts to the patient's EHR. These alerts include a wide range of information that is relevant to the patient's history and current condition. Based on the patient's data, alerts may be posted to alert the provider that there is an order that may be incorrect or that there is critical documentation that is missing. The importance of these alerts can range from critical to informational; however, there is some indication that many providers ignore the alerts or bypass the system, which means that Choice *C* is correct. Inventory charges are not generally included with the patient-specific data, which means that Choice *A* is incorrect. Choices *B* and *D* are issues for the agency but are not directly related to patient safety and the EHR, so they are incorrect.

20. B: Diffusion is the informal transfer of information about a proposed change in policy or process. Team leaders should be alert to the informal transfer of incorrect information. Dissemination is the deliberative process of informing specific groups about the new processes, so Choice *A* is incorrect. Using the new CAUTI bundles is an example of implementation; therefore, Choice *C* is incorrect. Choice *D* is incorrect because spread is defined in terms of the time it takes for a new process to be adopted. Spread can be measured in terms of the rate of compliance.

21. C: Stratified sampling requires separating the target population into two homogenous groups and then comparing random samples of each group. Male Medicare patients would be over 65, and annual prostate exams would be an appropriate metric for this relatively homogenous population. Choice *A* is an example of cluster sampling, which uses a random sample of heterogenous population groups. Choice *B* is incorrect because it is an example of systematic sampling, which involves selecting participants from a population according to a recurring interval with a randomly chosen starting point. Volunteer or convenience sampling is a form of non-probability sampling that is subject to bias and does not provide results that can be generalized to the population. This means that Choice *D* is incorrect.

22. C: The "time out" is a scripted check of critical details regarding the patient's identity and the intended procedure. It is required at least once before every invasive procedure. The protocol requires that all personnel in the treatment area pause all activity while the checklist is completed by the responsible provider. The "time out" is not to be confused with the consent for a procedure, which is required for all care interventions. This means that Choice *C* is the correct answer. The remaining choices require consent for treatment and two patient identifiers; however, the "time out" is required for procedures that are invasive and associated with possible patient injury. That means that Choices *A*, *B*, and *D* are incorrect.

23. A: Central line infection rate is a quantifiable outcome, which is the definition of an output. Dressing change modules are activities that are required to meet the proposed objective, so Choice *B* is incorrect. Demonstration of safe practice is an example of an overall objective; therefore, Choice *C* is incorrect. Patient report measures related to pain management are an example of a measurement tool used to evaluate each objective in the action plan, so Choice *D* is incorrect.

24. C: The goal of Meaningful Measures is to identify problem areas that have improvement potential. For instance, if the endoscopy department has frequent "no-show" patients, implementing a detailed reminder system could increase patient satisfaction with scheduling and save time and money on staffing. The Meaningful Measures address organization-specific problem areas that are often related to payment models. Choice *A* is incorrect because the promotion of patient and family involvement in care

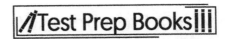

planning is one of the goals of the CMS National Quality Strategy for Healthcare, rather than the Meaningful Measures initiative. Choices *B* and *D* are incorrect because these measures are general organizing principles for the 2016 CMS National Quality Strategy for Healthcare rather than specific areas for improvement in a single organization.

25. C: The Pareto principle states that 80% of the variation in performance measures will be due to variations in only 20 percent of the areas that are measured. Application of this principle helps to identify the areas that require improvement; therefore, Choice *C* is correct. In healthcare, the application of the principle is related to variations in performance measures rather than financial details, so Choice *A* is incorrect. The Pareto principle addresses the variation in performance measures, not the size of the group; therefore, Choices *B* and *D* are incorrect.

26. A: Infants should always be transported in the bassinet for safety reasons and because it indicates that only authorized individuals are caring for the infant. That means that Choice *A* is the correct answer. The nurse educates the family on the importance of all safeguards related to the infant's security. Security tags may be attached to linens and clothing as well as the infant's umbilical clamp. Choice *B* is incorrect because there is no risk to the infant. Choice *C* is incorrect because the CMA reported the incident so that the infant's bracelet could be replaced immediately. Choice *D* is incorrect because the father would need to provide two forms of identification to receive a temporary badge for the duration of his visit. Additionally, infant abduction is most often committed by a stranger.

27. B: The Hospital Readmissions Reduction Program (HRRP) requires reporting of the thirty-day readmission rates for total knee and hip arthroplasty, chronic obstructive lung disease, coronary bypass surgery, acute myocardial infarction, pneumonia, and heart failure. Financial penalties may be assessed, and hospitals are also required to submit remediation plans for all deficiencies. The value-based program focuses on the need for improved discharge planning to eliminate preventable readmissions. Choices *A*, *C*, and *D* are incorrect because the readmission rates of the identified diagnoses are not currently tracked by Medicare.

28. D: The blame-free environment is critical to safety because, in a punitive environment, the errors that are not reported will be repeated. In light of recent events, nurses have legitimate concerns about the employer approach to error reporting that varies among healthcare systems. This means that Choice *D* is the correct answer. Each of the remaining choices is generally accepted as critical to a culture of safety, which means that they are incorrect.

29. B: The People mode addresses relationships with employees, stakeholders, and vendors. Employees from all areas are expected to evaluate work processes and to actively participate in the change process. The Lean principles suggest that the flow of information should not assume a top-down direction because employees at all levels are included in the evaluation of the work processes; therefore, Choice *A* is incorrect. Vendors are also considered to be part of the team, and the quality of the goods and services provided by the vendor would be important considerations in any contractual agreement, so Choice *C* is incorrect. In the Lean model, stakeholders would be involved in the evaluation of proposed process changes, making Choice *D* incorrect.

30. B: The HQP's primary job after a safety event is to analyze the incident report, determine the most significant risks that caused the safety event, and recommend a course of action to the leadership team. Choice *A* is incorrect because front-line staff who handled the event are required to document it. Choice *C* is incorrect because debriefing is the responsibility of department management, senior staff, or therapeutic personnel. Choice *D* is incorrect because reporting is the duty of the leadership team.

31. D: Value-based reimbursement schedules are based on analysis of patient-care data. Incomplete or inaccurate documentation affects the bottom line of a hospital. The remaining choices are important documentation functions; however, the critical outcome of adequate documentation is accurate data analysis and reporting of value-based care information. Therefore, Choices *A, B,* and *C* are incorrect.

32. A: Reducing the duration of an inpatient stay has high impact because the hospital can serve more patients, more quickly. Choice *B* is incorrect because the goal has lower impact than Choice *A.* Choice *C* is incorrect because the goal lacks appropriate specificity. Reducing patient mortality by a specified quantity would be an appropriate goal. Choice *D* is incorrect because the goal has high urgency but low impact.

33. C: Reliable evaluation results depend on the proper construction of the project goals. Goals should be measurable, specific to the project, achievable, and time-oriented. Choice *C* meets these requirements because it is possible to measure patient reports, and the stated increase in positive reports provides a standard for the evaluation of the goal. Also, while the feasibility of the 10 percent increase will be determined by the project team, the increase seems reasonable within the stated time frame. The remaining choices are either incomplete, not achievable or measurable, or not time-oriented. Choice *A* is incorrect because although it is possible that hospital readmission rates could decrease over the next quarter, specifying the rate of improvement would strengthen the evaluation of the goal. Choice *B* is incorrect because zero incidence of catheter-associated urinary tract infections (CAUTI) is not achievable in most inpatient healthcare environments. The final goal is not specific and not measurable as stated, so Choice *D* is incorrect.

34. D: Harm reduction refers to adverse events that occur in the actual patient-care environment. The reduction of medication administration errors is an appropriate outcome because it is measurable. The remaining choices are incorrect because the outcomes stated are at the organizational level rather than at the direct patient-care level where harm occurs.

35. D: The Gantt chart tracks each element of a project. The first step is the identification of the work breakdown chart, which typically includes all of the information identified in Choices *A, B,* and *C;* however, the work breakdown chart is based on the 100 percent rule, which requires the identification of the entire scope of the project from start to completion. Therefore, Choice *D* is correct.

36. A: Healthcare customer relations management (HCRM) system software collects and analyzes multiple forms of patient and population data from sources such as the EHR, social media, and consumer sites. This integration provides team leaders with information that can be used in marketing as well as patient care. Enterprise application software focuses on the needs of the entire hospital system as opposed to the care of the individual patient, so Choice *B* is incorrect. The EHR is a single source that collects and stores inpatient care documentation. The EHR does not integrate information from consumer sites, which means that Choice *C* is incorrect. Reliability-centered maintenance software assesses system-wide equipment performance. For instance, the software can estimate equipment maintenance schedules for the heating system and the risks and possible outcomes of equipment failure. The software does assess patient care, which means that Choice *D* is incorrect.

37. A: Communication defects are responsible for a disproportionate amount of error in the healthcare setting. The SBAR framework (situation, background, assessment, recommendation) was developed by physicians to standardize reporting from one individual to another. Recent research suggests that the model may improve communication, but any positive effect on errors in the clinical setting is lacking. The model has not had a significant positive effect on errors, so Choice *A* is correct. The remaining choices have demonstrated positive effects on the safety culture; however, the interventions are synergistic, which means that the solution to the problem requires more than one approach to safety. That means that Choices *B*, *C*, and *D* are incorrect.

38. C: The PDCA model was introduced in 1950 by Dr. W. Edwards Deming as a way to impose the rigor of scientific inquiry upon business practices. The original intent of the PDCA model was continuous quality improvement. Over time, however, Deming and others proposed the PDSA model because the Study phase was more effective than the original Check phase of the PDCA model. Deming felt that there needed to be additional reflection on the results of early testing. This means that Choice *C* is correct because the Study phase facilitates more reliable estimates of project outcomes. Choice *A* is incorrect because both models have been used in multiple settings. Of the two models, the PDCA was originally designed as a continuous improvement method, so Choice *B* is incorrect. Choice *D* is incorrect because the PDSA model was specifically designed to go beyond checking and comparing to reflecting on the test results.

39. B: A program champion is most often a senior manager who develops and maintains close relationships with existing and potential stakeholders who are interested in furthering the hospital's mission. The champion understands the growth and development plan and demonstrates knowledgeable enthusiasm for the future of the hospital by communicating effectively with all interested parties. Choice *A* is incorrect because cost reduction is the responsibility of financial managers. Choice *C* is incorrect because the program champion's efforts are directed to community stakeholders rather than "in-house" employees. Choice *D* is incorrect because risk reduction team members would be responsible for investigating adverse patient-care events.

40. A: The most critical risk to accurate and thorough data collection is the failure to use standardized data collection measures. For example, if narrative data entry in an EHR is not well understood, then that important information may not be retrievable. Standardized measures support better communication and improve the success of quality improvement efforts. Choice *B* is incorrect because the elimination of human error is not possible. Choice *C* is incorrect because data collection methods are hospital-specific, and what is appropriate for one hospital is not necessarily the best fit for another. CMS incentives may or may not be associated with any single element of data collection; however, the incentives are not the basic requirement or initial focus of data management process planning. This means that Choice *D* is incorrect.

41. A: The three-fold American Hospital Association (AHA) plan is aimed at providing better care, improved population health, and lowered healthcare costs. One of the approaches associated with this initiative is the formation of alliances among acute care, primary care, and specialty care organizations that allow financial risk and costs to be shared across all providers. In this model, patients would receive care across the lifespan from one or more of the alliance partners as necessary. Although decreased emergency room visits might result from patient care in an alliance, the primary focus of the alliance is to share financial risk, which means that Choice *B* is incorrect. Potential revenue increases are not the alliance's focus, which means that Choice *C* is incorrect. Employee retention is not an element of the alliance criteria; therefore, Choice *D* is incorrect.

42. B: The process champion is most often a middle or senior-level manager who promotes quality improvement and supports and mentors employees who participate in the process. The sponsor is commonly a senior-level manager who defines the specific details and requirements of the project. Choice *B* is correct because there is overlap in the roles of these group leaders, and there is often a single person responsible for both roles in a given project. The remaining roles are employee-level positions as opposed to managerial positions. The facilitator is a member of the organization who is certified as a Sigma black belt and is therefore qualified to coordinate the events of the change process and to communicate with the executive management team. Choice A is incorrect because in most cases, the facilitator is not a middle or senior-level manager. Choice C is also incorrect because the team leader manages the project and may also assume the duties of the facilitator, but the team leader would not be a senior-level manager. The scribe is responsible for maintaining a record of all team activities, and since this is an employee-level position, Choice D is also incorrect.

43. B: The healthcare system was fined for failing to blind the patient information that was added to the group websites or patient portals. The cookies attached to the websites allowed protected information to be shared with third-party analytic providers without proper notification of the patients using the sites. Patients stated that there was insufficient information for informed consent related to the use of cookies on the sites. Choice A is incorrect because data sharing between providers is appropriate with security protections. Choices C and D are incorrect because posting results and correcting data are not specifically related to website security.

44. D: All of the choices are necessary components of the priority-setting process; however, the availability of resources is the delimiting factor. That means that Choices A, B, and C are incorrect because, although they are all important elements of priority-setting, the availability of resources remains the highest priority.

45. D: Individual hospitals are required to develop and maintain a current detailed preparedness plan for likely disasters. For instance, hospitals in Boston are more likely to experience hurricanes, while hospitals in San Francisco are more likely to experience earthquakes. CMS publishes detailed checklists to assist the individual healthcare agencies but does not develop the plans. This means that Choice A is incorrect. The CDC issues alerts and care guidelines for specific illnesses but does not issue preparedness plans, which means that Choice B is incorrect. The AHA consults with the United States Department of Health and Human Services (HHS) and provides a forum for regional discussions among healthcare agencies; however, the AHA does not develop preparedness plans. Therefore, Choice C is incorrect.

46. B: A fishbone diagram helps team members visualize a problem's root causes and is therefore critically important to processes like root cause analysis. Therefore, Choice B is correct.

47. A: Every group in the organization must develop an action plan that identifies how the work of the group will contribute toward the achievement of the organizational objectives. Choice B is incorrect because the employee action plan is also focused on how the employee's work correlates with the organizational objectives. The organizational action plan includes identification of the organizational objectives, the timelines, and those responsible for each action. Choice C is incorrect because the description of the action plan does not include the organization's goals or timelines. The action plans for individual groups within an organization are required to reflect the group contribution to the achievement of the organizational objectives; therefore, Choice D is incorrect.

48. A: The project charter includes all details of the quality improvement plan, including the identification of team members, planned measurement tools, and a project timeline. The plan also reflects the mission of the healthcare institution. Choice B is incorrect because the project charter is not a legal document; it is a planning device that is used to organize the quality improvement effort. Experts encourage the use of existing measurement tools that meet the requirements of the new project because measure development is a lengthy process that could negatively affect the project timeline. This means that Choice C is incorrect. Quality improvement projects require broad-based institutional

184

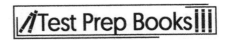

participation for success and sustainability. Employees at all levels should be included in the process, which means that Choice *D* is incorrect.

49. C: The purpose of the 2016 National Strategy for Healthcare initiative is to increase the participation of the patients and families in all aspects of healthcare delivery. The expected outcome is a healthcare agency that provides affordable, safe, and patient-centered care. Improved end-of-life care may be a result of this initiative; however, it is not the primary focus. Therefore, Choice *A* is incorrect. Providers are committed to lifelong learning; however, the focus of this initiative is the involvement of the patient and family, which means that Choice *B* is incorrect. The development of IT infrastructure would support patient-centered care, but since it is not the primary goal, Choice *D* is incorrect.

50. C: Computer systems are password-protected, but that protection only works if the nursing staff consistently follows the protocol. An idle computer that is not secured is a breach of confidentiality and a violation of the Health Insurance Portability and Accountability Act of 1996 (HIPAA). This means that Choice *C* is the correct answer. Choice *A* is incorrect because the accuracy of data input is a form of data integrity. Choice *B* is incorrect because restricted interdepartmental sharing is an example of faulty accessibility. This problem is seen as being responsible for costly duplication of services and failure to identify possible safety risks. Choice *D* is incorrect because if patients are not able to manage the connections between the online patient resources and their devices, patient access to agency information will be decreased.

51. C: The assessment of quality improvement measures includes three basic forms: outcome measures, which typically describe resulting behaviors in a target population; process measures, which assess how the improved process is functioning; and balancing measures, which add perspective to the outcome measures. Choice *C* is correct because the results of the customer satisfaction surveys put the product outcome measures in perspective. Choices *A* and *B* are incorrect because they are outcome measures that are not compared to any additional measure. Choice *D* is incorrect because it is a comparison between two outcome measures.

52. B: The scope of practice for licensed providers is mandated by the professional licensing board in the individual states. The leadership team must be aware of these requirements to properly credential professional providers. Choice *A* is incorrect because it describes the process of privileging, rather than credentialing. Choice *C* is incorrect because specialty certification and licensure are not generally required for all licensed providers. The leadership team can impose that requirement; however, it is beyond the definition of credentialing. The leadership team is responsible for credentialing, privileging, and oversight of licensed providers. Individual credentialing decisions are based on performance evaluations in addition to proper licensure, and not all applicants will be accepted. Therefore, Choice *D* is incorrect.

53. D: Special cause variations are conditions that affect the existing system. The wide range of the patients' ages is a special cause variation in the length-of-stay pathway because older patients would potentially present with additional co-morbidities that would affect their postoperative course. The effect of the special cause variation of patients' age could be addressed by revising the clinical pathway, the common cause variation, to reflect the situation more accurately. Choices *A*, *B*, and *C* are incorrect because they represent common cause variations that are inherent to the organization. The team leaders are responsible for the transfer protocol, the staffing levels and the number of available surgical suites, and common cause variations; however, team leaders do not have control over the ages of the patients.

54. D: Randomizing access codes and requiring agency attire increase the security of the nursing unit. Due diligence with the rules and situational awareness are essential to safe practice.

55. D: Indicators are measures that show the degree to which the action plan is meeting the overall objective. Choice *D* is correct because it provides a tally of the number of patients who received care. Choice *A* is incorrect because it is an overall objective of the action plan. Choice *B* is incorrect because, while it could be considered an outcome or an output, it does include a direct measure or time frame. Choice *C* is incorrect because it is an activity used to facilitate the plan outcomes.

56. A: Risk management increasingly represents the relationship between financial stability and patient-care *outcomes* that can affect the entire organization. Risk management has traditionally looked to protection from liability associated with adverse events. In contrast, value-based models put the entire healthcare organization at significant financial risk because payers only reimburse patient care that meets or exceeds established outcomes. The development of diagnosis-related groups (DRGs) in the 1980s was aimed at the reduction of healthcare costs by using the DRG codes, which identified patient categories based on the patient's diagnosis, existing co-morbidities, and surgical history as the basis for payment for the care of an individual patient. This means that Choice *B* is incorrect.

Value-based care models have expanded the focus to patient-care outcomes rather than simpler patient categories such as length of stay and age. These systems affect the entire organization and are designed to promote excellent patient care with commensurate reimbursement. Fee-for-service models that pay a predetermined fee for a specific service without regard to patient characteristics or care outcomes have been the long-standing reimbursement model, which was largely eliminated with the Affordable Care Act, which means that Choice *C* is incorrect. Risk management has always been associated with potential legal costs, and that potential continues to exist in value-based care models. However, one could argue that improved patient-care outcomes could lower legal costs, which means that Choice *D* is incorrect.

57. D: The facilitation of a quality improvement (QI) initiative requires an assessment of the stakeholder view, appropriate small-scale testing of the proposed change, and communication with those affected by the proposed change. Choice *D* is correct because it is an opportunity for two-way communication relative to the QI project. Choice *A* is incorrect because it is a "top-down" approach to QI. This decision-making style may be necessary for certain organizational decisions, but it is not viewed as the most productive approach to QI. Choice *B* is also incorrect because the employees were not involved in the planning or assessment of the proposed change prior to the announcement. Choice *C* is incorrect because the employees were not involved in any of the preliminary steps that led to policy changes.

58. B: The control chart has several functions: identifying processes for improvement, developing and implementing the new plan, evaluating the effectiveness of the plan, and monitoring the continued use of the plan over time. This means that Choices *A, C,* and *D* are incorrect. Root cause analysis is not one of the functions of the control chart.

59. C: The Agency for Healthcare Research and Quality (AHRQ) is a division of HHS that uses current research to develop toolkits or guidelines for the implementation of safe care practices in different care settings. TeamSTEPPS is an organizational communication plan developed by the AHRQ and the United States Department of Defense aimed at the successful implementation of the safety recommendations. The core competencies of the AHRQ are data and analytics, healthcare research, and quality and safety improvement, which means that the agency-specific improvement plans are an essential resource for any healthcare institution. However, Choice *A* is incorrect because the AHRQ only provides the research

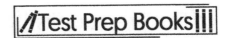

evidence and the voluntary implementation plan. Adoption of the plan by the healthcare agency is voluntary. Choice *B* is incorrect because, as mentioned above, the AHRQ is a division of HHS and is funded by the United States government. Choice *D* is incorrect because the AHRQ maintains a comprehensive website that provides access to a wide range of resources for all researchers.

60. B: The instrument was developed for smaller agencies and individual practices as an aid to meeting risk assessment requirements for HIPAA and CMS, so Choice *B* is the correct answer. The assessment is required by the HIPAA Security Rule, and it is used to identify potential risks and develop a plan to mitigate those risks. Therefore, Choices *A, C,* and *D* are incorrect.

61. B: The failure rate in some large organizations is as high as 60 percent. It is possible that the lack of success is due to errors in the conduct of the process rather than the process itself, which means that Choice *B* is the correct answer. Choices *A* and *C* address the expenses and training required for the implementation of the protocol. These are fixed costs that are not modifiable, which means that both choices are incorrect. Even when the initiatives are successful, customer satisfaction is difficult to predict, which means that Choice *D* is incorrect.

62. D: The effectiveness of the resulting diagram depends on an accurate definition of the problem. The detailed statement is defined as the "head" of the fish, so if the statement is detailed and complete, the bones of the fish are more accurately defined.

Consider the difference between the following statements:

Problem statement: "Patient falls."

Problem statement: "6/24/2022 1930 sixty-six-year-old male patient was found lying on the floor. No apparent injuries."

The second statement identifies the time of day as one of the issues that would not necessarily be identified in the first statement. The fall occurred during the change of shift, which would then be one of the "bones" on the diagram. The team members do not all have to be quality improvement experts; however, the team members should be knowledgeable about the process as well as the problem being discussed. This means that Choice *A* is incorrect. Human error is commonly identified by root cause analysis in healthcare, but identifying human error is not the primary purpose of the model. So, Choice *B* is incorrect. Punitive action is contrary to the purpose of quality improvement, which is better patient care. This means that Choice *C* is incorrect.

63. B: The Institute for Healthcare Improvement (IHI) is a private non-profit organization that is partially funded by grants from the AHRQ. The focus of the IHI is the worldwide implementation of safe patient-care practices. The Science of Improvement is based on identifying areas for improvement and testing new ideas according to the plan, do, study, act (PDSA) sequence rather than error analysis. This means that Choice *A* is incorrect. Implementation of IHI improvement plans is voluntary and not associated with CMS reimbursement, so Choice *C* is incorrect. The IHI improvement plans apply to all patient-care environments, which means that Choice *D* is incorrect.

64. A: Pareto analysis identifies the areas that require intervention; however, identification of the costs associated with the proposed actions is not addressed in the analysis. The remaining activities are included in the Pareto model, which means that Choices *B, C,* and *D* are incorrect.

65. A: High-reliability organizations are complex systems with inherent risk potential that function without reported errors for extended periods. This means that Choice *A* is correct. Choice *B* is incorrect because system processes are streamlined but not simplified; simplification can potentially hide risks associated with the process. Choice *C* is incorrect because "deference to expertise" is one of the identified characteristics, which means that every individual in the system is an expert in their work and is therefore responsible for risk reduction. Choice *D* is incorrect because near-misses are viewed as system failures that identify areas for improvement rather than successes.

66. D: The National Quality Forum (NQF) is a non-profit, non-partisan research foundation that develops measurement tools for safe practice evaluation in multiple care settings. For instance, if a hospital implements a new protocol for surgical site wound care, an NQF measure could be used to evaluate and report the outcomes of that new protocol. CMS consults with the Measure Applications Partnership, a division of NQF, to provide measures that accurately reflect an agency's healthcare quality. Choice *A* is incorrect because the NQF is funded by donors. Choice *B* is incorrect because the NQF develops evaluation measures rather than communication plans. Choice *C* is incorrect because the NQF includes a wide range of stakeholders, including patients, measurement experts, and healthcare professionals, in the development of the evaluation measures.

67. C: Root cause analysis categorizes causes as physical, human, or organizational. Choice *C* is correct because the cause of the discrepancy was directly related to the failure of the institution to identify the proper protocol for controlled substance reconciliation. Choice *A* is a human issue because only a single licensed person verified the count when two signatures were necessary, which means that Choice *A* is incorrect. Choice *B* is incorrect because the computer malfunction is a physical cause. Choice *D* also describes a human cause, so it too is incorrect.

68. C: Risk-adjustment methods are mathematical projections of the care costs for a population of patients based on demographics and diagnoses, which are beyond the control of the provider. The models are used for CMS and third-party payer reimbursement. Choice *A* is incorrect because the development of the models was commissioned by CMS in the 1990s as a provider reimbursement framework. The projections and the reimbursement rates are now published annually by CMS. As noted, the models adjust outcomes for demographic status and medical diagnoses, which means that Choice *B* is incorrect. The risk models are also used by third-party payers to set rates for enrollees, so that means that Choice *D* is incorrect.

69. D: A sentinel event is any patient safety event that occurs during or soon after a patient's stay at a healthcare facility. To be considered a sentinel event, the event must be unrelated to the natural course of a patient's illness or condition. Therefore, Choice *D* is correct.

70. A: The World Health Organization (WHO) is a division of the United Nations that is charged with overseeing worldwide health concerns. WHO focuses on the dissemination and use of research aimed at a wide range of issues from infectious disease control to the health effects of climate change. Choice *B* is incorrect because WHO decisions can be and are challenged by member nations. Choice *C* is incorrect because WHO provides practice guidelines for infectious diseases but does not provide case management for individuals with the disease. WHO provides worldwide alerts regarding infectious diseases; however, WHO is not responsible for the actual development of vaccines. Therefore, Choice *D* is incorrect.

71. A: The scatter diagram is used to display pairs of numerical data. In the example, patient age groups and the number of clinic visits would be compared and displayed. The fishbone diagram is used to

188

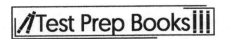

determine cause and effect, which means that Choice *B* is incorrect. The control chart is a detailed time-series view of an entire process, which tracks changes over time. Choice *C* is incorrect because the question does not specify a time-series model. The Pareto chart estimates the impact of multiple factors on outcome measures, which means that Choice *D* is incorrect; the example only requires the relationship between one pair of variables.

72. A: The purpose of the process control measurement is to prevent errors from reaching the customer. These measures should be identified for each possible cause identified in the failure mode and effects analysis (FMEA); therefore, Choice *A* is correct. Choice *B* is incorrect because identifying links is more common in a cause-and-effect study. The process control would not apply to employee performance criteria, which means that Choice *C* is incorrect. A time and motion study could ultimately affect customer satisfaction, but the focus is on the production of the product, so Choice *D* is incorrect.

73. C: Patient care visits that are canceled and not rescheduled often result in poor patient outcomes. The delay in rescheduling the appointment means that any changes in the patient's condition will be untreated for a longer period, and the patient's questions and concerns will not be addressed. Therefore, Choice *C* is the correct answer. Loss of revenue, staffing issues, and CMS reporting criteria are all significant issues related to canceled appointments that are not rescheduled. However, the greatest risk is poor patient outcomes resulting from substandard care.

74. C: Healthcare Effectiveness Data and Information Set (HEDIS) databases, a product of the National Committee for Quality Assurance (NCQA), are intended to provide a comprehensive evaluation of the effectiveness of healthcare plans. The NCQA determines performance standards for six domains of care, including effectiveness, access and availability of care, patient-care experiences, health-plan utilization and descriptive data, and the use of the electronic health record (EHR) for clinical data reporting. The HEDIS databases provide a comparison of established performance standards with performance data voluntarily submitted by individual healthcare plans.

This comparison provides the healthcare plan administrators with the identification of areas requiring improvement and also provides consumers with a reliable resource for comparing healthcare plans. Choice *A* is incorrect because the HEDIS database is used to evaluate healthcare plan effectiveness, not communicable disease tracking. Choice *B* is incorrect because the evaluation of environmental services would not be evaluated in the healthcare plan assessment. CMS has contracted with NCQA to establish performance standards for Special Needs Plans (SNPs) to be added to the performance evaluation of the healthcare plans. For instance, an SNP was developed to evaluate the plan's performance in medication reconciliation after hospital discharge. The performance standard would evaluate when and how the medication check was completed. Choice *D* is incorrect because the EHR use would be evaluated for accuracy of the medication list, patient access to the list, and verification of the post-discharge medication check.

75. D: Choice *D* is the correct answer because it is not objectively measurable. The remaining choices are incorrect because it is possible to assess each of the process champion's performances objectively. Choice *A* is incorrect because the relationship between the process champion and the patient can be measured objectively. Team members can report on the effectiveness of the process champion as a leader, which means that Choice *B* is incorrect. Choice *C* is incorrect because it is possible to measure the relationships between the process champions, senior management, and team members.

76. D: The point of ERM is that every aspect of a single healthcare system must be subject to ongoing critical analysis of risk potential. This whole-system approach doesn't deviate from an emphasis on

189

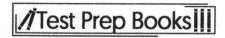

patient outcomes, but rather expands the scope of risk analysis to include every circumstance that could affect patient outcomes; therefore, Choice *D* is the correct answer. Choices *A* and *C* are more recent additions to risk assessment models, and Choice *B* has always been addressed in the risk assessment models.

77. B: A structural measure provides patients with information about the provider that can affect care choices. The number of board-certified providers is generally accepted as a measure of quality, which would be an important addition to the marketing strategy. Choice *A* is incorrect because glaucoma screening for all patients over forty-five years old would be a process measure. The screening affects the health of a patient population. Choices *C* and *D* are incorrect because they are outcome measures that reflect the quality of care.

78. B: When rates of innovation adoption by a group are plotted on a bell curve, the early adopters are 13.5 percent of the entire group. This group identifies the pros and cons of the proposed innovation and then decides to adopt the solution. Group leaders are most often identified as early adopters based on their assessment of the value of the innovation rather than on the "newness" of the innovation (innovators), or the need to "wait and see" how it works (majority). Choice *A* is incorrect because diffusion is often a slow process, even for changes that are widely anticipated. Choice *C* is incorrect because late majority adopters are slow to recognize the value of the innovation, and more commonly take a "wait and see" attitude before adopting the changes. Choice *D* is incorrect because the diffusion of an idea in a social system can occur informally without deliberate dissemination by system leaders.

79. C: Risk management provides value to a business, but the customer is not going to pay for it. That is the definition of a business value-added activity, which means that Choice *C* is correct. Choice *A* is incorrect because meeting government regulations is a required non-value-added activity. Choice *B* is incorrect because accommodating contracted customer requirements is a non-value-added activity. Choice *D* is a non-value-added activity that is considered a waste by Sigma standards.

80. D: Situation awareness means planning for "what if." The handoff report alerts the oncoming nurse to the possible development of pneumonia, which could be confirmed with a chest x-ray. This means that Choice D is correct. Choice *A* is incorrect because it provides a timeline and important information about the patient's condition for the oncoming nurse. Choice *B* is incorrect because it describes the patient's illness stability. Choice *C* is incorrect because it is an example of synthesis, or "talk back," in which the oncoming nurse repeats the summary.

81. A: Disease management is a form of case management that constructs a care plan for patients with largely predictable outcomes. The elderly female patient who has a knee arthroplasty generally follows a predictable course that facilitates care planning. The remaining choices are incorrect because the diagnoses are either potentially evolving or at least unpredictable. Hemorrhagic strokes and posterior wall MIs can extend, and tumor lysis syndrome can produce unpredictable effects, which means that Choices *B, C,* and *D* are incorrect.

82. D: The Pareto chart is used to identify areas for potential quality improvement. It is based on the 80/20 rule, which states that 80% of the effect is due to 20 percent of the causes. For instance, if the team identifies ten problems that cause patient complaints, the 80/20 principle predicts that 80% of the patient complaints are related to only two of the identified problems. The control charts or run charts examine variation; however, the Pareto chart cannot identify either common cause or special cause variation effects. This means that Choice *A* is incorrect. The Pareto chart is relevant for the initial quality improvement planning; however, the resulting data can also be used in the analysis and evaluation

190

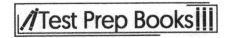

phases to assess the continued success of the innovations. This means that Choice *B* is incorrect. The Pareto chart only measures variables on the categorical, nominal, or ordinal level, which means that Choice *C* is incorrect.

83. A: A fluctuation in environmental conditions is identified as a common cause variation that is expected and acceptable, which means that Choice *A* is correct. The remaining choices are incorrect because they are all special cause variations that are unexpected and not acceptable.

84. A: The I-PASS mnemonic stands for the following: illness severity (I), patient information (P), action list (A), situational awareness and contingency plans (S), and synthesis by the receiver (S). The patient experiencing chest pain is unstable, which is the first element of the I-PASS report. There are additional details related to the patient's pain that will be reported in subsequent sections of the protocol; for example, the patient's medication history or EKG patterns will be reported in the patient summary (P) or the to-do list (A). However, the critical element will be reported first. This means that Choices *B, C,* and *D* are incorrect.

85. B: The 5 Whys focuses on identifying the root cause as opposed to a solution that may or may not provide long-term improvement in the situation. Choice *A* is incorrect because the purpose of the technique is to solve the problem. Choice *C* is incorrect because there is no certainty that countermeasures or solutions would be less difficult to implement. The team charged with using the 5 Whys technique does not require management approval of the identified countermeasures, which means that Choice *D* is incorrect.

86. A: Three choices define illness severity in the I-PASS model: stable, watcher, or unstable. The watcher category includes patients that require close observation because their conditions have inherent risk. For example, the patient being treated for atrial fibrillation with anticoagulant therapy has a risk of bleeding, and the patient with a mild cognitive deficit has increased safety issues. The stable category includes patients who require routine monitoring that is appropriate to their condition, and the unstable category includes patients who require emergency management. This means that Choice *A* is correct. Choice *B* is incorrect because it describes a timeline according to the mnemonic. Choices *C* and *D* each describe situation awareness, looking ahead at possible patient needs.

87. B: Registries are databases that focus on a single disease, condition, or patient characteristic for research purposes related to treatment effectiveness, tracking of implanted devices in case of product recalls, or comparing the patient-care outcomes of different healthcare organizations. Choice *A* is incorrect because failure to share data between systems is one of the most critical shortcomings of current EHR systems. Capturing care costs is a routine function of the EHR system and the information would not be included in a patient-specific registry, which means that Choice *C* is incorrect. Registries are focused on patient data for improved patient care, which means that Choice *D* is incorrect.

88. A: The CMS Meaningful Measures 2022 initiative is focused on identifying areas for quality improvement and providing a comprehensive list of assessment measures. The remaining choices may be addressed in individual measures included in the list; however, the focus of the initiative is the identification of both the healthcare issue and the assessment measures. That means that Choices *B, C,* and *D* are incorrect.

89. C: Scorecards and dashboards are both used to identify data that require additional action by the hospital. Experts argue that unused data shouldn't be collected. Scorecards are a detailed long-term picture of the strategic plan for the organization. The scorecards are used by senior managers for institutional-level evaluation and planning. In contrast, dashboards are real-time measures of systems operations that are used by frontline managers to direct workflow. Choice A is incorrect because scorecards address the long-term strategic view of the organization rather than the identification of a single quality improvement effort. Dashboards address the issues associated with the real-time performance of process and outcome measures, which means that Choice B is incorrect. Drill-down capability means that the data-entry system allows current data to be instantly connected to comparative or historical data. Scorecards that take the long-term view do not require this capability; however, this function is a requirement for dashboards that are used for real-time comparisons by the frontline managers. This means that Choice D is incorrect.

90. C: Direct messages are the best indicator of the conversions for a site. Conversions are defined as the number of people who visit the site and become customers. Likes, follows, and social shares indicate different levels of engagement with the product or the corporation; however, the conversion rates from website viewer to paying customer are lower than the direct messaging metric. This means that Choices A, B, and D are incorrect.

91. B: Two HIPAA safeguards address access to PHI. Audit controls track access to PHI over time, while access controls identify the procedures that restrict access to PHI. Integrity controls refer to procedures that protect PHI from unauthorized edits or data loss, which means that Choice A is incorrect. Choice C is incorrect because transmission security refers to the protection of PHI that is sent to another device, such as sending data by email to another provider.

92. C: The thirty-day readmission rate is a long-term measure that would be checked as an element of strategic planning, which is consistent with the use of the scorecard by senior management. Choices A, B, and D are measures used in real time by frontline managers, which means that these choices are incorrect.

93. D: The Institute for Healthcare Improvement (IHI) initiative was a response to earlier reports by the Institute of Medicine (IOM) of widespread errors and inequities in healthcare in the United States. The primary interest of the IHI initiative was improved quality of care for all patients (including timeliness, effectiveness, and efficiency) rather than cost containment. That means that Choices A, B, and C are incorrect.

94. B: Choice B is correct because ISO 9000 focuses on production standards, but it does not include any assessment of the finished product's quality. ISO 9000 standards do address the importance of stakeholder involvement in terms of client satisfaction and proper use of employee talent and expertise, which means that Choices A and C are incorrect. Senior management's approval and support are essential to the successful use of this product improvement framework; therefore, Choice D is incorrect.

95. B: Non-probability sampling methods are prone to bias and do not use random assignment. Probability sampling methods require random sampling of some form designed to eliminate or limit bias. This means that Choice A is incorrect. Voluntary sampling does not include any form of random assignment, which is required for probability sampling; therefore, Choice C is incorrect. Non-probability sampling methods do not include random assignment, which means that Choice D is incorrect.

96. C: The time from the decision to admit an ER patient to the patient's arrival on the nursing unit is a reportable electronic clinical quality measure (eCQM) that demonstrates quality care. Choice A is incorrect because the actual measure assesses the number of infants who are *breastfed* from birth to discharge, which is evidence of the quality of patient education related to the importance of

192

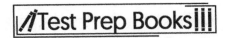

breastfeeding. Choice *B* is also incorrect because the eCQMs are measures of patient-care quality that would be expressed as a positive outcome (e.g., an eCQM might be the number of non-ambulatory patients with documentation of skin assessment every shift). Choice *D* is incorrect because opioid documentation is mandatory and must be submitted in addition to the voluntary reports.

97. A: Choice *A* is correct because Lean is focused on removing wastes, which are also described as non-value-added activities. Lean uses simpler methods, such as reorganization of the production process and workplace analysis techniques such as the 5 Whys, while Six Sigma employs hypothesis testing; therefore, Choice *B* is incorrect. Six Sigma is focused on process variation while Lean is focused on waste reduction, which means that Choice *C* is incorrect. Choice *D* is incorrect because Lean is the suggested first step in process improvement; progression to Six Sigma analysis occurs as needed depending on the situation.

98. D: The most frequent issues associated with imported data sources are formatting problems. Hospital managers must assess all aspects of the imported data for errors. Authoritative data sources that meet the needs of the hospital plan would be expected to be bias-free, which means that Choice *A* is incorrect. The costs of data analysis vary according to the specific needs and resources of the organization, which means that Choice *B* is incorrect. Experts caution hospitals to examine the data before the creation of objects such as tables and graphs due to the possible effects of inaccurate information. Therefore, Choice *C* is incorrect.

99. C: PDCA—which stands for Plan, Do, Check, Act—is a methodology for problem-solving that emphasizes variation reduction and process improvement. PDSA replaces "Check" with "Study" and has the desired goal of encouraging more reflection on how metrics for measuring improvement are selected and utilized. Therefore, Choice *C* is correct.

100. A: Cyber experts voice concerns about the level of protection afforded by compliance with HIPAA standards. The weakness lies in the cyber security levels of the healthcare system's business associates, such as vendors and primary care partners. For instance, if the security of the all-care primary practice is less than secure, breaches of that system can extend to the general hospital system, and that potential risk is not addressed in the HIPAA security standards. Therefore, Choice *A* is correct. Choice *B* is incorrect because the critical issue in cyber security is the need for continuous surveillance for gaps and initiation of protection updates. Choice *C* is incorrect because all systems are vulnerable to cyber breaches, and protection against the threats is a continuous process. Choice *D* is incorrect because two-factor authentication (2FA) is considered the minimum standard, and multi-factor authentication (MFA) is the preferred standard for all partner systems that interface with the hospital system.

101. A: Benchmarks may be imposed externally by the Joint Commission on Accreditation of Healthcare Organizations (JCAHO) and CMS, or they may be identified by senior managers for internal monitoring. Effective benchmarking depends on input from a broad range of stakeholders. Senior managers can identify benchmarks for internal audits in addition to the benchmark reports required by JCAHO and CMS. This means that Choices *B* and *C* are incorrect. Benchmarking is required for all healthcare facilities that are reimbursed by CMS, which means that Choice *D* is incorrect.

102. A: The sale of the protected health information (PHI) is consistent with the intent of the most severe criminal offense because the PHI was accessed under false pretenses, and the staff member intended to sell the information for personal gain. Choice *B* is also a criminal violation because the information was accessed without a "need to know." This violation is also commonly associated with agency dismissal rather than a prison sentence. The nursing assistant's error described in Choice *C*

193

would be considered a civil violation related to lack of knowledge rather than criminal intent, which means that Choice C is incorrect. Choice D is an example of a civil violation identified as willful neglect. The nurse was aware of the correct procedure; however, these violations are not assessed penalties if the violation is corrected within thirty days of the occurrence. In this instance, the hospital might be required to schedule additional information sessions, or the IT department might be required to modify the default "timeout" for active patient pages in the hospital's EHR system. This means that Choice D is incorrect.

103. C: By definition, an external-helpful factor would be something that benefits the organization but is not under its control. That means that Choice C is correct because the funds are beneficial to the organization, but the organization did not have control over the award of the benefit. Existing organizational resources would be considered a helpful benefit; however, the control would be internal rather than external, which means that Choice A is incorrect. Knowledge gained from past failures is regarded as internal and helpful as well, so Choice B is incorrect. Losing customers due to supply chain issues would be an external-unhelpful factor because the loss is detrimental and not controlled by the organization, which means that Choice D is incorrect.

104. D: Conflicts and lack of cooperation between departments in a healthcare system are viewed as socio-organizational environmental barriers in the PETT model. Choices A and B are incorrect because they are identified as people issues in the model. Choice C is also incorrect because the model considers the complex interface as a tool, and it is a barrier when people find it difficult to use.

105. B: Meaningful Use criteria address the use of the EHR in three specific areas that include providing a tangible patient service such as e-prescribing, facilitating the electronic exchange of information between providers or healthcare systems, and communicating the quality-of-care indicators. Financial schedules for reimbursement of any service are not included in the Meaningful Use criteria because the criteria are focused on the direct enhancement of the patient's care experience. The use of the EHR for e-prescribing can positively affect the patient's experience, which means that Choice A is incorrect. The patient's care experience and engagement in the treatment plan are positively affected by using an EHR system that can successfully share information with another system. This means that Choice C is incorrect. EHR systems that can be used to transmit the quality-of-care data such as A1C results meet the third Meaningful Use objective; therefore, Choice D is incorrect.

106. C: The most common "ribs" of the fishbone diagram are materials, methods, equipment, environment, and people. The model is focused on identifying the root cause of an error by tracking the information associated with these categories. This means that Choices A, B, and D are incorrect because they are classic categories associated with the model.

107. B: Quality and process improvements both stem from systems thinking, but they differ in the outcome measurement they seek to improve. QI examines processes, whereas PI addresses human performance. Therefore, Choice B is correct.

108. D: State licensing boards in thirty-seven states restrict physicians from telehealth visits across state lines; however, there were accommodations made by most states during the COVID-19 pandemic. Currently, some states are again requiring licensure in the state where the care is provided. For instance, during the pandemic, a physician in New Jersey could provide telehealth care for a patient in Connecticut. Presently, both states have rescinded those rules and reverted to the pre-pandemic requirements for MD licensure in the state where the care was rendered. The remaining states have either accepted temporary waiver applications or adopted the alternative licensure rules.

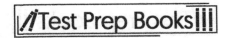

Nurse licensure rules also vary from state to state. Except for California, Oregon, Nevada, and Hawaii, the states have established compact licensure, which allows a nurse registered in a "compact" state to work in another compact state without obtaining a license in the second state.

Choice A is incorrect because the main issue with technology is sufficient funding, which would not affect interstate delivery of care. Choice B is incorrect because software licensing is between the developer and the healthcare agency rather than the geographic scope of practice. Choice C is incorrect because Medicaid payments are set by the states, while Medicare payments are set by CMS.

109. A: Although the two terms are often used interchangeably, Lean is focused on reducing areas of waste within an industry or system, while Six Sigma uses metrics analysis to minimize defects in a system and ultimately reduce variation. Therefore, Choice A is correct.

110. A: Multi-stage sampling is a form of cluster sampling that samples large populations efficiently. Stratified sampling is used effectively with homogenous groups, which means that Choice B is incorrect. Bias can only be statistically controlled, not eliminated, with random sampling, which means that Choice C is incorrect. There are no sample size requirements for multi-stage sampling, so Choice D is incorrect.

111. C: The theory suggests that praising small steps toward the desired behavior increases the rate of change and success of the desired behavior. Choice A is incorrect because the group must have a workable strategy in place to identify possible barriers. The members of the coalition must include all stakeholders to promote effective change. The group will include senior management; however, staff members, patients, and families must also be included as appropriate. This means that Choice B is incorrect. Communicating the vision must occur before any change can be expected. Individuals affected by the proposed changes must see the need for the change, or at least agree that some form of change is required, which means that Choice D is incorrect.

112. C: The first step for any process improvement in healthcare is to review current guidelines and procedures. This is done first so that the process can be understood and areas of weakness can be properly assessed, using methods such as FMEA. Therefore, Choice C is correct.

113. D: Gantt charts are bar charts that use timelines to represent the flow and progress of tasks needed to complete a project. They provide a high-level overview in which all members can track dependencies and maintain realistic expectations. Therefore, Choice D is correct.

114. B: High-reliability healthcare organizations (HROs) demonstrate resiliency by using errors that occur to shape mitigation plans for the next untoward event, which means that Choice B is correct. HROs also defer to the expertise of the individual closest to the task to identify risks and mitigation strategies for that process, which refers to the HRO characteristic of deference to expertise, which means that Choice A is incorrect. In addition, the employees are provided with the appropriate educational resources, and they have a strong voice in risk management activities. These choices relate to the HRO characteristics that include sensitivity to operations, which means that Choices C and D are incorrect.

115. C: The virtual private network (VPN) masks the hospital's internal information while protecting against unauthorized access to the system. The use of the VPN meets HIPAA regulations and facilitates the safe transfer of PHI. The VPN provides a password-protected email system for the entire organization rather than only senior managers, which means that Choice A is incorrect. A VPN would not be required to support a remote position or to stream patient teaching modules, so Choices B and D are incorrect.

116. B: Even though the United States spends more than twice as much money on healthcare as other developed nations, healthcare outcome measures are worse and life expectancy is shorter. CMS is moving to a value-based reimbursement plan to address rising costs and declining quality of care. Providers are advised to identify and measure the effectiveness of KPIs such as hospital readmission rates, patient satisfaction, and ER visits as evidence of the quality of care. The financial risk assumed by the provider varies with the design of the value-based care model used by the practice. There are three basic models—the accountable care organizations, bundled payment plans, and patient-centered medical home model—and each model assumes some but not all of the financial risks; therefore, Choice A is incorrect. Value-based modifiers address provider care, not hospital care, which means that Choices C and D are incorrect.

117. A: Choice A is correct because the value stream map traces the availability of all required resources at each step in the process. The map is also used to identify wastes or redundancies in the process. The basic flow sheet is useful at the beginning of the project to provide an overall view; however, the chart does not assess the availability of resources, which means that Choice B is incorrect. Choice C is incorrect because, while the value chain map is focused on identifying the steps of a process, it is not designed to track the availability of resources or to identify areas of waste. The cross functional map identifies connections among the processes and the people. The map identifies what resources are required; however, it does not document the availability of the resources. That means that Choice D is incorrect.

118. C: Value-based care models are associated with financial risk for the provider. Generally speaking, upside risk means that if the provider meets the patient-care goals set by CMS or a private payer, the provider shares the savings with the payer, and downside risk means that the provider is penalized for failing to meet the patient-care goals. Although there are greater rewards for quality patient care by providers in models with downside risk, many providers, especially groups that include hospitals, are not joining these models.

CMS saves more money with downside risk models and for that reason, it is currently promoting participation in hybrid, or two-sided, risk models that limit participation in models with only upside risk. Providers that participate in a downside risk model such as the Medical Home must be well coordinated to avoid the penalties associated with the model. Choice A is incorrect because upside risk is not associated with penalties for failure to meet metrics. CMS benefits from the penalties associated with downside risk models and would not limit provider participation in the model, which means that Choice B is incorrect. Downside risk models are associated with penalties for care outcomes that do not meet CMS standards, which means that Choice D is incorrect.

119. B: Stratified sampling is designed to increase sampling efficiency, which is a measure of the quality and amount of data obtained from the analysis. The sampling strata must contain mutually exclusive groups of participants, while the contents of the individual stratum should be homogenous. The homogeneity of the individual stratum decreases the variability of the sampling results, which improves the quality of the data analysis. Stratified sampling has greater sampling efficiency than random sampling due to the homogeneity of the individual stratum and the contrast between the mutually exclusive groups. This means that Choice A is incorrect. Volunteer sampling is a non-probability method that is not part of stratified sampling, which means that Choice C is incorrect. Stratified sampling is not dependent on sample size, which means that Choice D is incorrect.

120. D: BPM requires a continuous exploration of processes in an organization, especially those important processes that exist only in the heads of the people who developed and used the process.

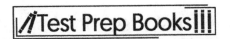

BPM focuses on the identification, evaluation, and appropriate implementation of all organizational processes that affect outcomes, which means that Choice *D* is correct. BPM is an organizational philosophy of continuous evaluation of processes that is shared with employees and management; therefore, Choice *A* is incorrect. BPM relies on the ability of the business process champion to look to the future and communicate that plan to the entire organization. The business process champion looks forward rather than backward, which means that Choice *B* is incorrect. The success of BPM is enhanced by team members who can employ the principles of Six Sigma; therefore, Choice *C* is incorrect.

121. D: Control charts provide a time-series view of system processes that highlights areas for improvement. The chart tracks process and outcomes measures; however, structural measures are not included in that chart, so Choice *A* is incorrect. Stable processes often indicate areas for improvement such as increasing the performance benchmark for a process. For instance, if the nursing staff is meeting the benchmark for 80% documentation of the use of the IV infusion, that process should be re-evaluated and improved to meet a higher benchmark. This means that Choice *B* is incorrect. One of the purposes of the control chart is to identify the effects of special cause variations on system processes, which means that Choice *C* is incorrect.

122. A: Choice *A* is correct because it is the outcome measure of Choices *B, C,* and *D*. Drops in readmission rates for high-risk diagnoses such as chronic heart failure have been contributed to increased focus in the following areas: attention to patient education, medication management, and comprehensive post-discharge care. This means that Choices *B, C,* and *D* are incorrect.

123. B: A mission statement is more concrete than a vision statement, and it is less precise than goals and objectives. Providing a quality product is a broad statement that includes more specific details than the vision statement, which means that Choice *B* is correct. Choice *A* is incorrect because it is a vision statement that broadly defines the reason that the company exists. Choice *C* is a goal that is timed and measurable, and more specific than a mission statement. That means that Choice *C* is incorrect. The eighty-twenty rule is a measure of variances that are used when determining the action plan and it is not related to the mission statement; therefore, Choice *D* is incorrect.

124. B: The Enterprise Application software addresses the data management requirements for hospital-wide processes such as OSHA compliance rather than individual patient-care outcomes. The Reliability Centered Maintenance (RCM) system evaluates risks associated with equipment costs and maintenance, which means that Choice *A* is incorrect. The EHR effectiveness surveys and the HCRM survey are patient-specific records that do not track compliance with system-wide measures, so Choices *C* and *D* are incorrect.

125. D: Economists suggest that integrating social services with healthcare interventions will decrease overall care costs. The plan proposes that federal funding of all Medicaid patients should be contingent upon the enrollment of covered patients in appropriate social services such as Head Start, nutritional support, and housing assistance. The major change is the federal funding of the plan for all Medicaid patients, rather than Medicare patients. This means that Choice *A* is incorrect. Choices *B* and *C* are incorrect because the unique part of the plan is applying the changes to federal funding of all Medicaid patients, rather than reporting patient data.

126. B: Choices *A* and *D* are incorrect since they both assist with collecting health outcomes data. Choice *C* is incorrect since it helps collect environmental data. Choice *B* is the correct answer because state health departments are a means for collecting vital statistics data.

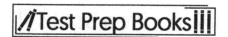

127. B: Younger populations are more likely to be engaged in managing their health conditions when using smartphone apps and smart watches. Choices *A, C,* and *D* could all help manage chronic conditions, but they are incorrect because they are not specifically targeted to the teenage patient. Therefore, Choice *B* is the correct answer.

128. D: Choices *A, B,* and *C* may be helpful topics to teach during a health fair; however, the question states that the purpose of this health fair is to raise awareness of health risks. Therefore, Choices *A, B,* and *C* are incorrect, and Choice *D* is correct since it provides education on health risks.

129. B: Choice *A* is incorrect because it is too broad and not specific to disease prevention. Choice *C* is helpful, but it does not directly promote disease prevention within the community; therefore, it is incorrect. Choice *D* is incorrect since it does not focus on disease prevention. Choice *B* is correct because it allows individuals, who may not have any symptoms of disease, to detect potential health problems, thus assisting with disease prevention in the community.

130. D: Choice *A* is an intervention that does not assist in reducing costs, so it is incorrect. Choice *B* may help reduce costs but only if it is accompanied by follow-up actions; therefore, it is incorrect. Choice *C* is incorrect, as it relates to improving social determinants of health (SDOH). Choice *D* is the correct answer since it provides a safe and data-driven way to reduce costs.

131. A: Choices *B* and *D* are both incorrect because they are examples of SDOH. Choice *C* is incorrect, as it refers to equity data. Choice *A* is the correct answer since EHRs contain patient diagnoses, treatments, etc., all of which assist in analyzing clinical data.

132. C: Shift handoff occurs between two healthcare providers in order to allow consistent care for the patient. This signifies a transition of responsibility between healthcare providers and ensures that all tasks and information have been relayed to the incoming provider. Choice *A* is incorrect because this would signify a transition of care, not a standardized shift handoff. Choice *B* is incorrect because the purpose of a shift handoff is not to update the physician. Choice *D* is incorrect because addressing family member needs is not the priority of a shift handoff.

133. D: Choices *A* and *B* do not directly impact the flow of work. Choice *C* allows for new experiences, but it does not guarantee an improvement of care. Choice *D* provides staff with the ability to assume a new responsibility when needed and is therefore the correct answer.

134. A: Choice *B* is informative, but it does not indicate how adherent the patient is to their prescribed medication regimen. Choice *C* does not provide any insight into the patient's eating habits, only the frequency with which they go shopping. Choice *D* is incorrect since it doesn't reflect a patient's health behavior. Therefore, Choice *A* is correct since it gives the provider an understanding of the patient's activity level.

135. C: Choice *A* is incorrect because an emergency department is a healthcare facility, and it only provides short-term care. Choices *B* and *D* could be appropriate, but the question asks for a resource outside of a healthcare facility; therefore, they are incorrect. Choice *C* provides the patient with a resource to promote their health and wellbeing outside of a healthcare facility; therefore, it is the correct answer.

136. A: Health equity, Choice *A*, refers to a group or an individual's ability to access the care necessary to obtain good health regardless of non-medical factors. Access is only a small part of what health equity encompasses, and amenities are simply an element of care aimed at increasing patient satisfaction,

198

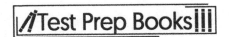

regardless of clinical effect. Responsiveness to patient preferences is a similar idea, but refers to a healthcare organization's ability to engage with a patient and their personal desires or beliefs in terms of care.

137. B: Cultural competency training is usually implemented to help address health disparities between different groups and subsequently promote healthcare equity by helping providers to better understand and respect the cultural beliefs, values, and general backgrounds of diverse patient populations. Improving cultural competency allows providers to ensure that all patients receive the same level of care regardless of their cultural backgrounds. While this training may increase patient satisfaction scores, the administrative process and cost of care are largely unaffected, so Choice *B* is the best option here.

138. C: The ISO offers accreditation and certification for healthcare facilities, which can help those companies improve their quality and safety.

139. B: FPPE (focused professional practice evaluation) looks at a practitioner's performance over a shorter, limited time period, whereas OPPE (ongoing professional practice evaluation) looks at a practitioner's performance over a long period of time. Therefore, Choice *B* is correct.

140. B: Healthcare compliance is the practice of complying with federal healthcare regulations. Choice *B* is correct because healthcare compliance is the responsibility of every healthcare worker, not just the heads of administration.

CPHQ Practice Tests #3, #4, and #5

To keep the size of this book manageable, save paper, and provide a digital test-taking experience, the $3^{rd} - 5^{th}$ practice test can be found online. Scan the QR code or go to this link to access it:

testprepbooks.com/online387/cphq

The first time you access the tests, you will need to register as a "new user" and verify your email address.

If you have any issues, please email support@testprepbooks.com

Index

Accreditation, 25, 34, 66, 109, 110, 136, 151

Action, 16, 40, 162, 173

Adjourning, 38

Adverse Event, 23, 60, 61, 103, 179, 182, 186
  Adverse Events, 88, 90

American Health Care Association (AHCA), 38

American Medical Association (AMA) Code of
  Medical Ethics, 101

Anchor the Change, 41

Balancing Measures, 69

Benchmarking, 17, 69, 74, 80, 115, 170, 178,
  193

Bias, 71, 138, 152, 159, 169, 171, 180, 192, 193

Brainstorming, 15, 81, 130, 140, 153, 157, 178

Bruce Tuckman's Model, 37

Bundled Payments, 60, 130, 147

Cause-and-Effect Diagram, 70, 94
  Cause and Effect Diagram, 48, 78

Certification, 109, 110, 133

Champions, 26

Change, 15, 23, 26, 33, 36, 40, 41, 43, 50, 66,
  81, 83, 99, 102, 112, 134, 151, 153, 156, 159,
  160, 164, 167, 172, 177, 180, 181, 184, 186,
  187, 188, 195, 197

Check Sheet, 70, 135, 150

Cluster Sampling, 72

Clusters, 72

CMS Meaningful Measures, 22, 168, 191

Common Cause Variation, 80, 136, 139, 151

Confirmation, 51

Consumer Assessment of Healthcare Providers
  and Systems (CAHPS), 96

Contemplation, 40

Continuous Data, 69

Control Chart, 70, 128, 135, 146, 166, 173, 197

Core Quality Measures, 97

Credentialing, 28, 34, 102, 123, 144, 163

Critical to Quality Measures (CTQs), 16, 121

Dashboards, 75, 124, 145, 168, 192

Data Management, 104, 144

Decision, 51

Department of Health and Human Services
  (HHS), 100, 113, 184

Diffusion, 20, 41, 50, 140, 146, 148, 158, 167,
  190

Diffusion of Innovation, 41

Discrete Data, 69

Dissemination, 41, 180

DMAIC, 46, 48, 51, 85, 127, 128, 129, 147, 148,
  149

DMAIC Model, 48, 51, 85, 127, 147

EHR, 24, 39, 66, 76, 84, 87, 97, 104, 128, 137,
  151, 158, 160, 161, 163, 169, 170, 171, 173,
  174, 182, 183, 189, 191, 194, 197

Electronic Health Record (EHR), 39, 104
  Electronic Health Record, 39, 84, 100, 101,
    104, 158
  Electronic Health Records (EHRs), 76

Enterprise Application Software (EAS), 77

Episode of Care (EOC), 60

Episode-Based Payments, 60

Ergonomics, 88, 119, 149

Evidence-Based Practices (EBP), 96

External Handoffs, 60

Failure Mode and Effect Analysis (FMEA), 47,
  145
  Failure Mode and Effect Analysis, 47, 91, 145

Fairness, 101

False Claims Act, 100

Fee-for-Service System, 60

Fiduciary Duty-of-Care Rule, 23

Fishbone, 48, 54, 70, 78, 145, 171, 188, 194

Five-Step Decision-Making Process, 51, 153

Form a Coalition, 40

Forming, 37, 54, 69, 139, 144, 152, 153

Group Process, 14

Health Information Technology for Economic
  and Clinical Health (HITECH) Act, 24

Health Insurance Portability and Accountability
  Act (HIPAA), 66, 100
  HIPAA, 24, 66, 112, 164, 168, 170, 185, 187,
    192, 193

Healthcare Customer Relations Management
  (HCRM), 76

Healthcare Data Management, 76

Healthcare Effectiveness Data and Information
  Set (HEDIS), 132, 149, 166, 189

Histogram, 70, 78, 135, 150

HITECH Act, 24, 100

Hospital Consumer Assessment of Healthcare Providers and Systems (HCAHPS), 102, 147

Human-Factors Engineering, 88, 149

Implementation, 41, 44, 51, 150, 187

Innovation, 22, 39, 50, 127, 146

Institute for Healthcare Improvement (IHI), 67, 96, 164, 187

Key Performance Indicators (KPI), 21, 134

Key Performance Indicators (KPIs), 16, 75, 137, 156, 158, 177, 179

Knowledge, 51, 170, 194

Lean Six Sigma, 44, 45, 49, 52, 85, 121, 129, 130, 133, 136, 138, 143, 145, 147, 149, 151, 152

Maintenance, 40, 161

Mean, 71, 74, 79, 80, 83, 127, 146

Measurement Error, 71

Mechanistic Organizations, 26, 177

Median, 74, 79, 80, 83, 127, 146

Mistake-Proofing, 22, 49, 137, 151, 152

Mode, 46, 79, 83, 127, 139, 146, 160, 181

Multi-Stage Sampling, 72, 195

National Committee for Quality Assurance (NCQA), 96, 110, 166, 189

National Health Service Sustainability Model, 33

National Patient Safety (NPS), 25

National Quality Forum (NQF), 96, 102, 165, 188

Need-to-Know Rule, 105

Never Event, 103

Non-Probability Sampling, 72, 152, 192

Norming, 38, 53, 138, 144, 152

Office of Inspector General (OIG), 100

Office of the Inspector General, 100

Organic Organizations, 26, 132, 177

Outcome Measures, 69, 73, 136, 151

Oversight, 28, 60, 123, 144, 185

Pareto Analysis, 20, 165, 187

Pareto Chart, 50, 70, 77, 128, 130, 136, 148, 166, 167, 189, 190

Pareto Diagram, 50

Patient Protection and Affordable Care Act (PPACA), 106

Affordable Care Act, 22, 102, 112, 113, 165, 186

Patient Protection and Affordable Care Act, 100, 106

Pay for Performance (P4P) Method, 106

PDSA Cycle, 42, 43, 44

Performing, 37, 38, 48, 54, 78, 101, 103, 117, 139, 144, 146, 147

Persuasion, 51

Physician Value-Based Modifier System (PVM), 106

Precontemplation, 40

Preparation, 28, 34, 40, 97, 110, 116, 117, 118, 177

Privileging, 28, 102, 123, 144

Probability Sampling, 71, 192

Process Champions, 51, 126, 189

Process Measures, 69, 73, 145

Qualitative Research, 87

Quality Chasm, 96

Quality Compass, 96

Quantitative Investigation, 87

Random Samples, 72

Random Variation, 80

Range, 70, 79, 80, 158, 180, 187, 188, 193

Refreeze, 40

Reliability Centered Maintenance (RCM), 77, 197

Requirements for Improvement (RFI), 117

Risk Assessment, 92

Risk Assessment Test, 112

Risk Management, 28, 87, 90, 92, 94, 186, 190

Risk of Harm Standard, 112

Risk-Adjustment Methods, 73, 188

Root-Cause Analysis, 91, 124, 140, 153

Sampling Error, 71

Scatter Diagram, 70, 166

Scorecard, 75, 115, 169, 192

Seasonality, 80

Sentinel Event, 28, 85, 87, 88, 89, 90, 91, 98, 115, 125, 134, 139, 145, 153, 167

Smoothing, 80, 139

Social Security Act, 100

Special Cause Variation, 80, 185

Spread, 39, 41, 50, 78, 94, 95, 97, 98, 123, 125, 130, 132, 134, 135, 136, 138, 140, 150, 151, 153, 180

Standardized Shift Handoff, 60

Statistical Process Control (SPC), 79, 137

Storms, 37

Strata, 72, 173, 196

Strategy Phase, 17, 149, 156, 177

Stratification, 71

Stratified Sampling, 72, 180, 195, 196
Structural Measures, 73
Systematic Sampling, 72, 157, 179
Systems Thinking, 89, 94, 132, 135, 149
Telehealth, 39, 194
Telemedicine, 24, 39, 146
Termination, 40
The Joint Commission (JTC), 25, 34, 35, 89, 92, 102, 109, 110, 115, 117, 121, 123, 124, 143, 144, 145
    The Joint Commission of Healthcare Organizations, 92
Theory of the Diffusion of Innovation, 50
Training, 32, 33, 45, 117
Transitions of Care, 60

Transtheoretical Model, 40
Trend, 80
Trend Analysis, 80, 127, 146
T-Test, 79
Unfreeze, 40
Value-Based Care, 60, 182, 186, 196
Value-Based Modifier Program (VBM), 106
Value-Based Payment, 99
Value-Based Purchasing (VBP), 106
Values-Based Leadership, 26, 148, 177
Variance, 79
Voice of the Business (VOB), 16, 146
Voice of the Customer (VOC), 16, 17, 130, 143
VPN (Virtual Private Network), 75

Dear CPHQ Test Taker,

Thank you for purchasing this study guide for your CPHQ exam. We hope that we exceeded your expectations.

Our goal in creating this study guide was to cover all of the topics that you will see on the test. We also strove to make our practice questions as similar as possible to what you will encounter on test day. With that being said, if you found something that you feel was not up to your standards, please send us an email and let us know.

We have study guides in a wide variety of fields. If you're interested in one, try searching for it on Amazon or send us an email.

Thanks Again and Happy Testing!
Product Development Team
info@studyguideteam.com

Online Resources & Audiobook

Included with your purchase are multiple online resources. This includes practice tests in an interactive format and this book in audiobook format. There is also a convenient study timer to help you manage your time.

Scan the QR code or go to this link to access this content:

testprepbooks.com/online387/cphq

The first time you access the page, you will need to register as a "new user" and verify your email address.

If you have any issues, please email support@testprepbooks.com.

Thank you for letting us be a part of your studying journey!